"*Neurodiversity-Affirming Therapy* is a must-read for therapists seeking to provide inclusive and affirming care to neurodivergent clients. This comprehensive guide offers practical strategies, evidence-based techniques, and a deep understanding of neurodiversity. Equip yourself with the tools to build stronger relationships, improve your understanding, and make a positive difference in the lives of your neurodivergent clients."

—**J. E. Moyer, LPC,** author of the weekly newsletter *Letters from a Psychotherapist*

"Amy Marschall has written a must-read for anyone working in the mental health field. She explains beautifully the language, empathy, and understanding required for working with neurodivergence and how getting this right can be life-affirming and, indeed, lifesaving. I shall be buying copies for my peers."

—**Iain Lee, MNCPS, ACC,** broadcaster, counselor, and ADHD coach

"As a neurodivergent therapist, I find Amy Marschall's book provides essential insights into neurodiversity-affirming therapy. It offers valuable guidance on creating inclusive spaces for neurodivergent clients, emphasizing respect for lived experiences and client empowerment.

The strategies are easy to integrate into your practice, enabling you to provide more ethical, effective care. The book is an essential resource that contributes to the paradigm shift in supporting and empowering neurodivergent individuals. Whether you're new to the field or a seasoned professional, this book will challenge you to grow and better serve your neurodivergent clients."

—Stephanie Cartwright-Karlsson, MA, MSW, LICSW

NEURODIVERSITY-
AFFIRMING
THERAPY

What Every Mental Health Provider
Needs to Know

NEURODIVERSITY-
AFFIRMING
THERAPY

AMY MARSCHALL

Norton Professional Books

An Imprint of W. W. Norton & Company
Independent Publishers Since 1923

Note to Readers: This book is intended as a general information resource for professionals practicing in the field of psychotherapy and mental health. It is not a substitute for appropriate training or clinical supervision. Standards of clinical practice and protocol vary in different practice settings and change over time. No technique or recommendation is guaranteed to be safe or effective in all circumstances, and neither the publisher nor the author can guarantee the complete accuracy, efficacy, or appropriateness of any particular recommendation in every respect or in all settings or circumstances.

Any URLs displayed in this book link or refer to websites that existed as of press time. The publisher is not responsible for, and should not be deemed to endorse or recommend, any website other than its own or any content that it did not create. The author, also, is not responsible for any third-party material.

For information about permission to reproduce selections from this book, write to Permissions, W. W. Norton & Company, Inc., 500 Fifth Avenue, New York, NY 10110

For information about special discounts for bulk purchases, please contact W. W. Norton Special Sales at specialsales@wwnorton.com or 800-233-4830

Manufacturing by Versa Press
Production manager: Ramona Wilkes

ISBN: 978-1-324-05407-8

W. W. Norton & Company, Inc., 500 Fifth Avenue, New York, NY 10110
www.wwnorton.com

W. W. Norton & Company Ltd., 15 Carlisle Street, London W1D 3BS

1 2 3 4 5 6 7 8 9 0

This book is dedicated to every mental health provider committed to providing neurodiversity-affirming care to their clients

CONTENTS

ACKNOWLEDGMENTS

First, I want to give a huge thank you to Dr. Deborah Malmud, my editor at Norton, who reached out to me last year with the idea for this book. I had just submitted the final edits to my *Clinician's Guide to Supporting Autistic Clients*, and she had no idea at the time that I wanted to create a resource on neurodiversity-affirming mental health care that encompassed the entire neurodivergent community. I am so glad that we could connect and work together on this project.

Next, I want to thank my husband, whose willingness to constantly listen to my rants about the system is the reason my manuscripts end up coherent and not just a disorganized jumble of angry yelling.

Third, I of course must thank our cats, Armani and Vera. Vera's insistence that no one go into my office while I am working gave me the focus to complete this project, and Armani's insistence on joining me every time I was writing was so motivating. Armani, I am sorry that your contribution of "000000000000" was removed from the final manuscript.

Fourth, I want to thank my followers on Mastodon for hyping me up as I shared daily word counts. Being able to body double without actually physically sharing my space is the reason why this book is coming out now and not in five or ten years.

Finally, I want to give a shout out to my friends and colleagues who keep supporting me and continue acting interested no matter how many projects I take on. You are the best.

INTRODUCTION

The mental health field was built on the concept of a professional expert with training and knowledge treating an individual with a diagnosis. Treatment plans are based on evidence developed and selected by experts, and clients are expected to defer to the professional's judgment. Committees of these professionals develop lists of diagnostic criteria that describe different diagnoses, emphasizing how the symptoms look to an observer, with research predominantly focused on Western, white, cisgender, male experiences and presentations. Clients who push back against this model are labeled noncompliant or resistant. This model has harmed countless clients, particularly those with multiple marginalized identities.

Over the years, there has been an increase in community voices, leading to a shift in the field of psychology and mental health as a whole. Providers are learning to listen to the needs of their clients, those with lived experience, rather than clinging to the idea that only an expert who has not lived with a diagnosis can know what an individual needs. Many in the field are learning to recognize the ways in which neurodivergence can be part of someone's identity and that while many have support needs, they are not broken or needing to be fixed or cured of their neurodivergence. This is known as the neurodiversity-affirming model of care. Providers who refuse to learn and adapt to this model of care face pushback and are called out for harm caused by the paternalism of the expert model.

Neurodiversity-affirming mental health care is not a specific set of therapeutic interventions, assessments, or steps a clinician must take to fit into this model. Instead, it is an underlying philosophy that recognizes individuals as the experts on their own experience, experts who can collaborate with professionals who have expertise from our training. It additionally recognizes that the provider/client duality is false, as many providers are also neurodivergent. It acknowledges that, while neurodivergence can come with challenges, and many neurodivergent individuals are disabled, the spectrum of neurodiversity is an asset to humanity. Neurodivergence is not a problem to be extinguished but a naturally occurring variation in humanity, just like physical abilities and other individual strengths and weaknesses. Additionally, no human being's value or worth is tied to their ability to be productive or contribute in a specific way. Everyone deserves appropriate support and freedom from expectation to conform to neurotypical standards.

This book is for any mental health professional who wants to understand the historical, practical, and clinical context of neurodiversity-affirming care and why this philosophy of mental health care is vital for supporting our neurodivergent clients. It is not specific to one type of neurodivergence, and providers would benefit from enhancing their knowledge of neurodiversity-affirming care in the context of any specific populations with whom they work. This book provides broad information on the philosophy behind neurodiversity-affirming mental health care and how it applies to those who engage with the mental health system.

Through this book, readers will learn the history of neuro-divergence and diagnoses, how this has historically been framed in the mental health field, and how this approach has perpetuated harm and stigma against our clients. It will additionally address ongoing issues if stigma and harm in the system, including the harm that comes with nonaffirming care for clients across the life span. It explores the nuances of affirming care in practice and considerations that any provider should be aware of when working with neurodivergent communities.

No single book can encompass all aspects of every human experience. Use this book to expand your knowledge of neuro-divergence and neurodiversity-affirming mental health care, but read other books on this topic, attend trainings, and most importantly, listen to the stories, needs, and opinions of the communities you serve. Maintain an overarching approach to your work that is affirming, and individualize everything you do to the needs of the person in front of you in your practice.

We will all make mistakes in our efforts toward being affirming, but with a solid knowledge base and good intentions, we can make the field better for our clients.

Note: The author of this text makes efforts to be as affirming as possible with the language used. However, as language evolves, the terms in this book may become dated. Additionally, the author may use the terms that seem most affirming but be mistaken about a given community's preferences. In instances where data about community trends and preferences are available, the author will make every effort to use this language throughout this text. For those communities who do not have a tendency toward one preference or where the data was not available, the author will alternate between identity-first and person-first language.

NEURODIVERSITY-
AFFIRMING
THERAPY

1

What Is Neurodivergence?

Before we can become neurodiversity-affirming, we first must understand what neurodiversity and neurodivergence are. First, *neurodiversity* refers to the full spectrum of human neurotypes, all the varied, diverse, and different ways our brains can develop and function. One person cannot be neurodiverse because diversity refers to a variety of presentations, and each person only has one brain.

Neurodivergence, on the other hand, refers to when someone's neurotype diverts from the umbrella of what has socially been deemed typical. What falls under *neurotypical* versus *neurodivergent* is essentially a social construct, in that the way in which someone compares to general definitions of *normal* determines whether their neurotype is deemed typical versus divergent. The majority of people fall under the neurotypical category; according to a review of the literature from medical, psychiatric, psychological, and sociological studies, approximately 20% of the population has some form of neurodivergence, meaning that 80% are neurotypical (Doyle, 2020).

We can compare neurotype to handedness: studies show that approximately 90% of the world's population is right-hand dominant, 10% are left-hand dominant, and a very small percent-age are ambidextrous (Pfeifer et al., 2022). Differences in hand dominance are a natural part of human diversity. Because there are more right-handed people than other groups, much of our world is built to accommodate right-handed dominance. This does not mean that being left-handed is inferior or bad, and left-hand dominance can even be an asset in completing some tasks, but this causes stress and difficulty for left-handed people who need to constantly operate with their nondominant hand as they go about their day. As a result, left-handed people have a shorter life span than right-handed people.

Neurodivergence, like left-handedness, diverts from the expected. It can be disabling, like any trait or quality, and man-ageable with appropriate support. Unfortunately, Western society places value on having low support needs, and those neurodiver-gent people with more needs are often labeled as having less value.

Sometimes, a difference is disabling regardless of the envi-ronment, but we can structure society in a way that seamlessly (or nearly seamlessly) accommodates everyone who needs it. For instance, almost two-thirds of Americans wear some kind of glasses (Vision Council, 2021). Vision impairment is a disability, and not being able to see can present challenges, but glasses are so normalized today that many do not think about this regularly. People today are not shamed for wearing glasses, although they once were when glasses-wearers were a minority. They are usu-ally not asked, "Are you *sure* you *really* need them?" We simply accept that some people need glasses to see better. There is still a lag in health care coverage, but needing glasses is no longer stig-matized like needing a mobility aid or needing accommodations for mental health.

In order to become neurodiversity-affirming, we must first break away from the mindset that neurotypical equals good, and neurodivergent equals bad, and that abled equals good, and disabled equals bad. The goal is not to invert these two ideas (to place neurodivergent in the superior role and neurotypical as inferior), but to recognize that an individual's inherent value is not tied to their neurotype. Everyone deserves the care and support that they need, and we can tear down existing systems to accommodate a broader range of neurotypes, thus reducing the need for external support to begin with.

To become neurodiversity-affirming, we must first break away from the mindset that neurotypical equals good, and neurodivergent equals bad."

As a starting point, we will define these terms in order to understand what it means to be neurotypical and neurodivergent. We will explore the language around these terms and communities, noting the importance of affirming language in these conversations. Finally, we will dive into community voices, as centering those with lived experience in these domains is central in providing affirming care and approaching mental health from a neurodiversity-affirming standpoint.

It is important to note that one single text cannot sufficiently encompass every aspect and nuance of a topic. Additionally, individuals within a community will have their own experiences, perspectives, and opinions. While affirming language makes efforts to prioritize community trends and preferences, individuals within those communities have the right to disagree with the majority. Providers should always consider the individual's needs and stated preferences in one-on-one treatment and conversation and defer to majority preference in other settings. When in doubt, ask.

Defining Neurodivergence

For a long time, neurodivergence is the term that has been used to refer to people who do not fit into the spectrum of what is considered typical. Neurodiversity, on the other hand, refers to the full spectrum of neurotypes, the various ways human brains can develop, and includes everyone, neurotypical and neurodivergent alike.

An individual's brain impacts how they perceive and interact with the world, how they form and recall memories, how they communicate, essentially all aspects of behavior. As humans have evolved, we have built a society intended to allow people to function and exist in community. However, the rules, requirements, and expectations of our society mean that some individuals have an easier time engaging with these expectations than others. Expectations tend to be built around what works for the majority (or at least those in power), and those who do not fit into this box are penalized and ostracized. As we have learned more about neurodivergence, many have pushed for a more inclusive world.

The term "neurodiversity" was first published in an academic setting by Judy Singer, an autistic sociologist, in her thesis paper. Singer has been credited with coining this term. While it is true that she was the first to use the term in a publication (Singer, 1998), it is also true that many communities were using the term long before Singer's thesis was published (Botha et al., 2024). Additionally, Singer later clarified that her definition of "neurodivergence" specifically applied to autistic individuals who met criteria for Asperger's syndrome rather than the full umbrella of individuals whose neurotype does not fit into societal definitions of "typical" (Lutz, 2023). For this reason, various neurodivergent communities have rejected her narrow definition of the term.

Asperger's syndrome is no longer recognized by the *DSM* as a diagnosis distinct from autism spectrum disorder. Psychologists generally struggled with distinguishing the two conditions, and Asperger's was often considered *higher functioning* autism based on observed behavior rather than the individual's internal experience. Furthermore, Asperger was a Nazi whose research focused on categorizing autistic children as those who could be put to work and those who should be exterminated—hardly a neurodiversity-affirming approach to assessment!

The term *neurodivergence* was actually coined by Kassiane Asasumasu, an autistic rights advocate and blogger (https:// timetolisten.blogspot.com/). Her work is often incorrectly attributed to Singer or erased altogether, a common occurrence for women of color that needs to be named and addressed. White supremacy in mental health, research, and academia downplays or erases these contributions all the time. Kassiane Asasumasu has repeatedly stated that the term refers to everyone whose neurotype differs from typical or societal expectations (Thompson, 2020). This text uses her definition and emphasizes intersectionality and inclusion.

According to an analysis by Botha et al. (2024), "Going forward, we should recognize the multiple, collective origins of the neurodiversity concept rather than attributing it to any single author." In other words, like many things, the very idea of neurodivergence is not attributable to a single person or small group of people, but to communities and group efforts at self-understanding.

There are many ways that an individual's neurotype can divert from societal expectations, and over time neurodivergence has been embraced as a wide term for a variety of communities (Doyle, 2020). One benefit of taking a wide definition for this term is that neurodivergent individuals who want to communicate a need for support resulting from their neurodivergence can do so while maintaining privacy around their specific diagnosis. Of course, many institutions that can provide appropriate accommodations will ask for more specific diagnostic information anyway, but in some cases the individual can preserve their privacy.

Neurodivergence can be acquired or lifelong. For example, neurodevelopmental disorders as defined by the *Diagnostic and Statistical Manual of Mental Disorders*, Fifth Edition, Text Revision (DSM-5-TR), including autism, ADHD, intellectual disabilities, and learning disorders have early childhood onset, and much research indicates that these traits have an onset at or before birth.

Some forms of neurodivergence tend to develop later in life; for instance, schizophrenia and bipolar disorders both tend to onset in early adulthood. An individual may appear neurotypical until the onset of these symptoms, which are a form of neurodivergence. These diagnoses can be triggered by a stressor but also have a genetic predisposition.

Head traumas resulting in brain injuries cause acquired neurodivergence that is not caused by an individual's genetic makeup. Some forms of neurodivergence can also cause neurological changes over time, such as manic episodes, psychosis, or seizures.

If we accept that neurodivergent refers to anyone whose neurotype causes them to fall outside of typical expectations for brains and behaviors, this category would include:

ADHD

Anxiety disorders

Autism

Bipolar disorders

Cerebral palsy

Communication disorders

Dementia

Down syndrome

Dyspraxia

Epilepsy and other seizure disorders

Fetal alcohol spectrum disorder

Intellectual disability

Intellectual giftedness (high IQ)

Learning disorders

Major depressive disorder

Multiple sclerosis

Neurological disorders caused by environment

Obsessive compulsive disorders

Other genetic conditions that impact cognition

Other mood disorders

Other neurodevelopmental disorders

Other psychotic disorders

Other trauma disorders

Parkinson's

Persistent depressive disorder

Personality disorders

Posttraumatic stress disorder (PTSD)

Processing disorders

Schizophrenia

Schizophreniform disorder

Tic disorders

Tourette syndrome

Traumatic brain injury

This list is intended as a comprehensive overview of many conditions that could be considered neurodivergent; however, other individuals whose neurotype falls outside of typical expectations may also be considered under this definition of neurodivergence.

Essentially, neurodivergence is a wide term that encompasses many people with different presentations, symptoms, and needs. When approaching mental health care from a neurodiversity-affirming standpoint, we must be aware that these individuals form several communities, all with different needs and preferences, and each of those communities is made up of individuals whose values and needs may differ from what the majority of the group prefers. An affirming therapist will be aware of overall community trends and stated preferences, while ensuring that each individual client we see has space to make their voice heard.

These individuals form several communities, all with different needs and preferences."

This is not an easy task! Not only do community preferences change over time, but individual clients may indicate preferences that do not fit with majority trends. For example, the autistic community previously indicated preference for person-first language (person with autism) but presently prefers identity-first language (autistic person) in recent surveys. Another example can be seen in the community of neurodivergent individuals who do not communicate by speaking with their mouths. These individuals have previously been referred to as *nonverbal*; however, some in the community have expressed that professionals sometimes interpret this as "unable to communicate or understand communication." This is often used as an excuse to not attempt to communicate directly with the individual, to deny them autonomy, and to violate their human rights. Many in this community have indicated a preference for *nonspeaking* to underscore the importance of helping them communicate in ways that work for them, such as by providing access to augmentive and alternative communication (AAC), rather than assuming that they are incapable of self-expression.

This means that we as providers need to continuously listen to the communities we serve and be aware of changes. We must continuously publicize our commitment to centering their voices in our work and education. We must also ask each client about their individual needs, never assuming that our education is finished and that we know everything we need to know for our jobs. Lead with good intentions, be prepared to make corrections when you inevitably make mistakes, and center lived experience.

Language

It should always be a clinician's intent to use inclusive and affirming language. This is something that applies to sessions with clients and our lives outside of our jobs. While it is true that therapists have days off and get to clock out like everyone else, in order to truly embrace what it means to be neurodiversity-affirming, we must accept these values as fundamental in our world, not just our work.

The National Association of Social Workers (2017) ethics code states: "Social workers pursue social change, particularly with and on behalf of vulnerable and oppressed individuals and groups of people." In other words, a clinical social worker must act in ways that promote social justice even outside of each client's individual session. Although the American Psychological Association does not have a comparable line in their ethics code, it only makes sense for psychologists to share this value as well. The same is true for counselors and marriage and family therapists. How can we claim to be helping clients when systemic oppression is often a component of their mental health concerns, if we do not also loudly address these issues both in our sessions and outside of them?

It would be hypocritical, for instance, for a therapist to claim to be queer-affirming and support LGBTQ+ clients, and then donate money they earned from those clients to organizations seeking to take away marriage equality. The same is true for being neurodiversity-affirming. If a therapist's personal values indicate that they support eugenics toward autistic people, it does not matter how they talk or act in any sessions, or how they treat their clients. That therapist is not and cannot be neurodiversity-affirming.

Our words reflect our values, and they also inform them. If I make a conscious choice to change my language, over time, I will start to think differently about that topic. If I go out of my way to use language that is affirming, language that reflects the preferences of the communities I serve, it will help me consciously think about those community members first and prioritize their needs rather than seeing myself as an expert who knows what is best for them. It will help me stop myself from speaking over them, and it will help me be a better provider to my clients.

What Makes Language Affirming?

Since neurodivergence is such a wide, encompassing term, there is not a short and simple list of neurodiversity-affirming terms to pepper into your conversations. Like all aspects of creating a neurodiversity-affirming practice, it is not simple or easy.

First, language changes and evolves over time. Terms that might have been appropriate or even affirming 10 years ago might currently be dated at best, if not outright harmful. The solution is to always be learning and always be listening. Be aware that there will be times that language has shifted, and you are not yet aware of it, so you might need to be open to correction. Surround yourself with community voices, and both listen and amplify what you hear. Make adjustments, and apologize sincerely and without centering yourself when you make a mistake.

Even the language in this text will become dated over time. I have made an effort to reflect affirming language for all communities discussed, sought out community members for consultation and support, and reviewed surveys of communities in an effort to reflect what is currently considered most affirming and best practice. However, the so-called right language in 2024 is unlikely to still be correct in all areas in 10, 20, or more years. The philosophy behind a neurodiversity-affirming approach to mental health care remains the same: take steps to avoid harming clients, and address and acknowledge past harm caused by nonaffirming approaches.

Second, ask questions. Therapists have a duty to engage in ongoing consultation—all ethics codes have statements about this, and one reason why consultation is so important is to help each other provide the best, most competent services we can to our clients. Have trusted professionals who you know will point out if you fall short and who will help you continue growing throughout your career. Additionally, make sure you are consulting directly with members of the communities you serve. This involves reading articles and books by and for the community as well as forming professional relationships with community members. If you regularly request labor and education from someone, it is appropriate to compensate them. Members of marginalized groups are often expected to educate for free, even though this task can be incredibly draining. This goes double and triple for Black, Indigenous, and other People of Color (BIPOC), gender minorities, disabled individuals, and those at the intersection of multiple marginalized identities.

Intersectionality

As noted previously, we cannot be truly affirming of neurodivergent communities without taking an intersectional approach and being affirming of other marginalized groups in our society. This means it is insufficient to strive for language that is neurodiversity-affirming if we do not simultaneously strive for language that is antiracist, antimisogynistic, antihomophobic, antitransphobic, antiheteronormative, anti-ableist, and so on. Not only are many neurodivergent individuals simultaneously marginalized in other ways, but there is an inherent hypocrisy to striving for justice in one group while disregarding or actively harming others.

For example, one cannot be considered neurodiversity-affirming when using affirming language when talking about people with learning disabilities if they simultaneously intentionally misgender trans people. Inclusion means inclusion of all identities, not just neurotype.

One issue that is particularly prevalent in neurodivergent communities is ableism in language. One example of this is a phenomenon often experienced by those with ADHD as *paralysis*. For someone with ADHD, they may feel paralyzed when they struggle to start or continue an important task, or they may become stuck with making a seemingly basic and small decision. However, many in physically disabled communities have pushed back on this kind of language. They note that paralysis is a real medical condition, and while an individual's neurodivergence might make them feel frozen or immobile, they are not literally paralyzed. Comparing these experiences can be harmful to physically disabled individuals who experience invalidation in their struggles or feel erased in conversations centering the experiences of able-bodied neurodivergent people.

This does not mean that, if a client in their own appointment says, "And then I experienced decision paralysis," the clinician needs to cut them off and explain why that language is problematic in that moment. However, in our own conversations and publications, we have a responsibility to lead the way and set an example with the terms we use to describe different neurodivergent experiences. I might reframe the statement as, "You felt stuck," and make a point of avoiding the term paralysis when writing or speaking about neurodivergence.

> *We have a responsibility to lead the way and set an example with the terms we use to describe different neurodivergent experiences."*

People tend to get defensive around their language choices. Many feel that this is not an important topic to consider, but remember that our goal is to create an affirming space that supports *all* people. Just as society has historically marginalized and pushed out neurodivergent people, the same has happened to many other groups. (Again, many members of these groups are neurodivergent as well!)

When this topic comes up in professional settings, pushback is common. People will hear, "Here is a small way your language can be more inclusive," as "You are not allowed to speak that way." I cannot control how others choose to communicate, and I am not here to police anyone's language. This is simply information about how certain language may come across to some communities, informed by my conversations with these communities. You can choose to ignore this input, and as a result some might not trust you or feel safe communicating with you.

It is simultaneously true that all words are made up, and the words we use matter. So much of our language has implications we do not even think of in day-to-day life, with ableism in particular baked in so deeply that it is easy to overlook. (When is the last time you referred to something as "lame"?) You can choose to do better now and have compassion for your past self who did not know better. We do not need to be perfect in our language choices; all that is asked is that we do our best to be 1% more inclusive, paving the way for a better world.

Talking About Language

Although there is not a set list of terms and phrases that are automatically neurodiversity-affirming in all contexts, there is some general vocabulary that providers who seek to be neurodiversity-affirming should be aware of. Due to the fluid nature of language, these terms are unlikely to be all-encompassing. As always, no one text is the be-all and the end-all for any conversation, so when you finish reading this book, seek out other authors speaking to neurodiversity-affirming mental health care as well.

Identity-First/Person-First

There has been much debate about identity-first language (IFL) and person-first language (PFL). For neurodivergence, IFL is language that centers the neurotype (autistic person), and PFL centers the person (person with autism). For some time, there was a push for PFL because providers would use IFL to dehumanize patients and decenter their perspective on their lived experiences. However, in more recent years, some communities have felt that PFL removes them from their identity. For instance, many in the ADHD community have begun referring to themselves as "ADHD-ers" rather than as "people with ADHD."

In particular, surveys conducted around the time this text was published show that approximately 80% of the autistic community prefers IFL because many see autism as part of their identity, in the way that one's nationality or religion is part of their identity. (It would sound odd to say "person with Christianity" versus "Christian," for example.)

However, IFL is not a universal preference for all neurodivergent communities. Many communities unfortunately do not have handy surveys available to indicate majority preference; however, a 2021 study from the *Journal of Counseling & Development* found that providers treated patients diagnosed with schizophrenia with more benevolence and tolerance when they referred to the patient as a "person with schizophrenia" versus as a "schizophrenic person" (Granello & Gorby, 2021). In that case, when community data is unavailable, PFL would be most appropriate in order to avoid potential harm to the client caused by our own bias or the bias of other professionals who access our records.

There is not one set, right answer regarding IFL and PFL with regard to neurodivergence. When there is a notable community preference (as with the autistic community) or documented best practice to avoid harm to our clients (as with the study on clients with schizophrenia), use these terms in general. As always, you can ask individual clients about their preference and honor that preference on a one-on-one basis.

Of course, these preferences are likely to change over time—autistic, for example, used to be used as a dehumanizing term, leading to a time when PFL was preferred in this community before shifting back to IFL. Knowing this history and continuing to educate yourself can ensure that the language you use regarding your clients reflects your commitment to affirming care and practice.

Nonpathologizing Terminology

As clinicians, we walk a delicate tightrope when talking about and to our clients about their diagnoses and challenges. The neurodiversity-affirming movement has rightly pointed out that much of the language around neurodivergence tends to be overly medical and pathologizing. At the same time, there are moments in our work when we are required to use certain language and terminology in order to support our clients.

For instance, there are some in the ADHD community who feel the term *disorder* does not accurately capture their experience as neurodivergent individuals. Some refer to ADHC (attention-deficit/hyperactivity condition), feeling that *condi-*

tion is a less pathologizing term. A client who feels that disorder does not accurately or appropriately describe their experience has the right to self-refer with alternate terms and ask that their treatment team respect and honor their preferred vocabulary. At the same time, ADHC is not a recognized DSM or ICD code that can be submitted to insurance for reimbursement or for workplace accommodations under the Americans with Disabilities Act (ADA) (Americans with Disabilities Act, 1990). If a client needs these supports (insurance coverage for their treatment or ADA accommodations), I have to use the term *disorder* in the client's diagnosis, even if they do not resonate with this terminology.

When discussing affirming language with clients, we can explain the requirements of our professional role and honor their needs whenever possible. Letting them know, "This is what I have to input for you to receive this support, even though we both understand and recognize its limitations," can assure the client that you see them and respect their experience. As providers, we can recognize limitations and problems in our line of work, respect and honor our clients, be neurodiversity-affirming, and still operate within the system as it requires in order to give our clients access to the best resources for them.

In practice, always defer to the preferences of the individual in front of you when managing their care, and defer to your best knowledge of community preferences when speaking publicly. Within this text, there are times when I must use clinical terms to indicate a specific diagnosis or quote exact diagnostic criteria. Communicate with your client about the times when you also might have to use nonaffirming language and your reasons for doing so.

Functioning Versus Support Needs

One common language debate that comes up in neurodivergent communities is the way we talk about an individual's needs. For example, many diagnoses in the DSM include specifiers for severity. Someone with a diagnosis of ADHD or major depressive disorder is typically assigned a mild, moderate, or severe specifier.

Historically, this specifier has focused on how the individual impacts the people around them. Especially for neurodivergences that emerge in early childhood, it may be appropriate to include this information for the purpose of screening clients for assessment and access to needed support; however, this is only one small piece of the picture. With the example of ADHD above, the severity of one's symptoms is often described by how disruptive those symptoms are to others. Someone experiencing distress as a result of their neurodivergence but successfully camouflaging those traits successfully would be considered mild without considering their needs. Additionally, conversations that center the impact of an individual's neurodivergence on those around them tend to ignore that person's needs. We stop discussing what might help the individual thrive and instead focus on how they inconvenience others in their environment. That conversation quickly becomes, "How do we fix them?"

The autistic community in particular has discussed at length issues around functioning labels. In the past, autistic individuals were divided into categories including Asperger's to indicate those who were high functioning and autistic for those who were considered lower functioning. As noted in the introduction, this division was started by Hans Asperger, a Nazi scientist who was determining which autistic children could be put to work (the high functioning children) and which should be put to death (the low functioning children) (Czech, 2018).

I hope I do not have to explain why this system is horrifying and should be rejected outright.

Functioning labels also traditionally focus on an individual's ability to survive in a capitalistic environment. Often, a neurodivergent individual who is capable of working full-time hours is labeled high functioning and considered not needing support regardless of the toll it takes on them in order to sustain those work hours or what accommodations they require in order to function within that system. Depressive disorders typically have specifiers of mild, moderate, or severe. An individual who is suffering significantly but is still forcing themselves to attend work would be labeled as having less severe symptoms than someone who is unable to work due to their symptoms. Both of these individuals may be struggling significantly, but one would be seen as needing less support. While it is not a contest to determine who is struggling the most, downplaying someone's needs because their symptoms are less observable perpetuates harm. Many who mask, camouflage, or hide their neurodivergent traits are labeled high functioning because they can appear neurotypical to the people around them. Essentially, high functioning means, "You are not causing a problem for me, and therefore you are not struggling."

Instead, in being neurodiversity-affirming, we focus on support. When the DSM shifted over to autism spectrum disorder as a label for all autistic individuals, it continued to use a levels system, with Level 1 indicating "Requiring support," Level 2 indicating "Requiring substantial support," and Level 3 indicating "Requiring very substantial support." The shift to support needs means that, instead of looking at how an individual functions in their environment, we look at what supports they need in order to live their best life.

The levels system is still flawed, however. First, it is oversimplified. A neurodivergent individual (autistic or other) may only require a small amount of support in one area but substantial or very substantial support in others. Additionally, the autism spectrum disorder levels are generally considered consistent throughout one's lifetime, but research shows that an individual's support needs can change substantially in response to an episode of autistic burnout, trauma, or even unmasking (when an individual realizes they were previously ignoring their support needs) (Barger, Campbell, & McDonough, 2013). Thus, the levels system used for autism diagnoses is insufficient for this community and would not be beneficial as a universal system for all neurodivergent individuals to identify support needs.

Instead, a neurodiversity-affirming approach to diagnosis and support recommendations accounts for the individual as a whole person, both directly related to their neurodivergence or neurodivergences and their personal values, life goals, and needs. For example, many providers would see a child client experiencing frequent meltdowns and recommend a treatment goal of "reducing the frequency of meltdowns" by reinforcing the child for alternative responses to stressors. An affirming provider would instead focus on what is triggering these meltdowns and reducing the stressor or teaching the child's caregiver to support the child in communicating needs before they reach the point of meltdown and then meeting that need. Additionally, many providers assume that certain symptoms, traits, or presentations necessitate certain treatment goals. In the example above, a provider might assume that the top priority is to change the behavior, while the child or their caregiver might have other treatment goals. An affirming provider will develop goals collaboratively, listening to the client and crafting a treatment plan that reflects what the client wants.

This is much more difficult to code in a book like the DSM, as it does not lend itself to simple, easily defined categories we can assign to each client. It is a big task that we take on when we commit our careers to helping these individuals and communities.

> *An affirming provider will develop goals collaboratively, listening to the client and crafting a treatment plan that reflects what the client wants."*

It is important to remember also that, while many neurodivergent individuals reject the notion of levels or functional labels outright, some find these designations helpful. Continuing to use the autistic community as an example, some individuals with more significant support needs have reported the levels system has helped them communicate what their needs are, what specific difficulties they experience, and what supports would be beneficial in their day-to-day life. Some have even shared feeling that autistic individuals with fewer or less significant support needs are used as examples for why their support needs are not valid, which is incredibly harmful.

Another example of functioning and support needs labels causing harm plays out in the intellectually disabled community. (Autistic individuals can also be intellectually disabled, but these are two distinct neurodivergences with different diagnostic requirements.) Many intellectually disabled adults require a supportive living environment to ensure that their needs are met. In the United States, this may exist in the form of group homes where individuals can have freedom around aspects of their lives but still have staff available to assist with things like medication management, scheduling, transportation, and other tasks with which they might struggle.

Intellectual disabilities are also categorized in the DSM and can be considered mild, moderate, severe, and profound, with support needs varying based on the severity indicated with the diagnosis. While this might help staff understand the individual's support needs, the labels are again limited and might not accurately reflect individual needs, instead focusing on how the individual's neurodivergence places demands on support staff.

Additionally, in some cases, adults who require a supportive living environment are removed from group homes if they are perceived as too high functioning. Functional labels (which we have seen are limited, flawed, and rarely reflective of the individual's needs) can be used to deny support if those interpreting these labels feel that the client's presentation is not severe enough to justify support.

At the other extreme, those whose intellectual disability is perceived as significantly impairing their functioning might be placed in conservatorships and not permitted to make decisions about their finances, medical treatment, or personal life. While such conservatorships are described as helping protect those who are not competent to make their own decisions, they often result in the conservator abusing the disabled person and overreaching. Behaviors that would just be considered mistakes if a neurotypical made them are labeled as proof that the conservatorship is necessary to protect the individual from themselves. We will discuss conservatorships in more depth in the next section of this book.

Again, an approach to care that centers the individual and documents needs based on their unique experience would mitigate accusations like this. One person's support needs do not determine another person's support needs regardless of whether those two individuals share a diagnosis. At the same time, an awareness of how these dynamics play out in the existing system is essential in providing neurodiversity-affirming care to all clients and preventing further harm as a result of the system's many flaws.

Plain Language

For many providers, it is tempting to implement the jargon we learn in graduate school, research, and continuing education when we talk to and about our clients. However, the National Institute of Health recommends using plain language when talking to our clients (U.S. Department of Health and Human Services, n.d.). This does not mean that we talk down to them, but that we are making a point of using accessible, clear language that someone who does not have our training can understand.

This is important in our client interactions because clients might feel intimidated or nervous to acknowledge that they require clarification. It makes us approachable and communicates that we are a resource they can use for their learning. Unfortunately, although the internet makes information more available, it also makes misinformation more available. That is why it is essential that we use language and communicate with clients in a way they can understand so they can engage with us.

Clients deserve to understand their diagnosis, medical record, and information about their neurotype.

Community Terms

Thanks to greater awareness around neurodivergence and more options for communication, neurodivergent individuals are connecting to each other at unprecedented rates. Communities have formed, promoting affirming resources, language, and support, and neurodivergent individuals can connect with others who share their neurotype, identity, and experience.

If you specialize in supporting a specific neurodivergent community, immerse yourself in the language of that community. If you do not share that identity, be mindful of how you engage with these spaces. Many neurodivergent people have experienced harm in their interactions with the mental health system and might understandably feel mistrust of a provider coming into community spaces. Additionally, if you do not share the identity, you might not be welcome in some spaces. Understand your role, lead with curiosity, and avoid taking up space that is not yours.

Connecting with the community outside of client sessions reminds us of our clients' humanity. Of course, hopefully clinicians are maintaining awareness of this without reminders, but we can get caught up in the technical aspects of our job and begin focusing on a client's symptoms, diagnosis, clinical presentation, and so on and lose sight of their underlying humanity.

Additionally, community involvement helps us take our plain language a step further. While it is good to ensure that clients understand what you are communicating to them, you can signal that you are affirming of their neurotype and that you are providing a safe space to unmask by using the preferred language of that community. This is not limited to things like knowing if the community prefers person-first or identity-first language. It includes other terms that the community uses to share different experiences.

For instance, the DSM refers to autistic clients having "Highly restricted, fixated interests that are abnormal in intensity or focus." This phrasing is incredibly pathologizing with the indication that the individual is restricted, and fixated and that their interest is abnormal. The autistic community instead refers to this quality as having a *special interest*. If you are evaluating an individual, you can show your commitment to neurodiversity-affirming care by asking about special interests rather than about interests approached with abnormal intensity. When required, our documentation will reflect professional and clinical requirements. However, in our direct communications, we can reflect this affirming language to the client. We make ongoing efforts to understand current preferences and affirming language.

Neurodivergence and Disability

The concept of disability in neurodivergence is sometimes a point of disagreement and contention. For example, some in the ADHD community feel that their neurodivergence is not disabling, sometimes even referring to their ADHD as a superpower because it is the source of their creativity. This is valid and true, but it is also true that other aspects of their neurotype can be and are disabling for many. Impulsive behavior, executive dysfunction, distractibility, and so on can all be disabling.

Some neurodivergent communities have pointed out that some aspects of neurodivergence that can be disabling are only disabling in the context of how our society is structured. Continuing to use ADHD as an example, one of the hyperactive-impulsive symptoms in the DSM is "Often leaves seat in situations when remaining seated is expected." In a world where body movement is not seen as disruptive, where you are not expected to remain seated for long periods of time, this would simply be a personal quirk and not an issue to be addressed.

On the other hand, executive dysfunction is not limited to societal expectations. It can cause the individual to need support and continuous reminders to complete hygiene tasks necessary to care for their body is not limited to societal expectations, even if they are impacted by these expectations.

One person with ADHD might not experience disabling symptoms, and as a result they might not personally identify as disabled. This can happen for many reasons. Some might not feel comfortable identifying as disabled when the label feels as if it does not apply, as they do not want to take up space or pull focus from those whose symptoms are disabling. (This self-invalidation might reflect underlying schemas that need to be addressed.) They might just not relate to that term. They may have internalized ableism that they need to work through and do not want to be someone who is labeled disabled. (That is something the client would need to work on and address in themselves, though we cannot force someone to make changes for which they are not ready.)

Clients have the right to self-identify, and we empower them by honoring the terminology they claim for themselves. At the same time, an individual whose neurodivergence meets diagnostic criteria is legally considered disabled, at least in the United States. Again, this may come down to telling the client that you respect and affirm their personal decisions but are required to document using certain language.

> *Clients have the right to self-identify, and we empower them by honoring the terminology they claim for themselves."*

This may also involve identity work and insight building that leads the client to realize that they are experiencing a disability. Some neurodivergent individuals who are high-masking are often out of touch with their own needs, and the process of unmasking causes them to realize how much they were compensating in the past. As they pull back these masks, they may suddenly realize that they are experiencing more difficulties than they previously allowed themselves to acknowledge. This is not a guarantee, and if an individual continues to feel that they are not disabled, we honor and respect their identity. However, they may experience an identity crisis as their understanding of their needs shifts, which is something a mental health provider can help them navigate.

For some, societal changes would eliminate their disability. Others would experience impairment regardless of context. Of course, both groups would benefit from a world that offers appropriate support to all, a world that has eliminated ableism, but that world does not presently exist.

Disabled does not mean bad, inadequate, insufficient, a burden, or any of the other terms that an ableist society associates with it. It simply reflects an individual's support needs, just as neurodivergent simply means that one's brain does not fall under the neurotypical umbrella. Many neurodivergent individuals are disabled as a result of their neurodivergence, and both neurodivergent and neurotypical individuals can be disabled in ways unrelated to their neurotype.

As providers, we need to unpack our own biases and thoughts around what it means to be disabled and the nuance around this concept. We can educate our clients about the social constructs as well as objective impairments that contribute to disability while honoring their preferred language, and we can educate ourselves and the public on this topic. Addressing ableism is part of the intersectionality required to be truly neurodiversity-affirming.

Sanism

As noted, language cannot be neurodiversity-affirming if it harms other communities. Ableist language refers to language that is harmful to disabled communities, including both neurodivergent and neurotypical disabled people and neurodivergent people both with and without disabilities unrelated to their neurodivergence.

A subcategory of ableist language is sanist language. This is language that is harmful to neurodivergent individuals with mental health diagnoses. Language that is derogatory, hostile, or harmful to communities with mental health diagnoses is sanist. Examples of sanism in language include, but are not limited to:

- Referring to someone as "crazy" or "insane" based on unusual behavior
- Terms like "idiot" and "moron" aimed at insulting someone's intelligence
- Euphemisms for mental illness such as referring to someone as "off their rocker" or having "a screw loose"
- Use of diagnostic terms to insult someone, such as saying that someone is a "narcissist" or "so borderline"

Sanist language is harmful because it perpetuates negative stereotypes about neurodivergent people. It assumes that neurodivergent people are bad, dangerous, or undeserving of the same respect and consideration as neurotypical people. Eliminating this language from one's vocabulary is difficult, but committed providers can seek alternatives to sanist terms that encompass the meaning of their message without engaging in sanism. Of course, there may be times that it is difficult to find a nonsanist term for what you are trying to communicate because your underlying message is inherently sanist—in this case, take the opportunity to challenge your bias.

Making Your Language Affirming

As noted above, each individual may have their own preferences around the language of their neurodivergence and their experience. This is valid and correct, and individuals have the right to self-refer in the ways with which they are most comfortable.

This does not mean that all language they use is affirming, but simply that they have the right to self-identify and self-refer. Just as professionals can choose to ignore requests about making their language affirming and intersectional, individuals might prefer language that others in their community find problematic. This might result in them struggling to find a place within that community. For example, while some see their neurodivergence as a superpower, others find this language invalidating of the difficulties that can come from existing while neurodivergent. Someone who finds the superpower language off-putting or even harmful might not feel comfortable interacting with someone who sees their neurodivergence as a superpower. That does not mean either individual is wrong, but that they might not be the best fit to interact with or have any type of relationship with each other. There are billions of people in the world; no one will connect with every single other person perfectly.

If you provide individual therapy or other one-on-one services, you can ask clients about their preferences at the start of services and note how they prefer for you to refer to them when speaking to them or in your documentation of your interactions.

Just as I would ask a client what pronouns I should use when referring to them, I can ask how they would like me to refer to and talk about their neurodivergence. Sometimes, they might give an answer that I know goes against community trends and preferences. Again, this is their right, and I can respect and honor their choices in their sessions. I might let them know if their preference is different from the language I am used to using. For example, surveys show that approximately 80% of autistic people prefer identity-first language over person-first language. If an autistic client asks me to refer to them as a "person with autism," I will respect their choice, but I might let them know that I may slip up, as I am used to using the community-preferred terminology. That does not mean their preference is wrong, but that they have the right to correct me if I make a mistake, which is more likely when I am using language that is less familiar to me.

Some clients might not have thought about language preferences before discussing it with you. It is okay if they are unsure how to answer or if they change their minds over time. Part of our job is to help them explore their identity, which can include trying on different language and seeing what fits. When in doubt, ask. If they are not sure, defer to community trends until or unless they tell you differently.

Uplifting Community Voices

In order to be an effective mental health provider, we must possess a certain drive to want to help our clients. This is not a line of work that we can go into halfheartedly. Every article, training, and book I write for clinicians comes from the assumption that those consuming what I create want to do right by those with whom we work. We are not simply trying to create value for shareholders; rather, we are actively making the world a better place, one client at a time.

Unfortunately, the voices of the communities we serve are often overlooked when it comes to researching and determining the best ways to support these individuals. Glenn Patrick Doyle, psychologist and trauma expert, says this about supporting trauma survivors: "The best minds in mental health aren't the docs. They're the trauma survivors who have had to figure out how to stay alive for years with virtually no help. Wanna learn how to psychologically survive under unfathomable stress? Talk to abuse survivors" (Doyle, 2020).

This is true not only for survivors of trauma, but all neurodivergent communities. Want to know how to support someone going through psychosis? Talk to the people who live with psychotic symptoms. Want to know the best way to support someone with a mood disorder? Talk to people with mood disorders. Want to know how to best support someone with ADHD? Talk to ADHD-ers. And so on. You cannot know what is best for someone without listening to them about their experience and their personal values, goals, and needs.

Uplifting community voices may sound simple but becomes complex in practice. Communities are comprised of individuals who each have their own unique experiences, perspectives, and opinions. Generalizations can be incredibly harmful, and while many communities may show trends (e.g., the overwhelming preference for identity-first language in the autistic community), individual preferences remain. Regardless of how many books and articles you have read, how many trainings you have attended, or how much research you have done, the individual in front of you will come with a history and perspective you have not seen before. We must listen to trends and center the voice of the individual in front of us for their treatment.

This additionally means that it is vital to listen to a *variety* of community voices. You cannot put together a committee on neurodivergence that has a single neurodivergent participant, and then pat yourself on the back for listening to the neurodivergent community. First, as we have already discussed, the concept of neurodivergence is far too broad for a single individual to represent everyone. Second, even within smaller neurodivergent communities, a sample size of one cannot possibly represent a variety of experiences and views.

The author of this book, for example, is autistic and a member of the autistic community. While this means that I can advocate for my community as a member, it *does not* mean that I am the voice of all autistic people. I represent exactly one autistic person: myself. No single aspect of my identity, other than the fact of my autism, is universal to all other autistic people. For instance, my support needs are relatively low (or at least I have the financial resources that allow me to present as having low support needs). An autistic person with more support needs will have a vastly different perspective and likely different opinions on autism advocacy and support. I am also white, which means that my interactions with the health care system and society as a whole are influenced by privilege that comes with my skin color. Within the autistic community, voices like mine are usually the most prominent. While autism is still incredibly stigmatized, and autistic people as a whole face discrimination, prejudice, and abuse from the system, my experience of these systems will be nothing like that of someone who does not have my privileges. If you only listen to my perspective, you are looking at a single brush stroke and overlooking almost the entire painting.

Even if you are neurodivergent, and even if you are a member of the specific neurodivergent community you serve, you still have a responsibility and obligation to seek out other community voices. This is especially true regarding voices with less privilege than your own.

Seek out a variety of perspectives. Continuing to use the autistic community as an example, seek out stores from BIPOC autistic individuals, those with varying support needs, AAC users, those who are nonspeaking or semispeaking, those who are unable to work full time, those with co-occurring disabilities and conditions, and others. Read this book, certainly, but read all of the other books also.

Apply this to every other neurodivergent community. Listen to community members from a variety of different backgrounds with various identities and life experiences. Unfortunately, traditional publishing tends to center a specific type of experience. However, the internet has created opportunities for anyone to have their voice heard. Forums, social media, blogs, podcasts, self-publishing, and other forms of expression make it so that you can find a huge variety of community voices if you are willing to look for them.

If you enter an online neurodivergent community, remember your place in relation to that community. If you are not neurodivergent (or you are not the specific type of neurodivergent being centered in that space), do not center your own voice. It is acceptable and recommended to sit back quietly and learn. When appropriate, you can certainly ask questions, but remember that you are not entitled to free emotional labor or a polite tone. Only go into spaces where you are welcome. For example, there is a Facebook group for nonautistic people who want to be able to ask questions about autism, and autistic community members provide responses to these questions. A nonautistic person wanting to learn how to best support an autistic loved one would be welcome here! There is another private group specifically for Black autistic adults to support each other navigating the world as Black and autistic. As a white autistic person, it would be inappropriate for me to enter that space, even if I just wanted to observe.

Neurodiversity-affirming mental health care is a journey, not a destination. You will never be done learning about these communities or listening to community members. Prepare yourself to continue learning, and be prepared to rectify your errors when you make mistakes. Be humble. Let go of defensiveness, especially if you say or do something that is harmful to a community member even if you did not intend harm, as many neurodivergent individuals have experienced harm, abuse, and trauma in the system. Spend enough time within the community, and you will witness (and likely cause) a trauma trigger at some point. Do your best to avoid causing harm, but be prepared to make amends if it happens.

At the same time, you might also carry your own trauma, or you might be on the receiving end of harm or abuse. You are allowed to set boundaries in these communities. Once on social media, someone told me that I was violating my ethics code because I have a policy of blocking users who repeatedly comment on my posts saying that I did not deserve to make a single penny for the work I do because if I really cared, my services would be free for anyone who needed them. And yes, this happens often enough that I have a policy around it.

Blocking someone who is harassing or verbally abusing you is not shutting down their voice. Those people are still allowed to make as many social media posts as they want about how all therapists are evil for taking a salary, and I am allowed to choose not to see those posts or let them show up on my page. And I hope anyone making such posts is able to access the support they need.

To sum up: listen to the communities you serve, and make efforts to listen to a variety of perspectives from these communities. Do not take up space or center yourself if you are there to listen and learn. Ask questions when appropriate, and stay humble. Set boundaries. And never stop learning.

CHAPTER 2

Neurodivergence and Mental Health: The DSM, Assessment and Diagnosis, and Therapy

Neurodivergent people have infinite experiences, presentations, and perspectives, and the one thing we all have in common is the fact that our brains do not fit into typical expectations for how we should function, think, communicate, and interact with the world around us. Every human being experiences challenges as well as strengths, and some traits can both cause challenges and reflect strengths depending on the context.

As a personal example, my ability to hyperfocus allows me to complete projects efficiently, but it also causes me to forget to attend to my body's needs. I am sure my editor likes to hear that I have put out another 10,000 words on a manuscript, but it is not healthy to forget to drink water for 10 straight hours. I know many people who have a strong desire to help others (a positive quality and one that is essential in living in a cooperative society) who burn themselves out because they did not know when to say "no."

Some qualities are challenges regardless of the context. Most would agree that executive dysfunction, catatonia, panic attacks, and so on cannot be reframed as strengths. This is important to remember, as neurodiversity-affirming care often involves strengths-based work. Strengths-based therapy is an approach to mental health treatment that focuses on the individual's inherent abilities and strengths rather than their deficits. This can help build confidence and autonomy, and it can assist in reframing traditionally pathologized traits. For instance, autistic children are often pathologized for playing with their toys the wrong way when they line things up. A strengths-based approach might emphasize the child's dexterity or organization rather than trying to teach the child to play correctly. Another example of this can occur with learning disorders. For some, their academic difficulties come from the way the material is presented in a mainstream school setting. When permitted to learn in the way that comes naturally to their brain, many of these individuals thrive and even excel. Individuals diagnosed with oppositional defiant or conduct disorders are labeled defiant or resistant to authority, and at the same time, every revolution in history is led by people who were defiantly willing to resist authority.

At the same time, if we become too focused on finding the hidden strength associated with a trait, we may find ourselves engaging in toxic positivity. Toxic positivity is when we insist on only feeling or expressing positive emotions all the time, thus invalidating or repressing negative emotions. No one is happy every second of every day, and unpleasant emotions have their place. Anger can be motivating; fear lets us know we may be in danger; grief reminds us how much we loved what we lost.

Additionally, toxic positivity can mean insisting that *every* trait has underlying strengths when this sometimes is not the case or does not reflect an individual's reality. Both ADHD and autism have been described as superpowers because of the hidden strengths associated with these neurodivergences. Although many ADHD-ers and autistic individuals do identify strengths directly resulting from their neurodivergence, most also identify that there are ways that their neurodivergence causes difficulty and are disabling. Sometimes the disability is due to the structure of society, and other times the disability would be present regardless of social norms and structures. In other words, we do not want to overlook the ways that neurodivergence can be disabling. Even if an individual has no personal strengths that they can identify, they are still a human being, and their worth or value is not determined by whether or not we can identify strengths or reframe their difficulties in a positive way.

Their worth or value is not determined by whether or not we can identify strengths or reframe their difficulties in a positive way."

On the other hand, the traditional medical model goes to the opposite extreme of toxic positivity. Neurodivergence is framed as an inferiority, something to be either tolerated or fixed but not something to be supported. This is why many neurodivergent communities have faced eugenics. It is also why many neurodivergent individuals who are able to mask their neurodivergent traits or function under a capitalistic system are invalidated if they seek an official diagnosis or support.

The *Diagnostic and Statistical Manual of Mental Disorders* (DSM) is built on the medical model, pathologizing neurodivergence. Additionally, many diagnoses require that symptoms cause difficulties that are clearly observable to other people, such as personality disorders, learning disorders, ADHD, and autism. The clinical terms for many types of neurodivergence are not affirming and are linked to discrimination and mistreatment, and many neurodivergent communities have rejected these terms. For instance, research shows that individuals with a diagnosis of borderline personality disorder experience significant stigma and discrimination, including mistreatment by medical and mental health professionals, as a direct result of the diagnosis appearing in their medical history (Stiles et al., 2023). Similarly, many in the autistic community reject the clinical term autism spectrum disorder, as they conceptualize autism as a neurotype that is not inherently disordered.

As we have discussed, affirming providers honor the language preferences of the communities we serve and take steps to mitigate the harm these individuals face at the hands of the medical system. At the same time, we operate within the system as it exists, and a big part of our job is helping clients access appropriate support. Sometimes, this means using pathologizing clinical terminology, biased diagnostic criteria, or flawed assessment measures. The sections in this chapter explore the issues within the DSM and other components of the mental health system, as well as how we can navigate this system in a neurodiversity-affirming way.

Neurodivergence in the DSM

The DSM includes many forms of neurodivergence. It is not an exhaustive list of ways that an individual can be neurodivergent; Down syndrome, epilepsy, cerebral palsy, and other neurodivergences are not included in the DSM. This section looks at the language and conceptualization of the forms of neurodivergence included in the DSM, but it is important to remember that not every neurodivergent person meets criteria for a diagnosis listed in the DSM.

The medical model used to develop the DSM makes the text inherently pathologizing and nonaffirming. Of course, having consistent, agreed-upon clinical terms for things can streamline understanding an individual's possible challenges and support needs, and it can make it easier for treatment teams to be on the same page regarding the client's presentation. At the same time, though, the DSM is designed to identify what it refers to as mental disorders. While some might conceptualize their neurodivergence as a disorder, for many in neurodivergent communities, the term disorder is itself stigmatizing and misleading, as it implies that the person with the diagnosis is less than or inferior.

Misdiagnosis

The wording of many diagnoses listed in the DSM leaves room for clinician bias and misinterpretation, as well as misdiagnosis. In an interview with this author, Hannah Owens (2024), a schizoaffective social worker who agreed to be interviewed for this book, shared that she had "a long road" to finding her diagnosis. She was initially diagnosed with major depressive disorder, which was later updated to bipolar I disorder with psychotic features. Ten years after receiving that diagnosis, she learned that she actually has schizoaffective disorder, bipolar type. Receiving a correct diagnosis helped her receive the support she needed, and it took multiple providers over a decade to reach that point.

Unfortunately, misdiagnosis is common for many neurodivergent communities. Ayano et al. (2021) found that approximately 39% of clients with disorders considered severe according to the DSM were misdiagnosed before learning their true diagnosis. In fact, 75% of those with schizoaffective disorder (like Owens) were misdiagnosed. More than half of those with major depressive disorder were initially misdiagnosed, and almost one-quarter of those with schizophrenia were initially misdiagnosed.

These numbers show glaring problems in the field. Although a client's diagnostic category does not ultimately determine their needs or serve as a be all and end all for treatment planning, it is an important starting point in helping the client understand themselves and their needs. Until these diagnostic issues can be addressed, we are doing our clients a disservice.

Distress or Impairment

Another limitation to the DSM is that many listed neurodivergences require that "the symptoms cause clinically significant distress or impairment in social, occupational, or other important areas of functioning." It is not technically essential that the neurodivergent traits cause impairments in functioning if clinically significant distress is evident; however, this is a vague term. Each person exists within their own brain, and we do not have the power to enter into someone else's mind and experience the world from their perspective. Many default to the assumption that their experience is typical, as it is the only experience they know.

For example, aphantasia is the experience of not being able to visualize things in one's mind. An internet search will bring up hundreds of forum posts of individuals learning that other people can conjure images with their thoughts. These individuals went their entire lives not imagining pictures and assuming that no one could, until learning that their experience was not typical. (Aphantasia is not a diagnosis on its own in the DSM, though autistic individuals and people with acquired neurodivergence through a traumatic brain injury experience aphantasia at higher rates than the general population.)

If my perspective is that my experience is the norm, I might not recognize and accurately label my distress as clinically significant. In that case, providers might also not recognize my distress because I am unable to communicate to them that I am experiencing something that is not part of typical human experience. After all, everyone is distressed sometimes!

Additionally, not every neurodivergent individual experiences clinically significant distress. Some simply do not experience distress as a result of their neurodivergence, which is valid, and some would experience distress if they were not in a supportive and accommodating environment. For instance, many neurodivergences like ADHD, autism, learning disorders, and communication disorders have a strong genetic component, and many members of the same family will share traits or diagnoses. Sometimes, a child may not appear impaired in an obvious way because their caregivers and other family members are simply meeting their needs appropriately. This is a wonderful thing, as every person (neurodivergent or neurotypical) deserves to have their needs met, but it can create a barrier to diagnosis when the individual does not appear to be struggling enough to require support. Sometimes, a neurodivergent child whose needs are appropriately met in the home struggles significantly when they enter a school system with very different expectations. Unfortunately, these children are often denied accommodations before they exhibit distress or impairment in the classroom. We could avoid stress and trauma if we could recognize the neurodivergence and provide adequate support before the child struggles, falls behind, or experiences trauma at the hands of the school system, but current diagnostic criteria technically prohibit this.

If clinically significant distress cannot be documented, many neurodivergent diagnoses in the DSM can still be diagnosed if impairment in functioning is evident. Although an individual might self-report functioning issues (e.g., "I struggle with remembering or getting myself to attend to my hygiene" or "I can't manage my finances independently"), functional labels have significant limitations and problems. First, they emphasize the individual's impact on other people rather than their own support needs. Second, it invalidates the experience of someone with low support needs, as someone who is high-masking or can camouflage their neurodivergent traits is considered higher functioning and therefore not needing support. Third, the ranking of neurodivergent people by functioning level creates a hierarchy with the higher functioning individuals deemed better than lower functioning individuals. Someone's value is not determined by their ability to complete tasks independently. Similarly, higher functioning is a label often attributed to someone who is able to work full time. This emphasis on participation in a capitalist system perpetuates systems that oppress disabled communities and individuals.

Some red flags that an individual might be experiencing more distress than what is obvious at first glance include:

- A client who works a full-time job but reports that they are completely drained after work, do not have hobbies, and spend days off simply recharging from work because they do not have the bandwidth for anything more.
- A client whose skills get them by, but they report taking

more time or effort than their peers to accomplish the same things.

- A client who gets by but has a built-in support system at home that allows them to compensate due to existing supports.
- A client who reports that things that they used to be able to do seem to be getting more challenging.

For neurodivergent individuals, "burnout" refers to when the individual reaches a point of extreme exhaustion, reduced ability to cope, and a loss of skills they had previously mastered. Because neurodivergent individuals experience increased stress from living in a world not designed for them, and many go without adequate support, many constantly stretch themselves past their limit. Over time, this wears them down and can cause burnout. Typically, burnout is long-term and requires rest and space for recovery. It can reoccur as well if preventative measures are not taken.

Note that burnout can seem to emerge suddenly, so if someone is beginning to have difficulty with things that they previously felt were easy, quick intervention is essential to prevent decompensation.

Other Limitations of the DSM

Requirement for distress and impairment are not the only issues with the DSM's conceptualization of neurodivergence. As noted, although there is a benefit to having a unified, consistent system for crafting a starting point for individual needs, the DSM has significant limitations. While many neurodivergent individuals express relief at receiving a diagnosis, gaining a sense of community, and getting a better understanding of how their brain works, the current DSM has potential to cause harm.

Although the committees that created the DSM indicate that they strove to create consistent, clear diagnostic criteria, there is significant variability in diagnosis. A client who has been evaluated by multiple professionals often has contradictory diagnoses—for instance, bipolar disorder cannot be diagnosed alongside major depressive disorder because the bipolar diagnosis accounts for the major depressive episodes, and yet many clients have both diagnoses indicated in their charts because different providers disagreed on which mood disorder best described their symptoms (Young, 2016).

Additionally, a number of diagnoses listed in the DSM indicate that they cannot co-occur with other specific diagnoses. For example, the DSM-5-TR (the most recent revision) indicates that one individual cannot be diagnosed with both reactive attachment disorder and autism spectrum disorder. Reactive attachment disorder is a trauma disorder that develops in early childhood and prevents the child from forming emotional bonds to other people or experiencing empathetic feelings. Autistic children are at higher risk for trauma and abuse compared to nonautistic children, and there is no evidence that an autistic child cannot develop an attachment disorder, but the current DSM indicates that it is impossible to meet criteria for both. A particular danger to this kind of rule out is that an autistic child with a reactive attachment disorder diagnosis may face barriers to an accurate diagnosis regarding their autism if their provider believes that it is impossible for an individual to be autistic if they have another diagnosis.

Past editions of the DSM indicated that an individual could

not meet the diagnostic criteria for both ADHD and autism. Although this did not stop some providers from assigning both diagnoses to the same client, or diagnosing a client already diagnosed as ADHD or autistic with the other diagnosis, a provider who closely followed the diagnostic criteria could prevent client from accurately labeling and understanding their neurodivergence.

Many mental health professionals have criticized the DSM and the committee that oversaw its development for prioritizing personal opinions and bias over hard scientific research. In fact, many members who contributed to the DSM have been criticized for being compromised ethically and making changes to the final version of the text, basing these changes on personal agendas rather than what is best for the field of psychology and the clients we serve (Young, 2016).

Every version of the DSM has received criticism for its limitations and bias. As a text developed by and for predominantly white, Western populations, diagnostic criteria are based predominantly on how conditions tend to appear with this specific population, leading to higher rates of misdiagnosis. Much of the diagnostic criteria additionally have gender bias. For example, "inappropriate sexually seductive or provocative behavior" is still listed as part of the diagnostic criteria for histrionic personality disorder. A provider determining whether or not a client's sexual behavior is "inappropriate" is likely to be biased by that clinician's personal beliefs and values around sex, which are not universal.

Additionally, many cultures have different experiences of neurodivergence, and Western bias in the DSM leads to pathologizing culturally appropriate behavior. For example, in the United States, individuals with schizophrenia and other psychotic disorders tend to experience anxiety-provoking, scary hallucinations, while people with schizophrenia in many African countries hear neutral or even enjoyable voices instead (Luhrmann, 2014). The DSM not only approaches neurodivergence from an inherently pathological lens, but it does so in a way that is culturally uninformed and often xenophobic and racist.

Allegations of Financial Conflict of Interest

In 2022, the DSM-5-TR revision was published, the most current version of the DSM at the time this book was written. The DSM is regularly updated, supposedly with the intent of ensuring that the diagnoses listed and criteria for those diagnoses reflect current research about presentation and appropriate treatment recommendations.

Since neurodevelopmental differences, mental health diagnoses, and neurocognitive conditions are not directly observable and quantifiable in the same way that genetic diagnoses and various medical conditions are, there is room for interpretation and debate when developing the categories in the DSM. Unfortunately, the discussions and decisions around inclusion, exclusion, and modification of existing criteria are left up to a task force who are the ultimate decision makers. While public information is not available about each task force member's neurotype and any diagnoses (or lack thereof), it is highly unlikely that this task force has representation of the communities being discussed. Of course, every person has the right to privacy and may choose not to disclose their neurotype publicly, but those in the role of making decisions that can allow or prevent access to support should be part of the communities they are discussing (Hoekstra, Girma, Tekola, & Yenus, 2018).

Lack of representation is not the only problem with the DSM task force, however. An analysis of compensation received by task force members for the DSM-5-TR showed that 60% received payments from industry, meaning that they had financial conflicts of interest that may have impacted or impaired their ability to make objective decisions. Additionally, 33% of task force members publicly reported these payments, meaning that 27% received financial incentive but did not disclose the possible conflict of interest (Davis et al., 2024).

In other words, these financial conflicts of interest may have determined certain decisions made about the DSM and the diagnostic criteria included and excluded. This calls into question the validity of the document as a whole, and yet providers rely on the DSM in informing their client's symptoms, presentation, and access to supportive services. Any provider who bills insurance *has* to assign an approved diagnosis in order to be reimbursed for services rendered, and any client who seeks supportive services *has* to have such a diagnosis in their medical record in order to access those services.

Essentially, with the system as it currently stands, we cannot be effective providers without utilizing the DSM in our practice, but the DSM is rife with problems and limitations. As such, we must be mindful and cautious in our use of this document.

Navigating the DSM as a Neurodiversity-Affirming Provider

Despite its significant limitations and issues, the DSM is the current bible in the fields of psychology and psychiatry. In the United States, many clients can only access mental health care if they can use their health insurance to offset the cost. In order to bill insurance, the provider must submit a diagnostic code from the DSM or insurance will not pay for therapy.

Neurodivergent individuals with certain support needs—including, but not limited to, financial support because they are unable to work enough to support themselves, live-in or regular in-home care from professionals, or school or workplace accommodations—must have a documented diagnosis in order to qualify. The systems and processes of securing these supports, resources, benefits, and accommodations are not straightforward or simple at all, and many who have the right to these supports are often denied for arbitrary reasons. However, in order to even start the process, they must have a diagnosis and documentation of traits and symptoms according to the DSM diagnostic criteria.

A neurodiversity-affirming provider operating in a flawed system will struggle to navigate and hold conflicting truths: "The DSM is significantly flawed, and the diagnostic criteria I assign to my client are pathologizing and often harmful," and "Refusing to name a diagnosis can create additional barriers to my client receiving the support they need," are two statements that are simultaneously and equally valid and true. If every affirming provider refused to comply with a flawed system, this would leave our clients only to providers who are not neurodiversity-affirming, who are more likely to cause harm and trauma to our clients. Thus, many providers choose to operate within the system as it exists.

As noted, neurodiversity-affirming mental health care involves collaboration and respecting the client's knowledge as an expert in their own life. This means that we are transparent with our clients about our process, including systemic issues and problems within our field. When the system requires non-affirming language or assessments in order for a client to receive needed support, have a conversation with your client. Reaffirm to them your commitment to providing neurodiversity-affirming care as well as your commitment to helping them access the support they need. Explain your concerns about the system and what nonaffirming things are required from you in order to help them access what they need. Tell them that you are committed to helping them, which will mean that you operate within the system as you need to and simultaneously remain committed to being neurodiversity-affirming.

This may not be a one-and-done conversation. Clients may sit with the information and have follow-up questions later. We must always be open to questions or concerns by our clients, and we have to remember that informed consent is ongoing. The client has the right to ask more questions, gather more information, or change their mind at any time. In this way, we collaborate with them in determining what is best for their mental health care and for their lives. By providing them with accurate and appropriate information, we can empower them to make the best decisions for their life.

Not only will this honesty help clients understand our clinical decisions, but also this will prevent misunderstanding in the future. Clients have the right to view their records and see what we have written or shared about them to other providers and in their medical chart. If I tell a client that I am neurodiversity-affirming, and then use nonaffirming language in order to operate within the system, but I do not communicate this to the client, they might view the records and believe I was dishonest with them about my commitment to affirming care. They might think that I deceived them. Explaining my decision making can reassure them of my stance and approach to their care.

Some examples of how we can discuss these things with our clients include:

- "You've shared that you need (service) to help you with (goal). I want to help you get the support you need. As you know, the system is incredibly flawed, and those who decide whether or not you can access these services have specific rules. If I do not carefully follow their rules, they can deny you the support that you need. Let's go over the requirements together. I want to make sure I answer any questions you have about the process."

- "Because I am committed to providing care that is affirming and has a social justice focus, I have taken time to learn about the limitations and problems with many psychological assessments. There is research showing that this assessment has racial bias. At the same time, it can give us some information about the things you have described to me and give more evidence about the supports you need. If you are comfortable, I will make sure I interpret the results keeping these biases in mind so that we can use the beneficial information to help you. Is that something you are open to?"

- "We have talked about your preferred language around your neurodivergence. I want you to know that I take your preferences seriously, and I recognize that you have the best perception of your own experience. As much as possible, I will use that language when talking to you or when documenting. So you're aware, the technical clinical terms are (relevant clinical terms). I know these do not reflect your experience, and I know that you do not agree with the people who determine clinical terminology. When I write your report, I have to use (relevant clinical terms) in order for you to have official documentation of your neurodivergence. Sometimes the language that we know is best is not what has to be documented for people to get the support they need. I want to make sure we have an open conversation about this so that you know what to expect and so that I can answer any questions you have."

In addition to this transparency, it is important to use affirming language whenever possible. For instance, a provider in private practice who has the freedom to format their progress notes in whatever way they see fit can use affirming language in these notes even if they have to use pathologizing language in a treatment summary or report to be submitted for disability services. Examples of affirming language include:

- While the diagnostic impression has to include the accepted clinical terms, providers can still use community terms elsewhere in documentation. For instance, a provider can write autism spectrum disorder in the diagnosis but refer to the client as autistic elsewhere in their report.
- Providers can choose to describe support needs rather than functioning labels.
- When using assessment measures that contain bias, providers can document these biases and note that they only used the assessment because it was required.

- Providers can include a note stating the client's preferred
  language, indicate what clinical terms that language
  refers to, and incorporate preferred language throughout
  the report.

Advocacy and Striving for Change

While there are moments when we have to operate within problematic systems in order to help our clients receive appropriate
supports and services in the short term, the long-term goal of the
neurodiversity-affirming movement is to break down these systems and remove the need to operate within nonaffirming parameters. In addition to providing clients support in the moment, we
can also advocate for systems changes. Although we are required
to follow laws and systems in our practice, we are not required to
remain complicit.

For instance, several states in America have autism registries. Exactly as they sound, an autism registry is a government
list of autistic residents. The registries have different rules and reg-
ulations, and North Dakota law NDCC 23-01-41 requires that any
provider who diagnoses autism to submit a multiple page form
including extensive identifying and personal information about
any autistic client to be included in a database maintained by the
health department for "complete epidemiologic surveys, research
and analysis, and provide services to individuals with ASD"
(North Dakota Health and Human Services, n.d.).

Naturally, any neurodiversity-affirming provider will be
opposed to putting their clients on a government list based on
their diagnosis. At the same time, noncompliant providers can be

fined up to $1,000 per client they did not report and can lose their license to practice. If the provider is licensed in multiple states, even if they have not violated any laws in those other states, they can lose their other licenses if their North Dakota license is revoked.

Any neurodiversity-affirming provider will be opposed to putting their clients on a government list based on their diagnosis."

Due to this legal requirement, a neurodiversity-affirming provider who can diagnose autism may refuse to conduct evaluations in North Dakota. They might encourage clients to travel to another state to get their diagnosis if this is feasible and if the client does not require services that would involve disclosing the diagnosis to a North Dakota provider. Or they might incorporate the database into their informed consent form and comply, knowing their clients made a decision based on accurate information and agreed to being involved in the database. Provider also might refuse to comply and hope they are not caught. All of these options acknowledge the systems issue and take steps toward transparency and fostering autonomy in our clients.

While this addresses the day-to-day operations within a harmful and nonaffirming system, whichever choice the provider makes leaves the system intact. Neurodiversity-affirming care goes beyond the day-to-day and individual office visits, and it is not enough to simply be affirming in our own practice. We must actively advocate for systemic changes to make the world as a whole neurodiversity-affirming, and not just our appointments. This will be discussed in more depth in the final section of this book.

Assessment and Diagnosis of Neurodivergence

Now that we have discussed how the DSM conceptualizes many neurodivergences, we can further discuss the tools and assessment measures used to identify when someone is neurodivergent and what diagnosis or diagnoses fit their presentation. Again, the system as it presently exists typically requires an official or medical diagnosis of neurodivergence in order for an individual to receive occupational support, housing, disability income, and other supportive services. Thus, we must operate within a system that is not affirming and can often be actively harmful to our clients.

When it comes to defining best practice in assessing and diagnosing, there are two competing ideals. On the one hand, many methods have a strong evidence base and research backing. In our efforts to provide the best standard of care, it makes sense to seek out methods and measures that have been proven effective. But what does this mean? Much of academic research is based on a narrow population, often white, male, and middle class. Additionally, very little of the available research takes a neurodiversity-affirming approach. A measure might appear to have strong evidence backing, but a deeper exploration of that research reveals significant concerns.

The Minnesota Multiphasic Personality Inventory (MMPI), for instance, is a staple in psychodiagnostics batteries for many different neurodivergences, including personality disorders, mood disorders, and psychotic disorders. However, for decades, the MMPI has been claimed to be racially biased the MMPI (Prichard & Rosenblatt, 1980; Schapiro, Ellis, & Golden, 2023).

Although newer editions have attempted to address this bias and have demonstrated progress, even the MMPI-3 (the newest version at the time of writing) continues to show higher anger scores in Latinx respondents (Shumaker et al., 2022) and higher paranoia scores in Black respondents (Dixon et al., 2023) compared to white respondents.

At the same time, MMPI-3 scales can validate client experiences by showing that they have support needs and challenges that go beyond typical expectations and life difficulties. Additionally, some clients might be required to complete an MMPI-3 as a condition of their disability claim, parole, child custody claim, or other reason. Vetting the research and interpreting the test results through a neurodiversity-affirming and culturally competent lens can get the client the support that they need while again operating within a flawed system.

Diagnostic Interviews

For most providers, an evaluation or therapeutic relationship starts with a diagnostic interview, also known as an intake. Although there are standard questions and components of a diagnostic or intake interview, each provider has their own style and the freedom to structure these appointments in the way that works best for them.

There is no one way to conduct a diagnostic interview that is inherently superior to all others. Providers will be most effective when leaning into the approach that plays to their strengths, and clients will have different needs and preferences when it comes to engaging. We need providers with all different styles in order to fit each client's needs. However, there are some approaches to these interviews that can be harmful, especially to neurodivergent clients.

Below are some general tips for what *not* to do in a neurodiversity-affirming intake appointment:

1. *Assuming dishonesty.* Unfortunately, many providers approach evaluations assuming that a client is going to exaggerate their symptoms and difficulties or try to deceive the provider. You cannot effectively build rapport with a client if you come from an assumption that they are lying to you.

2. *Assuming unmasking.* Masking, by definition, causes a client to present in a way that shows few neurodivergent traits. This means that a provider might not directly witness some of the traits a client experiences, and it may appear that they are not demonstrating experiences they describe in the session. Remember that masking is often an adaptive behavior developed in response to being penalized for authenticity! You cannot assume that a client will feel comfortable unmasking the first time they meet you, or that they have even begun the process of learning how to unmask.

3. *Trying to trigger behaviors.* Sometimes, a provider will want to directly observe certain behaviors that a client is not showing in the intake session and might attempt to bring out that behavior. Clients have shared stories of evaluators attempting to induce a meltdown during an intake in order to see what the client is like in this moment. It is inappropriate and unethical to deliberately cause a client severe distress, especially in a first session when you likely do not have the rapport established to support the client in de-escalating. No, you do not need to see the behavior to believe the client's experience.

4. *Arguing with the client about their experience.* Similar to assuming a client is being dishonest, many providers come from the assumption that the client might be trying to tell the truth but has fundamentally misunderstood their experience. Clients rarely develop trust in response to arguments with and invalidation of their description of their experience.

Conversely, some general tips for making diagnostic interviews affirming:

1. *Understand the power dynamic.* Although a neurodiversity-affirming provider approaches mental health care from a place of equality with the client, acknowledging that they are the expert on their own experience, there is an inherent power dynamic to any appointment. The provider has the power to diagnose, deny a diagnosis, or misdiagnose. They can modify the client's medical record to reflect their perception of the visit, impacting the individual's future access to care. By acknowledging and understanding this power dynamic, providers can avoid harm to the client due to our position.

2. *Follow the client's lead.* As clients are the experts on their personal life experience, following their lead in an intake can result in gathering robust and extensive information. This additionally builds rapport, making the client more likely to unmask and show their authentic self in the appointment.

3. *Be transparent.* Clearly explain to the client what your role is. If you are a therapist who cannot diagnose certain neu-

rodivergences, let the client know that. If you are conducting a diagnostic evaluation, detail your diagnostic process.
Encourage questions, and answer as comprehensively as
you are able.

4. *Prioritize emotional safety.* Clients who have had harmful
experiences with other providers might have increased difficulty trusting new providers. Be patient, and make efforts
to create an emotionally safe place for the client to open
up to you.

5. *Collaborate.* Remember, the provider is the expert on
the mental health field, and the client is the expert on
their unique personal experience. When we approach
intakes from a place of collaboration, we are likely to
get better information about the client, their needs, and
their experience.

Collateral Interviews and Self-Report

There are many circumstances in which a provider will seek collateral information about a client when formulating a diagnosis or
determining the individual's needs. These circumstances include,
but are not limited to:

- A client is either below the age of majority or has a court-
appointed guardian, and the provider is legally required to
involve the individual in this process.
- A young client is not able to provide firsthand information
about their experience, traits, or symptoms due to their
developmental level.
- A client struggles with perception and reality testing, and a

provider needs to gather information about symptoms and needs that the client is unable to directly provide.

- A support person or caregiver might have insight into a client's support needs.
- A client has a memory issue, and the provider needs more history information in order to confidently confirm or rule out a diagnosis.
- A client suspects a diagnosis that requires information about early developmental history that they do not personally recall.
- Observational data can inform how symptoms and traits manifest in the client's day-to-day life.
- A client specifically asks a provider to conduct collateral interviews.

At the same time, there are circumstances where it may be inappropriate or even impossible to gather collateral information:

- A client who was adopted in early childhood who has no contact with their family of origin, and records about early development do not exist or cannot be accessed.
- A client who does not have contact with their family for safety reasons.
- A client whose parents are deceased.
- A client who is isolated and does not have a close friend or partner to complete observer rating forms.
- A client who is very private and does not want to involve anyone else in their evaluation.

Certainly, this might limit the conclusions a provider feels confident drawing from the information provided. For example, ADHD, autism, learning disorders, and intellectual disability all have diagnostic criteria that require onset of neurodivergence in early childhood. If a client does not have memory of their early childhood, and they are unable to provide collateral information about their early developmental period, the provider might not be able to confidently conclude whether or not traits were present at that time. Testing measures and a thorough analysis of available information can be sufficient if the provider has appropriate diagnostic training.

Of course, some providers might feel that they cannot accurately determine certain diagnoses if the client is unable to provide access to collateral information. In this case, it is appropriate for the provider to operate within their scope of practice. We have an ethical obligation to only practice within our competency! In this case, the provider should include this requirement in their informed consent. Accepting an assessment, charging the client for services, and then indicating that a diagnostic conclusion cannot be reached because the client did not provide collateral information is unethical. Although, obviously, our consent forms must contain legally mandated language, we can explain these forms to patients along the following lines, depending on the provider's own policies and scope of practice:

- "Because (diagnosis) can include difficulty with perception or communicating one's internal experience in a clear way, I require clients to allow me to consult with someone close with them to gather information about how their traits appear to the people around them. You are the one who lives in your brain, so you know your own experience best, and also (diagnosis) can make it difficult to perceive the world around us, so it helps me to be able to get collateral information. Not everyone has someone they trust to provide this information, but this is information that I need in order to confidently confirm whether or not you have (diagnosis). Because of that, if you don't have someone who can provide collateral information, I will not be able to confirm if you meet criteria for (diagnosis)."

- "Part of the criteria for (diagnosis) is that it starts early on in your life. Because of that, I need to try and talk to someone who knew you when you were very young, like a parent or older sibling. If you don't have someone you feel comfortable having me talk to, we can use the information you can recall, but that might limit the conclusions I can make about your neurodivergence. If you do not want me to talk to anyone about your history, we can move forward with only the information you are able to tell me as long as you understand and are okay with the fact that that could limit the results."

- "Part of the criteria for (diagnosis) is that it starts early on in your life. Because of that, I need to try and talk to someone who knew you when you were very young, like a parent or older sibling. If you don't have someone you feel comfortable having me talk to, I unfortunately will not be able to confidently determine if you meet criteria for (diagnosis)."

- "When I assess for (diagnosis), some of the measures I use have observer rating forms. That means that someone who knows you well fills out the form so that we can see what your traits look like to someone close to you. When it comes to deciding whether or not you meet criteria for (diagnosis), your perspective is the most important. You are the one who lives inside your brain, so you know your experience best. At the same time, that additional information helps me see how your traits impact how you experience the world around you. I can complete the assessment if you aren't comfortable with anyone doing the observer form, but it might limit what conclusions I can make or what recommendations I can provide. Is that acceptable to you?"

Additionally, some providers who gather collateral information about a client's experience before determining a diagnosis will rely on the collateral information more heavily than on the client's self-report of their own experience. This comes from the assumption that the client is either deliberately misleading the provider or that the client is not competent to speak to their own experience. It additionally does not account for masking behavior. For example, many ADHD rating scales have observer rating forms, and clinicians might decline to assign a diagnosis to a client whose self-report is consistent with ADHD, but whose observer scores are lower than the client's self-report. If the client is proficient in masking, though, it would make sense that the observer cannot speak to the symptom severity that the client experiences.

Overall, collateral information can have its place in determining a client's diagnosis and neurodivergence. However, an overemphasis on collateral information can be a barrier to service access if a client is unable to provide this information or does not feel comfortable involving third parties in their treatment. Additionally, we must remember that the client (and *only* the client) is the expert on their internal experiences. Observers may be able to speak to difficulties the client experiences or to their behavior, but these observations will have limitations, as no one can climb into someone else's brain and experience the world from their perspective.

Assessment and Gender

As noted previously, much research on neurodivergent diagnoses that appears in the DSM is disproportionately reflective of the experience of white, cisgendered males. Anyone who does not fall into this identity category is at increased risk for misdiagnosis, including not being granted any diagnosis at all following testing. Clearly, this does not mean that no diagnosis is present, but simply that the existing measures do not adequately encompass the variety of experiences and presentation of neurodivergent individuals of all identities.

Some measures have an additional limitation that creates a barrier to receiving an evaluation based on gender, however. These measures cannot be scored unless the client or evaluator indicates either male or female gender. This overlooks the experiences of anyone who does not identify with a binary gender category, and the research behind this scoring overwhelmingly focuses on cisgender experiences, creating validity concerns for trans clients even if they identify with a binary gender.

Some assessment creators have updated their scoring criteria to address this. The Millon Clinical Multiaxial Inventory, Fourth Edition (MCMI-IV), for example, previously could not be scored without a binary gender. In response to feedback, the test developers added a third category, "Other." Similarly, when the Conners Adult ADHD Rating Scales 2nd Edition (CAARS2) was released, evaluators could score the measure without inputting any gender at all. However, at the time of this writing, there are still many common assessment measures that do not have nonbinary gender options for scoring. The Social Responsiveness Scale, Second Edition (SRS-2), is one of the few norm-referenced assessments that can be used to identify autism in adults and continues to require a binary gender before the assessment can be administered. As autistic individuals are more likely to be transgender and/or nonbinary than those who are not autistic (Warrier et al., 2020), this is a particularly important issue for the test creators to address.

(As an aside, one way that neurodiversity-affirming providers can advocate for our clients is to make a point of complaining to test developers every time this comes up in our practice. As we may not have the option to simply not use these measures and still offer this service, we can be the ones who pressure these companies into updating their services to better reflect our clients' diverse identities.)

Cognitive Assessments (Intelligence Quotient Tests)

Commonly known as IQ tests, cognitive assessments are a form of standardized tests that purport to speak to an individual's intelligence. However, like other standardized testing procedures, IQ tests have well-documented racial bias, which has been proven through decades of research (Epps, 1973). In fact, modern standardized tests (including IQ tests) are based on research from Carl Bringham, who openly published his belief that Black people have lower intelligence than white people and sought to prove superior white intelligence (Walker, 2021).

In short: IQ tests are inherently racist.

Additionally, there is disagreement within the field of psychology regarding what intelligence is and how to define this concept. In fact, the professor who taught this author how to administer an IQ test stated in a lecture that the only thing we have been able to agree on is that "intelligence" is the thing measured by an intelligence test. Certainly, IQ scores can correlate with things like education level, employment, and other things, but these are not definitive. Many who score highly on IQ tests experience challenges with thriving in society as it currently stands. Additionally, some who obtain lower IQ scores go on to perform well academically and achieve career success.

(Caveat: career success is not an indication of personal worth or value, but it is something that is valued in society and often used as a measure of functioning, which is why it is used as an example here.)

In other words, IQ tests have limited benefit and often do not speak to an individual's support needs, in addition to the documented racial biases. Despite these issues, many agencies and organizations require that a client have an IQ test on record in order to receive services. As noted in the previous section about language usage, sometimes a provider will use language that is not neurodiversity-affirming if that language is required for the client to receive appropriate support. This falls under the same umbrella of operating within a problematic system as it exists in order to provide individuals with the best care and support, while working to dismantle those systems when we are able.

Another important consideration is the opinions of neurodivergent communities. For instance, a diagnosis of intellectual disability requires an IQ score at or below 70, and this particular assessment measure is required in helping someone achieve an accurate diagnosis. Again, we work within the system as it exists to support our clients while naming the ways in which that system is insufficient and problematic. Some intellectually disabled advocates (advocates with lived experience, those who are intellectually disabled themselves) have pointed out that there is a utility to recognizing the concept of intelligence in determining their support needs and ensuring that those needs are appropriately met.

Essentially, the field of psychology needs to find a way to determine support needs for individuals with intellectual disabilities that does not have the racist roots and ongoing bias of intelligence tests. At the same time, we must not overlook the needs of this community, and we must ensure that we provide assessment options that allow these individuals to access appropriate support.

Functional/Adaptive Behavioral Assessments

A functional or adaptive behavioral assessment is a psychological testing measure that evaluates an individual's ability to perform certain tasks and thrive in certain environments. It will look at things like an individual's ability to maintain appropriate self-care, hygiene, and safety independently, their ability to manage finances, and their ability to form and maintain relationships.

As with many psychological assessments currently available, these measures often contain language that is pathologizing and nonaffirming. Many neurodivergent communities have rejected the notion of functioning labels because these labels emphasize the individual's impact on other people rather than their own needs. At the same time, the labels can provide valuable information about support needs. As with IQ tests, before providing support, many supportive services require that the client have a functional assessment on record.

Many functional assessments provide norm-referenced scores about an individual's ability to function in various environments, indicating the areas in which they would most benefit from support. They additionally often provide age equivalencies, which many neurodivergent individuals find harmful because they literally infantilize the client, comparing adults to children. Telling someone, "You likely have a difficult time with things like preparing meals or coping with stress compared to other people," is much more helpful than telling them, "Your functioning is equivalent to that of approximately a 6-year-old." For adult clients, this comparison to actual children can be weaponized to deny autonomy, something every neurodiversity-affirming professional strives to prevent. To create an affirming future for the field of psychology, these types of assessments need significant overhaul in language and framing of deficits in order to provide support to clients without denying autonomy or infantilizing them.

Furthermore, most adaptive behavioral assessments rely on observer reports. While individuals with higher support needs might benefit from caregiver input, some of these assessments do not provide a self-report option. This will be discussed in more depth in the next section, but abusive caregivers might overreport deficits in order to maintain control of an individual's choices, finances, or other aspects of their life.

While these assessments can have utility in informing support needs, they also present significant problems. Providers have a responsibility to protect our clients by using these measures with caution and being aware of their limitations and risks.

Malingering

The term *malingering* in the mental health field refers to when an individual is attempting to present themselves as having more severe symptoms than they actually experience. It is colloquially referred to as faking or lying.

The previous section has noted the harm that can come from assuming dishonestly from our clients. It inhibits rapport and trust both in the individual provider and in the system as a whole. It is not impossible for a client to be dishonest with a provider, of course, and there may be times when a clinician is required to speak to how they ensured the accuracy of the client's report of their symptoms.

At the same time, clients who experience extreme distress might flag malingering scales on certain assessment measures. They may truly be struggling that severely, or they might be used to providers not believing them or downplaying their symptoms, and in order to receive support they may feel that they need to make it very obvious that they are struggling.

Jumping to the assumption that the client is deliberately misleading the provider completely overlooks the factors that might lead to an elevated malingering scale on a psychological assessment. Remembering that behavior expresses needs, we can try to determine why this scale might elevate without automatically concluding malicious intent or dishonesty. If the scales elevate in such a way that the resulting scores are invalid, process this with the client, and work to identify alternative measures that might be more accessible to them. Explore what other factors might influence their approach to the assessment measure.

Invalid scores might mean that the provider cannot confidently determine a diagnosis. Inconclusive results can occur sometimes with any test or assessment battery. However, we can take the opportunity to work with the client rather than alienating them by assuming deliberate malingering with the intent to trick us.

"Not Better Explained by Another Diagnosis"

Every diagnosis listed in the DSM includes the criterion that the symptoms of the diagnosis not be attributable to another diagnosis. This gets complicated quickly, since many neurodivergent individuals have multiple diagnoses. According to Nierenberg (2023), 65% of individuals with bipolar disorder have at least one additional neurodivergent diagnosis. For those with ADHD, studies show between 60% to 100% have at least one additional diagnosis (Gnanavel et al., 2019). Some providers will not diagnose ADHD if any additional diagnosis is present, as they believe that those ADHD symptoms may be better explained in the DSM's terms by the other diagnosis. But if up to 100% of ADHD-ers have a co-occurring diagnosis, that would mean that no one meets criteria for ADHD by this definition.

It is true that symptoms and traits can look like multiple things, and many neurodivergences have overlap in their diagnostic criteria. We are not here to give clients a laundry list of dozens of diagnoses. Misdiagnosis and misidentification can be harmful, and accuracy is important. Continuing to use ADHD and bipolar disorders as an example, an individual can have both ADHD and a bipolar-type disorder, or one or the other. Many studies have shown that some with pediatric onset of bipolar disorder are misdiagnosed with ADHD (Afzal et al., 2023), and being identified later in life can prevent appropriate treatment. Since mood episodes can literally rewire the brain, early intervention can prevent irreversible neurological changes that can be disabling.

At the same time, many with ADHD are misdiagnosed as having bipolar disorder. While medication intervention can help many with the disabling aspects of a mood disorder, those same medications can be harmful and damaging when they are not appropriate.

Someone who has both a bipolar disorder and ADHD, but is only accurately diagnosed with one condition, is likely to only get some of their support needs met, as their treatment team is missing a big chunk of the picture. An evaluator with a rigid interpretation of not diagnosing if symptoms may be better explained by another diagnosis will decline to assign both diagnoses, as they may incorrectly assume that symptoms are all accounted for by one diagnosis.

Needless to say, this discussion calls for significant consideration and nuance: we do not want to assign too many diagnoses, listing conditions that are not relevant, because trait overlap means that all of those criteria are encompassed by other diagnoses. At the same time, we do not want to overlook co-occurring conditions when they are present, and the client deserves a full picture of how their brain works. We want to be thorough, but we do not want to make our assessment process so convoluted and excessive that it is inaccessible to clients who cannot afford an in-depth, several days

We want to be thorough, but we do not want to make our assessment process so convoluted and excessive that it is inaccessible to clients."

long neuropsychological evaluation that has components that are not necessary to answer their referral questions.

It is not easy to be accurate, be thorough, and consider every angle of each client we encounter. Neurodiversity-affirming care requires us to mindfully and carefully support each of our clients and their individualized needs and presentations, which means we cannot take a cookie-cutter approach to our jobs. It is not easy, but it is worth it.

Neurodiversity-Affirming Assessment Reports

Providers who conduct evaluations to determine a client's diagnosis or diagnoses typically have to write reports that summarize their findings. As noted in the previous two sections, in order to be clinically accurate and in compliance with various professional standards, these reports will likely have to contain language that is not affirming. For instance, many autistic individuals reject the idea that autism is a disorder regardless of whether the autistic individual is disabled as a direct result of autistic traits. While this is valid, in order to officially diagnose someone as autistic, they have to be labeled as having autism spectrum disorder in their medical chart. Again, transparent discussions with clients are appropriate to verify our stance as affirming while committing to correct language to ensure that the client's needs are documented.

At the same time, other aspects of assessment reports can include affirming language that validates the client's experience while accurately reflecting their needs. For instance, certain neurodivergences labeled communication disorders are conceptualized by those communities as communication *differences* that are not inherently disordered even if they are not consistent with neurotypical preferences and standards. An individual who communicates with sign language or augmentative and alternative communication (ACC) (communication cards, apps that speak for an individual, etc.) can communicate effectively and easily when given access to the proper device and/or support, but the diagnostic criteria continue to refer to this different approach as disordered.

When writing narrative information about the client's presentation and needs, the provider can use terms like "different communication style" or "communication that deviates from neurotypical expectations" rather than assigning pathologizing language like "communication deficits." In this way, a client reviewing their record will see that the evaluator took steps to clarify their neurodiversity-affirming stance by framing the client's communication needs as different rather than lesser.

When it comes to sharing the report directly with the client, and providing the client with a copy of their record, the principle of presuming competence includes the baseline assumption that the client has the right to view and maintain copies of their medical records, including mental health records. Historically, the mental health field has withheld this information. Often, the rationale was that it could be harmful for the client to have copies of their records. Harmful in what way? What professional is putting information in the client's chart that could harm them?

For example, many have assumed that clients with a diagnosis of borderline personality disorder cannot handle knowing their diagnosis. It is part of the provider's job to educate the client about their diagnosis, including addressing concerns, anxieties, and uncertainty. Additionally, a client cannot consent to treatment if they are not informed about what it is addressing. It is fully unethical to deny clients their own mental health information.

There may be limited instances where a provider chooses not to release copies of a record to a client. For instance, this author has previously worked in a shelter for women escaping abusive situations. At times, residents would leave the shelter and return to their abuser. Issues including but not limited to financial abuse, custody concerns, and emotional manipulation make it difficult to impossible to permanently leave an abuser on the first try, and we do not judge clients for making the decision that seems most appropriate for their life at that time. If a resident requested their records from their stay in the shelter with the intent of storing those records in the home that they share with said abuser, a provider might note the safety concern of the abuser potentially finding documentation of their victim discussing abuse with a mental health professional. In this very specific case, the provider can give the client the opportunity to review their records upon request, make a safety plan that allows the client to reach out and ask questions about the records as needed, but not provide a physical copy that the abuser could find.

Barring a specific, documentable safety concern, however, denying a client access to their own records presumes that the client is not competent to make decisions about their own care and treatment, and it fosters mistrust with the system. Assuming that other providers on a client's treatment team have the right to view the client's records, but not the client themselves, takes an authoritarian approach to care that is inappropriate for neurodiversity-affirming providers.

Essentially:

1. Neurodiversity-affirming providers make efforts to use affirming and nonpathologizing language in our assessment reports, while following professional standards for crafting these reports. (See the examples listed previously in this chapter as a reference for crafting reports using appropriate and affirming language.)
2. Neurodiversity-affirming providers communicate transparently with clients about times when we have to use nonaffirming language to help them get the support they need.
3. Neurodiversity-affirming providers do not put information in a client's record that could be harmful to the client if they viewed it.
4. Neurodiversity-affirming providers presume competence and understand that clients have the right to view their records and all information that the provider has written about them.
5. Neurodiversity-affirming providers understand that clients have the right to keep copies of their medical and mental health records, only denying this if there is a specific and documented safety concern for such release. In the event of such a concern, providers explain their reasoning to the client and make alternative arrangements to ensure that the client can access their records when needed, while maintaining safety.

Self-Identification/Self-Diagnosis

Except in circumstances where a client is exclusively seeking an evaluation at the request of another person (e.g., evaluations required for certain jobs or a client who feels that they do not have neurodivergent traits but are seeking assessment at the encouragement of a spouse or family member), every client that requests testing for neurodivergence has self-assessed to some extent before requesting the appointment. With the availability of information and firsthand experience on the internet, most clients arrive with a suspected diagnosis. Although not all information found online will be accurate, many clients have vetted various sources and come to have some understanding of their own traits prior to an intake appointment. In other words, every neurodivergent person with an official diagnosis was self-diagnosed or self-identified before they received their diagnosis.

Furthermore, there exist many barriers to obtaining an official diagnosis for many neurodivergences. For instance, very few qualified providers offer evaluations to diagnose autism in adults, and of those providers, even fewer have full understanding of the diverse presentations autistic people can have, leading to misdiagnosis.

If the client is able to find a qualified provider with whom they are comfortable, waiting periods can be extensive. Individuals seeking an ADHD evaluation, for example, have notoriously long wait times. According to a 2019 study by the National Institutes of Health, individuals seeking an ADHD diagnosis in the United States wait between 14 and 212 days for a first appointment and even longer for the official diagnosis (Bonati et al., 2019), and evaluation requests have increased significantly since 2019, so true wait times are likely much longer now.

In addition, psychological evaluations can be incredibly expensive. A brief evaluation with few components can still cost hundreds of dollars, and comprehensive neuropsychological testing typically costs thousands. If the client does not have insurance, they have to cover this cost out-of-pocket. If they do have insurance, deductibles and coinsurance costs may still leave them with a large bill. If a client has insurance, and their insurance says they will cover the cost of testing, the insurance company is not legally required to still provide coverage. The insurance company may say that the testing is not "medically necessary" (a fancy term with a vague meaning to get them out of paying), or they may say that a previous indication that testing would be covered is "not a guarantee of payment" (a fancy way of saying they cannot be forced to provide the coverage promised). Often, coverage is not guaranteed until several weeks after the provider bills insurance, so the client has to be prepared for a bill of indeterminate size when they seek testing.

All of this is assuming that the provider accepts the client's insurance, or accepts insurance at all. Due to unsustainable reimbursement rates, audits, clawbacks, arbitrary denials, and time-consuming billing requirements, more and more providers are decredentialing (leaving networks and ceasing to accept insurance) and declining to accept insurance. Some will still attempt to bill services out-of-network, but many plans will not accept out-of-network claims. Many providers offer super bills, or an itemized list indicating what the client paid for services so the client can request reimbursement directly, but this still requires the client to be able to pay for the evaluation in advance.

In other words, many clients who suspect they are neurodivergent simply do not have the option to receive an evaluation to confirm their neurodivergence.

Even if the health care system issues that bar many from receiving an evaluation were removed, some clients choose not to seek an official diagnosis due to concerns about discrimination and other risks that come with being identified as neurodivergent on their medical record. These risks include, but are not limited to:

1. *Medical discrimination.* As noted previously, for example, individuals with borderline personality disorder in their chart often report mistreatment by providers (including being told that they are untreatable, being denied access to their own medical records, and being denied services based on their borderline personality disorder) upon learning of the diagnosis (Klein et al., 2022).

2. *Government monitoring.* In several states, providers are legally required to submit lists of their autistic clients to the state government for research purposes even if the client does not consent to inclusion. Failure to comply can lead to fines or license revocation.

3. *Loss of autonomy.* This will be discussed further in the next chapter, but many neurodivergent individuals are given legal guardians or placed in conservatorships that take control of their finances and daily lives. While these arrangements can be supportive when appropriate, the system is rife with abuse and overreach.

4. *Loss of custody.* Many neurodivergent individuals with various diagnoses can lose custody of their children on the grounds of their diagnosis regardless of parenting ability.

5. *Loss of employment or career options.* Certain fields will not hire individuals with certain diagnoses in their medical records. While this may be considered discrimination, military and government positions in particular require the release of medical records to be considered for employment.

6. *Workplace discrimination.* The Americans with Disabili-

ties Act prohibits an employer from discriminating against employees for a diagnosis. However, almost every state has at-will employment in place, meaning that an employer can fire a worker without giving a reason. Unless the employer states, "I am letting you go because you are neurodivergent," it is on the employee to prove definitively that this occurred, which can be impossible.

7. *Barriers to immigration.* Many countries will deny work and residency visas to individuals with certain diagnoses.

8. *Insurance denials.* The law keeps changing. Technically, at the time of writing, insurance companies in the United States are not permitted to deny coverage due to pre-existing conditions, but this has not always been the case, and some companies continue to push to bring this provision back. Additionally, individuals can be denied life insurance for certain conditions. Having a diagnosis on record can interfere with the individual's ability to access these services.

Even those who have the option to be formally assessed and diagnosed often have very real, valid concerns about having the diagnosis in their medical record. At the same time, understanding their neurodivergent traits can help them self-accommodate and interact with a community that understands them. There is not a universal consensus, of course, and it can be difficult to accurately self-assess (this is why even qualified providers cannot conduct official evaluations on ourselves!), but overall, the risks of having an official diagnosis and the significant barriers to accessing them mean that many rely on self-identifying rather than getting official testing.

If a client cannot afford or does not want to pursue official testing, we can still validate their experience and work with them to identify accommodations and supports they can implement in their daily lives. Of course, there are limitations to self-diagnosis; for instance, many with ADHD or mood disorders benefit from medication to manage harmful symptoms associated with the diagnosis, and these medications are not accessible unless the diagnosis is in their medical record. However, interventions like finding a sleep schedule that fosters mental health, tweaking work hours to meet individual needs and abilities, or changing a communication style to fit what comes naturally to the individual are all examples of things a neurodiversity-affirming provider can support without having a specific diagnosis on record.

An example of what it might look like to affirm the client's experience:

"You have shared your experience of (details about client's perception of their neurodivergent traits). As you have pointed out, these traits are common for (neurodivergent diagnosis). You know more about your own internal experience than anyone else because no one else lives inside of your brain. At the same time, clinical diagnoses have to be assigned by a qualified provider so that we can be certain that the supports we offer people meet their needs. Not all supports need an official diagnosis, though. If you find that things that other (neurodivergent) people say is helpful also help you, then use those skills! Your self-identification is valid even if pursuing a formal assessment is not right or accessible for you at this time."

We affirm the client's experience, we recognize the system issues and barriers to seeking an evaluation, and we seek to protect our clients from harm in the way that best fits their needs. We additionally empower clients to make the best decisions for themselves regarding the best approach to getting appropriate support.

Therapy and Treatment With Neurodivergent Clients

Neurodiversity-affirming mental health care is not just the way that providers approach assessing and diagnosing our clients; it also includes ongoing mental health support and treatment. It is important to be aware of the different nuances and considerations with therapy clients when we are committed to providing affirming treatment and support. This section explores these considerations and how providers can become neurodiversity-affirming in their practices.

Mental Health and Neurodivergence:
A History of the Problem

Historically, many approaches to mental health treatment place the provider in the role of expert, and the client is expected to defer to their knowledge and training. While providers do complete years of training and study to understand mental health, support, and therapy, this still does not make us experts on the individual in front of us.

No one can exist inside someone else's brain and truly experience the world from another's perspective. We can listen, show compassion, sympathize, empathize, and mentally put ourselves in their shoes, but it is impossible to truly and fully immerse in someone else's experience. We must rely on each client to serve as an expert on themselves.

Unfortunately, traditional assumptions of who the true expert is in the therapy setting have led to providers talking over and disregarding our clients' experiences. Many impose their own values on the client, telling the client what they need or what they ought to desire from treatment rather than honoring the client's self-identified goals, desires, values, and needs.

What is the goal of mental health treatment? Each client usually has individualized treatment goals listed in their chart, but as a whole, therapy aims to help the client be the best version of themselves, achieve stable mental health, and self-actualize. However, values imposed by the system often lead to more harm than good.

For example, applied behavior analysis (ABA) has long been called the gold standard of treatment for autistic children because it leads to behavioral changes that make the child appear less autistic. Many in the autistic community have shared that their experience with ABA was abusive and traumatic, and there is a growing body of research demonstrating the harms of this therapy (Sandoval-Norton et al., 2019). Essentially, the goal is to eliminate the neurodivergence, and this goal is often set without any input from the client about what they want or need.

Some of the ways in which ABA can be harmful include:

- Many ABA protocols emphasize presenting in neurotypical ways rather than supporting the individual, and some autistic people report that they were taught to mask rather than being supported (Anderson, 2023).
- Some ABA protocols utilize punishment protocols that are abusive and harmful, including being treated like "they are a problem to be fixed" and being forced to change non-harmful behaviors (Anderson, 2023).
- Some autistic people who experienced ABA report that the

experience interfered negatively with their identity development (McGill & Robinson, 2021).

- ABA often includes compliance training, teaching autistic
  clients to obey and do what they are told even when they
  are uncomfortable (Sandoval-Norton et al., 2019). This both
  reinforces masking over meeting an individual's needs and
  increases risk for abuse when a child is taught that they
  must obey even when they are uncomfortable, as it teaches
  them to accept abusive behavior.

Another example is in approaches to treatment for trauma. While
many trauma survivors benefit from therapy to reduce their hypervigilance, flashbacks, and other distressing symptoms arising as a
result of their traumatic experiences, some treatment approaches
overlook the importance of validating the client's experience and
acknowledging ongoing fears. For instance, while there are cognitive behavioral therapy (CBT) interventions that can be beneficial
to trauma survivors, and many report a positive experience, there
are some trauma survivors who report that their CBT-oriented
therapist focused on correcting so-called cognitive distortions such
as "the world is an unsafe place." Someone who has had real threats
to their safety may realistically hold this belief and find direct challenges to the belief invalidating of their actual lived experience.

A third example of this trend is seen in many classrooms with
one or more neurodivergent students. Many neurodivergences,
including but not limited to ADHD, autism, other impulse-control
disorders, and sometimes trauma disorders, can lead to hyperactive
behaviors like fidgeting, making noise while working, getting out of
their seat, or talking out at inappropriate times. Often, the goal of
therapy and support for these children is to make them less disrup-

tive, forcing them to behave in the way that has been deemed appropriate for a classroom. While it is true that there are times when students need to listen to teachers, and sometimes excessive movement or noise can disrupt other students' learning, the sole goal of changing the problem child's behavior sends a clear message that this child is bad and wrong, and the adults who supposedly care for them bear no responsibility to meet their needs. Instead, the child must learn to force themselves to meet behavior standards (standards that are often unrealistic even for neurotypical children!) instead of changing the environment or learning to accommodate the needs communicated by the behavior.

Essentially, while mental health treatment is important for many neurodivergent individuals, too often it overlooks the individual's needs in favor of emphasizing how the client is causing problems for other people and how to make them stop. Instead of teaching them how to identify ways to accommodate their needs, we emphasize ignoring the needs altogether. Ignoring a need does not make it go away, of course, and it can lead to stress, further trauma, and burnout.

While mental health treatment is important for many neurodivergent individuals, too often it overlooks the individual's needs in favor of emphasizing how the client is causing problems for other people."

Treatment Versus Support

When it comes to therapy and other mental health services for neurodivergent individuals, a collaborative approach means putting the individual's needs and values at the forefront. This means that we cannot put together one outline or treatment plan that can be copied and pasted into each chart. There is no one approach because no two clients are identical.

Existing as neurodivergent in a world that is not built to meet your needs is exhausting, stressful, and often traumatic. Eugenicist messaging that it would be better if people like you did not exist wears on one's self-esteem, and constantly having to mask or be called out for bad behavior (even if that behavior is not harming anyone!) wears neurodivergent people down.

For some clients, appropriate therapy for their neurodivergence is actually support for the stress that comes from existing in their brain. They need space to be authentic and express frustration, as well as develop tools to cope with their challenges. This emphasis on coping with environmental stressors that we cannot change is much like giving aloe to someone who is on fire: it is not nothing, but it does not solve the underlying problem. This is one small part of why it is important for neurodiversity-affirming providers also engage in advocacy outside of our direct clinical work. In the meantime, this support is better than nothing, but it is not a sustainable solution. This will be discussed further in the final chapter of this text.

For others, there are direct aspects of their neurodivergence for which they want to seek treatment. It is not harmful to name that sometimes neurodivergence is disabling; disabled is not a bad word, nor is it something of which to be ashamed. Additionally, it is perfectly acceptable for an individual to want support for their disability that improves their quality of life. This can include therapy specifically aimed at reducing mood episodes that trigger dangerous or harmful behavior, breaks from reality, distressing trauma symptoms, and so on. When appropriate, therapy including goals of symptom reduction can help improve a client's quality of life. Again, this should be based on the client's personal values and goals, as well as their definition of quality.

Avoiding Toxic Positivity

As noted, there are times when neurodivergence is itself a strength or asset to the individual. This can simultaneously be true even when the individual experiences challenges directly resulting from their neurodivergence. It can be appropriate to name these strengths and even use them to guide an individual's decisions around support needs.

At the same time, strengths-based approaches to mental health treatment must be mindful of the trap of toxic positivity, discussed in a previous section. Additionally, clients are not required to have a positive outlook on their neurodivergence or abilities. It is possible for a client to feel that they have no strengths as a result of their neurodivergence. When this is their truth, this is valid. While the therapist can support a client in identifying personal strengths, pushing them to feel a certain way about their personal challenges is inappropriate and not client-centered.

It can be difficult to sit with a client's self-identified challenges, and the impulse to provide a positive reframe is understandable. However, this does not mean that every difficulty is secretly a strength, and it should not be presented this way to the client.

Support Needs, Client Autonomy, and Presumed Competence

Every single person, regardless of neurotype, has support needs. The poet John Donne said, "No man is an island," and while the language of the quote is not gender-inclusive in modern parlance, the sentiment is correct. Human beings are inherently relational and rely on each other for not only companionship but also support. Even those who live off the grid have communities, friendships, and alliances. At some point, we all need help from someone else.

Disabled people might need more frequent or broad support as a result of their disability. Some of these needs may be the result of a society that is not structured to provide this support, and some come from impairments directly resulting from the disability. Regardless, every human being deserves to have their support needs met. No one should have to manage reduced quality of life, shortened life expectancy, or mistreatment as a result of their support needs.

A neurodiversity-affirming provider strives to meet clients' support needs without overstepping or denying the client their own autonomy. Unfortunately, sometimes support needs are conflated with incompetence. Needing help with an activity of daily living does not mean that an individual is not competent to be in charge of their decisions or is unable to determine what their needs are.

Additionally, even in cases in which an individual needs substantial support, including supervision or guardianship, this must never mean that their autonomy is taken away. Maximizing autonomy can encourage growth, helping the individual develop skills for more independence if this is appropriate. Furthermore, regardless of an individual's support needs, they remain human beings with the right to make decisions about their own life.

Regardless of an individual's support needs, they remain human beings with the right to make decisions about their own life."

In practice, though, this is often not how things work. Often individuals with more support needs often see more and more of their autonomy stripped away. For example, many group homes for adults instill strict curfews and even bedtimes for fully grown adults who happen to need a supportive living environment. Those overseeing this care might argue the importance of a set sleep routine; however, a neurotypical adult who does not need such an environment has the right to stay up late even if it means they might be tired the next day. Rather than mandating a set bedtime, why not provide the tools and information to empower residents to make their own schedules? Insisting on controlling bedtimes only serves to strip away personal choice on the grounds of disability.

This is not limited to neurodivergent disabled individuals—the same denial of autonomy occurs probably with even more frequency for physically disabled individuals, both neurodivergent and neurotypical. This is not covered in this particular text but is important to address.

Medical and Mental Health Conservatorships

Denying disabled individuals (including neurodivergent individuals) autonomy perhaps takes its most obvious form in conservatorships, legal arrangements where an individual's rights and autonomy are stripped away, and they are put under the control of another person. Conservatorships vary, with some granting control over an individual's finances, and others giving the conservator the power to control other aspects of the individual's life, such as where they live, who they have relationships with, and their other activities.

As with everything, discussion about conservatorship requires nuance and careful consideration. As was seen in Britney Spears's case, a conservatorship can be misused to abuse and exploit an individual. For years, she was forced to work against her will (the literal definition of human trafficking) because her father was the conservator of her finances and her person (meaning that he had control over her money and activities). Regardless of whether or not that conservatorship was ever necessary, it took years for the system to identify and respond to the abuse she experienced before she was released. Additionally, the lawyer her conservator hired for her gave her false information about her options and rights, preventing her from advocating for herself (Spears, 2023). Clearly, a system that allows someone as well-known and public-facing as Britney Spears remain in such a situation for so long is not adequately protecting its citizens.

While it is clear and undeniable that there are cases where conservatorship perpetuates abuse and harm, this does not mean that conservatorships should never exist. For example, someone with dementia who falls victim to phone scams could benefit from having oversight of their finances to ensure that they are not sending money to criminals. Someone who makes reckless and life-threatening decisions while in a manic or depressive state may benefit from having an assigned supportive person to keep them physically safe. Someone with cognitive deficits that prevent them from effectively budgeting could use support in managing their money effectively.

To claim that neurodivergent individuals can never benefit from this kind of support is false, harmful, and falls into toxic positivity. It is not harmful to acknowledge someone's support needs or to take steps to get those needs met. At the same time, the harm that can come from a poorly implemented (or deliberately abusive) conservatorship is significant. How can we advocate for our clients' well-being and support needs? There is no one simple answer.

Considerations in ensuring the client's well-being and autonomy while providing appropriate support in the context of the conservatorship system include:

1. *Preserving autonomy.* Remember that support offered and implemented should emphasize the client's needs and be determined with their input. Support needs should not overreach into denying the client of autonomy.

2. *Overseeing the overseers.* Should a client require oversight on their financial affairs, for example, the guardian or conservator must also be monitored for accountability and to protect the client from abuse. Regular monitoring and oversight are essential, and the individual should have a streamlined process for reporting concerns or complaints.

3. *Reassessing need.* While some neurodivergent individuals require lifelong support, and independence is not always an appropriate or reasonable long-term goal, some may reach a point where the conservatorship is no longer needed. This should be regularly reevaluated. Even if lifelong support is appropriate, monitoring and reassessment can ensure that the current setup remains appropriate based on their needs at this time.

4. *Managing expectations.* In a perfect system, the goal of a conservatorship is to provide adequate support and protect the client from choices or behaviors that could harm them. Often, though, the system overlooks the fact that mistakes are a standard part of life for everyone. A neurotypical person who overspends on a fun weekend away and then has to scramble to pay their bills is not automatically thrown under financial conservatorship, but similar

behavior by a neurodivergent person may be used as evidence of their need for oversight. Bias might cause an individual to be perceived as needing more support because of their neurodivergence.

5. *Presuming competence.* Support needs can always be increased. Just because someone needs one type of support does not mean that other support will be essential. Our default assumption should be competence.

6. *Collaborating.* As a direct result of assuming that a neurodivergent individual is not competent to control their own life, too often the supports put in place or goals for independence are crafted without direct input from the individual in question. While some neurodivergent individuals may struggle to accurately identify what supports they need, this process should still be collaborative. They can still provide input and state their own preferences or values.

Values, Bias, and Capitalism

It has previously been noted that the client's input is vital in providing treatment and support to any neurodivergent individual. This is of course essential because they are a human being with autonomy and with the right to make decisions about their life, values, and needs. Too many have been pushed toward goals that are not appropriate for them, or that they simply do not want to pursue, because the expert provider assumes to know more than the individual about what they need or how to go about getting their needs met. In addition to overlooking the client, this approach inserts the provider's personal values into the client's treatment plan.

None of us is without bias. What I may deem the best approach to life is informed by my own experiences, messages I have received my entire life, and my own preferences, likes, dislikes, values, and so on. The assumption that I can somehow craft unbiased goals for my clients is false and harmful.

Currently, the United States operates under capitalist systems and values. This means that providers who grew up and were educated here (or in other countries with similar systems—there are many) are predisposed to these values. This is one way in which the system in place harms neurodivergent individuals. Capitalism values one's ability to contribute (to work), earn money, live independently, and afford basic necessities that are not guaranteed if you are unable to pay for them. Anyone who cannot function within the system as it currently stands is labeled less-than and ridiculed. Some examples of this include:

- Countless articles and think pieces indicating that anyone who cannot afford increasing rent is lazy if they only work one full-time job.
- Ridicule for any adult who continues to live with their parents, with the trope of the gross adult in their mother's basement.
- Stereotypes that those living on government assistance and disability are grifters who just don't want to work despite this assistance being well below the cost of living.
- Defining success as moving out, getting married, buying a house, and having children by specific ages.
- Blaming poverty on a poor work ethic.
- Claiming that mental health and supportive services are costing too much money while funneling billions into wars.

Due to lack of accessibility to accurate diagnosis, it is impossible to know for sure how much of the neurodivergent population is unable to maintain full-time employment, but Johns Hopkins University estimates the number to be 30 to 40% (Odukoya, 2022). Note that this is an estimate of those who are unemployed, not the number who cannot maintain full-time employment in a safe or healthy way but do so anyway because there is no alternative. These individuals often burn out or develop stress-related medical conditions.

Unfortunately, capitalistic values within society lead providers and support workers (and sometimes even the neurodivergent clients themselves!) to push for a goal of being able to work as much as possible. Rather than imagining a world where one's value is not linked to their productivity under capitalism, neurodivergent individuals are pushed to find ways to make full-time employment work, to figure out how to manage living alone even if this is not what is best for them, in order to meet this predetermined value of someone who contributes.

While acknowledging that many neurodivergent individuals may contort themselves into the capitalism box out of necessity, a neurodiversity-affirming provider names these systemic issues and the harm that they cause. When clients cannot fit into this box, we affirm that they are still human beings who are worthy of a comfortable, full life regardless of their ability to work or earn money. A neurodiversity-affirming provider unpacks their preconceived biases around what gives someone value and does not impose this on the client.

Money only exists because we all agree it does, anyway.

CHAPTER 3

Defining Neurodiversity-Affirming Care

With a thorough understanding of the need for neurodiversity-affirming care, the system issues that create barriers to support and treatment, societal issues that exacerbate the disabling aspects of neurodivergence, and a commitment to providing the best, most appropriate support possible to our clients, we can now dive into defining what makes mental health care neurodiversity-affirming. Neurodiversity-affirming mental health care relies on certain underlying philosophies as well as a specific approach to client interactions and treatment. While there is no one set of interventions that can be defined as affirming, the overarching approach to our clients can inform any intervention we choose (or that the client requests), allowing us to support clients in the most affirming ways we can.

In this chapter, we explore and clearly define what neurodiversity-affirming care means in the mental health system and what that looks like in real interactions with clients. We additionally explore the different components of what makes care neurodiversity-affirming and how mental health providers can uphold these standards in our practices.

What Does Affirming Mean?

To affirm refers to stating facts and also to offering encouragement and support. Affirming someone's identity means validating their personal experience and their knowledge of themselves. Affirming someone's neurotype means honoring their expertise and lived experience and acknowledging that they are not lesser for not falling under the umbrella of neurotypical. Affirming someone's support needs means honoring their self-stated goals and preferences and helping them take steps to receive the care they need.

Additionally, neurodiversity-affirming care means acknowledging the historic and ongoing systems issues that actively harm neurodivergent individuals we claim to support. As noted in the previous chapter, traditional conceptualizations of neurodivergence are often unnecessarily pathologizing and based on research that excludes huge portions of the neurodivergent community. Even those accurately identified are often subject to so-called treatments and therapies that actively harm them, or they face discrimination and mistreatment even from the providers who are supposed to exist to support them.

Neurodiversity-affirming providers not only promote the needs, values, and priorities of our neurodivergent clients, but we acknowledge the trauma and harm they may have faced as a result of interactions with a nonaffirming system. It is not guaranteed that every client will have this history, of course, but the current setup makes it likely that many of our clients have been treated in nonaffirming ways in the past. Furthermore, it is often the case that neurodivergent individuals have more than one provider within the system, whether for their mental health, other types of therapy, medical needs, or support for daily living. Even if they have not previously experienced harm from the system, we must be aware that this harm is always possible in the event that the client encounters a nonaffirming provider. We cannot break from these harmful systems without first acknowledging that they exist.

Components of Neurodiversity-Affirming Mental Health Care

Due to the individualized nature of client-centered practice and neurodiversity-affirming care, there is no one comprehensive list of boxes to check for a practice to be affirming. That being said, there are generally accepted components of affirming practice. Sonny Jane Wise, lived experience educator, author of *We're All Neurodiverse: How to Build a Neurodiversity-Affirming Future and Challenge Neuronormativity* and *The Neurodivergent Friendly Workbook of DBT Skills*, and neurodivergent individual, developed a list of core principles for a neurodiversity-affirming practice (Wise, 2023). According to Wise, in order for a practice to be truly neurodiversity-affirming, it must be based in and emphasize all of the following:

- *Intersectionality.* Sonny says, "When we do not see all of one's identities, we do not see the whole person. When we don't see the whole person, we can end up reinforcing barriers, discrimination and unfair expectations, standards and norms. When we don't see the whole person, we are missing the context that we need to understand and support someone" (Wise, 2023). Understanding each client's intersecting and complex identities helps us recognize the whole person as a unique individual. Additionally, intersectionality promotes breaking down oppressive systems for all individuals. One cannot be neurodiversity-affirming without also being antiracist, antihomophobic, antitransphobic, antisexist, and so on. Any other approach perpetuates oppression of multiply marginalized neurodivergent individuals.

- *Respecting autonomy.* This has been explored in previous sections. Respecting autonomy means giving the client the right to refuse treatments and interventions they have determined are not right for them, honoring their decisions about their support, therapy, treatment, body, personal values, and lives.

- *Presuming competence.* Again, this has been discussed in the previous chapter. This means providers start with the assumption that each individual has the capacity to understand, make decisions, and perform certain tasks. This does not mean they have no support needs, but it means that we come from a place of presuming they have some capabilities. It means talking directly to clients rather than to caregivers as if the client is not present, and it means directly educating them about their diagnoses and treatment options regardless of any notion of their ability to comprehend this information. Even if there are things the client is unable to fully grasp, refusing to take the time and make the effort disregards the client's humanity. Take steps to figure out the most effective ways to support the client and allow them to be as involved as possible in their care and decisions around their support needs.

- *Validating differences.* While it has been established
  that some neurodivergent traits can bring challenges,
  neurodiversity-affirming care also holds the truth that differences are not inherently bad or something to be fixed.
  Affirming providers recognize that neurodiversity, like
  all diversity, is a beautiful piece of the tapestry of humanity. This also means rejecting the notion that neurotypical
  brains are inherently better simply because they are more
  common or more accepted.
- *Rejecting neuronormativity.* "Neuronormativity," a term
  Wise coined in 2023, refers to "a set of norms, standards,
  and expectations reinforced through society [which] center a particular way of functioning, including thinking,
  feeling, communicating, and behaving. This way of functioning is seen as the superior and right way" (Wise, 2023).
  An extension of validating differences, rejecting neuronormativity means making room to recognize the value of
  different kinds of brains. It additionally means rejecting
  traditional definitions of value, such as contributions to
  capitalism (described in the previous chapter).
- *Reframing expectations.* As a direct result of neuronormative standards, neurodivergent individuals often feel less
  than and inferior. When you cannot live up to the expectations imposed on you, it hurts your self-esteem. By reframing expectations and helping our clients (and others in
  their lives) to reframe these expectations, we can respect
  diverse neurotypes.
- *Promoting self-advocacy.* While it is appropriate and
  often necessary for providers to advocate for our clients,
  a big part of neurodiversity-affirming mental health care

involves supporting the clients in advocating for themselves. Wise (2023) shares several examples of this in their work, including helping clients learn to identify their needs, understand their differences, making room for questions and concerns, giving choices, and respecting the individual's decisions about their own needs and priorities.

- *Prioritizing lived experience.* Since the individual is the expert on their own life, it is impossible to promote neurodiversity-affirming practices without centering these voices and experiences. This means listening to community members and centering their stories in any education about these experiences. It additionally means recognizing the right to define one's own experience, including respecting self-identified neurodivergence.

- *Nurturing positive self-identity.* Neuronormativity causes neurodivergent individuals to constantly receive the message of being less-than. Pathologizing and deficit models of neurodivergence foster poor self-esteem and sense of self-worth. Neurodiversity-affirming care attempts to reverse the impact of these negative messages.

- *Adapting systems and environments.* It cannot be stated enough that existing systems are not created with neurodivergent brains and needs in mind, and as a result many neurodivergent individuals experience challenges related to current structures that are not inherent to the neurodivergence itself. Instead of trying to change the neurodivergent individual so that they fit into existing systems (in other words, stop causing disruption to the neurotypical people around them), we must make changes to the systems themselves.

- *Honoring all forms of communication.* Many neurodivergent individuals experience challenges around communication, often because of systems that prioritize
neurotypical ways of thinking and communicating. When
we frame these communication styles as neutral differences rather than deficits, we can embrace the variety of
ways of communicating and open doors for neurodivergent individuals to communicate in ways that work for
them. This can mean using AAC if the individual does not
speak using mouth words (e.g., those with communication
disorders), giving cue cards or hand signals for those who
lose speech when overwhelmed or triggered (e.g., those
experiencing a freeze response during a trauma flash-
back), or accepting that differences in tone, facial expression, and so on are not inherently better, and individuals
should not be penalized for communicating differently
(e.g., many autistic individuals are told that they are rude
when this is not their intent).

As you can see, these principles include specific strategies that can
be implemented in a session (e.g., providing alternative communication options, fostering positive self-identity, and promoting
self-advocacy). Others involve pushing back against the overarching systems that harm neurodivergent people (e.g., rejecting neuronormativity and adapting systems). A truly affirming provider
must work toward both goals of helping the client and tearing
down systems that cause issues in the first place.

At the same time, these principles remain open-ended.
For instance, cognitive behavioral approaches to therapy may
help some clients with fostering positive self-identity by teach-

ing reframes of negative self-perception and challenging intrusive negative thoughts, but some clients might find challenges invalidating of their perception of their lived experience. When providers appropriately educate our clients about their treatment options, we can empower them to make choices about which approaches and which supports are the best fit for them as individuals. Additionally, we can prepare them to self-advocate in other situations where someone might not be committed to providing affirming care.

When providers appropriately educate our clients about their treatment options, we can empower them to make choices about which approaches and which supports are the best fit for them as individuals."

Again, no one list is exhaustive, but keeping these principles at the forefront in our approach to care will guide us in creating an affirming practice.

Challenging Training and Bias

Because the history of mental health care is rife with nonaffirming and harmful practices, and because many of these practices have been touted as gold standards of care, most if not all professionals operating within current systems were originally taught nonaffirming approaches to care. It is possible that we have even perpetuated these harmful systems. How can we go about challenging our training and biases and pave the way for a better future?

How can we go about challenging our training and biases and pave the way for a better future?"

Lowering Defenses

No one wants to hear that they have caused harm, and it seems safe to operate on the assumption that most mental health providers go into this field without the intent to hurt our clients.

Maya Angelou said, "Do the best you can until you know better. Then when you know better, do better." It is easy to become defensive when our preconceived ideas of what helps our clients are challenged, especially if that challenge means that the choices we made in the past were potentially harmful. It is also tempting to cling to what we were taught, as challenging our view of the world and how things work can be anxiety-provoking. Those feelings may be valid, but that does not mean that they are a good reason not to move forward or try to make things better for the future.

The very first step in changing harmful approaches to mental health care is to lower one's defenses and open oneself up to the possibility of past harm. If we are not open to the idea that we have done things poorly in the past, we are unlikely to be willing to change in the future. This will mean we continue to engage in any harmful practices that we need to unlearn.

For example, some providers believe that certain diagnoses can only be addressed if the individual uses medication to manage their symptoms. While psychiatric medication is life-changing for many, some clients choose not to go this path with their treatment. When we respect our clients' autonomy, we are open to the possibility that they will decide medication is not the correct route for them. However, within some systems, medication is compulsory, and clients may be pressured or forced to go this route even if they are unsure.

As with all things, balance is essential, and an opposite extreme is equally harmful. There are providers who firmly believe that any medication approach to mental health treatment is inappropriate. They may encourage clients to discontinue medication the client feels is truly helping them, or they may discourage clients from seeking medication consultation in which the client is interested. Again, empowering clients means presenting them with all options and respecting their decisions about which routes to pursue. It includes sharing the potential risks and benefits of all treatment approaches, including medication when this option is available to them.

Providers who mandate medication or who prohibit it both have the potential to harm clients by taking away autonomy and choice. Additionally, those who attempt to prevent clients from pursuing this option are barring clients from a resource that has the potential to truly help them.

Lowering our defenses as providers means acknowledging the potential for past harm. It also means acknowledging that we are not omnipotent, and we do not know everything. All mental health providers in the United States are ethically required to receive continuing education throughout our careers because it is understood that we are never done learning. We must apply this philosophy and be open to feedback without becoming defensive, digging our heels in, and refusing to make changes that could benefit our clients.

Challenging Cognitive Dissonance

Most mental health professionals are aware of the concept of cognitive dissonance, or the conflict that comes from incongruence between believes and behaviors. Many individuals who experience this struggle to tolerate awareness of when behaviors do not align with their values. When our choices do not reflect our stated values, it is easy to become uncomfortable. However, rather than changing behavior to align with what we claim to value, many people instead dig into their belief and claim that the behavior actually does not contradict that value.

It works like this: I believe I am a good person. Therefore, I strive to do good things. Therefore, the things I do are good things. Therefore, my behavior was not harmful. The logical fallacy that comes into play here is that no one's behavior is universally good—and there is no one coherent definition of "good" to base this on, anyway. Everyone makes mistakes, acts on misinformation or incomplete information, or does not realize the harm they caused until after the fact. But when the concept that we have done harm is distressing to us, we may refuse to acknowledge the mistake. Instead, we dig in and insist that the behavior was not actually harmful. In mental health, when it comes to light that a therapeutic intervention is actually harmful, many therapists who have used that intervention become defensive. "I'm a good therapist! I would never harm my clients! Therefore, what I did was not harmful! Maybe they're wrong about it being harmful at all, or maybe the way that *I* do it does not cause harm the way those other therapists do."

One example of this is seen in the autistic community. As previously discussed, many autistic people who underwent ABA therapy report the experience was abusive and traumatic, and research has shown that autistic individuals who received ABA have a higher rate of trauma symptoms compared to autistic individuals who did not receive this treatment (Kupferstein, 2018).

While research is still emerging in this area, there is evidence that ABA has the potential to cause trauma.

In response to this information, many who provide ABA have insisted that the way that *they* administer these interventions is in fact not harmful. There have even been claims within the industry that ABA *used to be* harmful, but they have changed the training and fixed the problems that made ABA traumatic for many autistic individuals. However, according to the 2022 Autistic Not Weird survey, as reported by Bonnello (2022), there has not been substantial improvement in autistic people's experiences of ABA following these supposed changes.

Similarly, hypnosis was once widely used as a treatment for trauma symptoms, often implemented with neurodivergent individuals as a result of behavior that was seen as atypical and therefore attributed to trauma even if no trauma was reported. In an effort to help the client uncover the trauma, therapists who used hypnosis would put the client in a suggestive state and encourage them to remember specific traumas they were clearly repressing. The hypnotists would suggest specific memories of trauma and abuse that the client had not reported. This led to clients developing false memories. (It is important to note that trauma impacts memory, and some trauma survivors do later recall traumas they had previously forgotten, but this is different from a therapist putting the client in a hypnotic state and suggesting memories. There is ongoing research and controversy around recovered trauma memories, and the fact that hypnosis was shown to lead to false memories does not invalidate the experiences of trauma survivors who remembered the trauma later.)

For several years, there was debate in the mental health field about this. While there was clear evidence that hypnosis could cause false memories of abuse, which in itself is traumatic, many therapists continued to use these techniques on the grounds that there were still times that they uncovered real memories.

Cognitive dissonance plays out here: "This thing that I do cannot be harmful because I am not a harmful person." Addressing this dissonance would mean changing the narrative: "There is evidence that this thing I do can and does cause harm. Because I strive to not cause harm, I need to stop doing this."

Currently, hypnosis is not seen as a standard treatment for uncovering traumatic memories, though ABA continues to dominate discussions of how to support autistic clients. This may be because the ABA industry generates five to seven billion dollars a year in revenue for large organizations that provide this service (KPMG, 2020).

While many mental health professionals are taught the concept of cognitive dissonance, it is difficult to recognize when this distortion plays out in your own life. As we lower our defenses, we can begin to recognize the dissonance in our own practice and take steps to be better for our clients, letting go of any practice that may be harmful, making adjustments where we need to, and admitting when we make a mistake.

Naming Our Deficits

While credentials vary by jurisdiction, any mental health professional has had specialized training in their line of work. Many are considered experts in the field, or at least in their specific niche of treatment. When one is considered an expert, it can be challenging to stay humble. When people defer to your opinions, it is natural to have a bit of an ego about your expertise. Sometimes, this expands into feeling like an expert on things more and more tangentially related to your specialty.

It is fair to say that many providers are highly knowledgeable. At the same time, this does not make us omniscient or above criticism. We must continuously assess our skills and knowledge, finding our deficits and gaps. This does not mean we have to fill every gap we come across—it would be impossible for any one human to become an expert in every single thing, or even every single aspect of one field. However, we need to know our limitations and not speak out of turn. We need to be aware of any possible biases resulting from our own limitations.

This includes communicating those deficits to clients. As each human is a complex individual, someone might come to a provider who is an expert in one aspect of their mental health or life experience and that therapist will likely lack knowledge in another aspect of the client's identity or experience. This is okay! We must simply be aware of our limitations and communicate those limitations clearly to clients as part of our informed consent.

Identifying Gaps in Training

One might assume that a program that takes several years, dozens of credits, and extensive vetting and testing to complete will be thorough and comprehensive. We do not know what we do not know, and it can be challenging to determine what we do not know *because* we do not know it. Most mental health professionals attended accredited programs that are held to specific training standards. We are taught by recognized experts in our field, and we understandably assume the information that we are paying hundreds of thousands of dollars for is comprehensive.

Sometimes, gaps in training present themselves easily in the critical setting. For instance, this author received extensive training in psychological assessment and diagnosis for ADHD and autism but did not realize until postlicensure that none of this training focused on adult presentations and support needs. I quickly had to expand my postdoctoral education to include information relevant to adult populations. Similarly, in the therapy setting, a training focus on evidence-based care was helpful in determining which interventions have research backing to indicate effectiveness. However, when a client presented who was not a good fit for that method, I had to quickly problem solve and learn to adjust to the different needs of the client in front of me.

The reason why mental health professionals ethically must continue our education for as long as we are in practice is because we are never done learning. We must continue to gather up-to-date information relevant to our work, and also we need to be aware that we will never know everything there is to know about our line of work.

Identifying Falsehoods in Training

It is possible to be open to one's weaknesses and limitations but still struggle with identifying exactly where those limitations fall. Just as it is easy to assume that an accredited, years-long graduate program is comprehensive, it is easy to assume that such a program also arms its students with accurate information about the mental health field. Unfortunately, this assumption causes us to unquestioningly accept what we were taught, and we perpetuate harmful systems rather than fixing them.

Appeal to authority is a logical fallacy that assumes that

someone's role as an authority figure automatically means that their claims are true. At the same time, it is also true that many professionals uncritically assume that the things their professors told them must be true. When professors perpetuate misinformation, students may absorb this information and carry it into their careers without realizing that the professor is misinformed or has presented something harmful.

Some so-called facts I was taught as a graduate student that I later had to unlearn include (but of course are not limited to):

- People with personality disorders cannot lead functional, happy lives, and their distressing mental health symptoms cannot improve.
- Vaccines cause dementia.
- Autistic people cannot benefit from therapy.
- Client-centered care cannot be effective because clients do not have the therapist's training.
- If a child does not have conscious memory of the trauma, their mental health issues are not related to that trauma.
- Several false and hateful statements about transgender clients that I will not put into print.

There are likely some that I did not list because I still have not realized that the information presented to me was inaccurate. Learning is lifelong, and so is unlearning.

There is significant need for nuance in this conversation, of course, because extensive training and knowledge is not meaningless, and many individuals have rightly earned the title of expert. Additionally, the appeal to authority fallacy unfairly favors the authority of cisgendered, white, heterosexual, financially privileged males. Experts in their field who do not fit into these privileged identities face disproportionate ridicule and questioning of their expertise, and these microaggressions add up, leading to burnout.

When working to counter misinformation learned in a graduate program or in postgraduate training, question what is being presented to you. Who is saying it, and do they have any vested interest in maintaining their stance regardless of its accuracy? Are they a member of the community they are discussing? If not, how do they justify themselves being at the front of this discussion instead of a member of that community? How do they address their own biases and incorporate community voices into their research and education?

Whenever possible, seek training from members of the community you are learning about. Of course, this may not always be available due to gatekeeping and ableism in the training programs that grant necessary credentials. In these instances, seek out allies identified by nonprofessional members of that community as valid sources of this information.

Be wary of trainings that prioritize values that go against preferences stated by the community as a whole. Additionally, be wary of any training that does not clearly indicate its limitations and potential risks. This text, for instance, is written by a neurodivergent author but references many neurodivergent communities of which the author is not part. This is why readers must consume information by a variety of experts and not just one text such as this in isolation. Additionally, while it would be inappropriate for the author to overlook how the intersection of racism and neurodivergence specifically impacts different neurodivergent communities, as a white individual this author would never claim to be an expert on the experience of minoritized ethnicities. In texts and trainings, this author makes a point of reminding readers and students to listen to the firsthand experiences of members of these communities.

Furthermore, research is always evolving. Interventions that were initially thought to be the gold standard of treatment often turn out to be unhelpful or even harmful over time as more information emerges. A true expert speaking based on the best information they have at the time might later be proven wrong. Going back to our need to lower our defensiveness, we need to be open to the possibility that we will be proven wrong in the future.

Addressing Nonaffirming Practice in Our Colleagues

In our journey to becoming neurodiversity-affirming in our clinical practices, we will encounter colleagues who do not share this value. Colleagues might cling to inaccurate or harmful information presented in their training programs or simply not feel that neurodiversity-affirming care is appropriate or necessary for their clients. When challenged about these attitudes, cognitive dissonance may cause them to become defensive and fail to make necessary changes.

Watching someone perpetuate harmful systems can be rage-inducing. Seeing this behavior from someone we have previously respected, even more so. At the same time, it is difficult to call someone out and correct harmful attitudes and practices. While it is unlikely that anyone's mind has ever been changed as a result of name calling and yelling, there is no appropriately kind way to criticize someone who does not want to receive such feedback.

Tone policing refers to refusing to accept the content of a message because the tone or emotion behind the message is deemed rude, cruel, or mean. It is an effective way to dodge accountability because one can say, "It's not that I don't want to listen! I am always open to feedback! But the way you present it is so angry that I can't focus on the content of the message. If only you presented it in a kinder way, I would be able and willing to listen." But this is a vague and always moving bar. There is not a nice way to call out harmful behavior, and frankly those who want to enact positive change will be open to receiving feedback even if the messaging is imperfect.

As with all interactions, we cannot control how the feedback is received or what the other person will do with the information. We can only control our message and how we express it. If they choose not to accept it, it can be counterproductive to keep pushing, as this can cause many to dig their heels in and reinforce their preexisting beliefs.

This does not mean we should not try. We need to be prepared for our efforts to be ineffective, but we can also continue to nudge, provide educational materials, and share resources by and for the communities served to expand our colleagues' knowledge.

Building a Better Generation of Providers

Because established providers may struggle to let go of preconceived notions about best practice and unlearn established standards of care, another way that we can strive for neurodiversity-affirming shifts in the mental health field is in the next generation of practitioners. New professionals are trained every year. Neurodiversity-affirming providers who are open to educating new providers may seek out roles as adjunct professors (or associate, tenured, etc.) to educate new providers, supervise students in clinical rotations, or provide mentorship. By helping colleagues start their career with a grounding in neurodiversity-affirming mental health care, we can continue to improve the field as a whole. We can weave the philosophy of neurodiversity-affirming mental health care into the training programs themselves and start providers from an affirming standpoint when they begin their careers.

Additionally, if we are in positions to review applications for incoming students, we can use our awareness of biases and intersectionality to work to reduce disparities in higher education. This applies to a myriad of historically marginalized identities and specifically to neurodivergent individuals. For example, when I applied for my graduate program, I was not aware of all the ways I am neurodivergent, but I spoke to one aspect of my neurodivergence. My advisor informed me that I would not get accepted into any program if I acknowledged this in my application, so I took the information out of my application. How can the mental health field claim to promote representation when we will not even accept neurodivergent providers into training programs?

While it is not essential that a provider share aspects of every client's identity, clients have the right to seek providers with whom they have things in common if they want to seek this out. Databases and directories exist that allow clients to seek providers who share their gender, race, sexual orientation, culture, and neurotype. Increasing prospective students' access to training programs gives clients the option to seek providers who truly get them and relate to their lived experience.

At the same time, not every provider is in a position to share this information. After I learned I was autistic, for instance, I did not share this publicly until I was self-employed, due to concerns about discrimination. The United States has few employment protections, and while it is technically illegal to terminate someone for being neurodivergent, it can be impossible to prove discrimination. By fighting the stigma in the field that led my advisor to tell me not to disclose my neurodivergence in my graduate school application, we can create a world where more providers feel safe being open about their neurotype. This is not limited to neurodivergence—providers might feel unsafe disclosing their gender, sexual orientation, religion, cultural background, or another aspect of their identity due to potential discrimination. Again, just because discrimination is illegal does not mean it does not happen, and workers rarely have recourse after being mistreated by an employer.

An ideal world would allow providers to share as much about their identity as they choose. Some professionals might simply feel that this information is personal, and they do not wish to share it publicly. This is their right as well; some clients might not care or might prefer not to know personal details about their mental health provider. If we can effectively eliminate stigma against neurodivergence in the mental health field, providers can disclose at their own comfort level rather than withholding out of fear or disclosing out of a sense of obligation to fight this stigma.

Addressing Stigma Within and Outside Neurodivergent Communities

It is indisputable that neurodivergent individuals experience ableism and stigma, both as a result of their diagnostic labels and as a result of neurodivergent traits that others consider weird or inherently dangerous. Those with psychotic symptoms are often assumed to be violent, resulting in individuals with visible symptoms being denied services and support with the rationale that the denial is for safety purposes—even though research shows that people with psychotic disorders are no more prone to violence than the rest of the population (Varshney et al., 2016) and in fact are more likely to be victims of violence rather than perpetrators.

Another example of neurodivergent stigma is seen in the ADHD community. ADHD-ers who seek medication treatment for their symptoms are often assumed to be dishonest and labeled as drug-seeking. While individuals with ADHD are at higher risk for substance dependence than the rest of the population (C. Davis et al., 2015), this is not a guarantee. In fact, some research suggests that ADHD-ers who receive appropriate medication treatment for their symptoms (including stimulant medication) may be *less* likely to develop dependence (Mariani & Levin, 2007), as the medication appropriately treats the traits that make those with ADHD more likely to develop dependence. Furthermore, stigmatizing substance dependence makes those who struggle with addiction less likely to seek support for fear of judgment. Many neurodivergent individuals, both with and without ADHD, may turn to substances as a way to cope with or self-medicate for challenges they experience existing in a world not designed to meet their needs. Stigma around substance use disorders is incredibly harmful to all neurodivergent communities.

Not only does stigmatizing substance use and dependence impede help-seeking, but it contributes to mistrust with the medical field. If as a client my providers assume I am trying to do something wrong and do not trust me, how can I be expected to extend trust to them? Fighting stigma allows neurodivergent individuals to receive appropriate support for their needs.

The experience of stigma varies for different communities within the neurodivergent population. Some are assumed dangerous, deceitful, abusive, incompetent, and so on. Although ableism and mistreatment are not a contest, stigma differs. Much as a neurodivergent individual's experience of oppression is impacted by other aspects of their identity, the specific neurodivergence or neurodivergences impact how the individual experiences the world and how they are likely to be treated by oppressive systems.

For example, while there is some documented progress in reducing stigma, the improvements are not universal to all neurodivergent individuals (Pescosolido et al., 2021; Schomerus & Angermeyer, 2017). Reduced stigma is not the same as eliminated stigma; less stigma does not mean that these communities do not experience discrimination or ableism as a result of neurodivergence. Although recently it has become more socially acceptable to acknowledge a diagnosis of depression or anxiety, for example, other neurodivergences have not seen this progress. Furthermore, co-opting of clinical language outside of the clinical setting has arguably led to increased stigma for some neurodivergent communities.

For instance, people with narcissistic personality disorder are neurodivergent. In recent years, the term *narcissistic abuse* has emerged to describe emotionally abusive behavior, including gaslighting, controlling behavior, mood swings, and ridiculing the victim of the abuse. The term emerged from the assumption that those with narcissistic personality disorder are automatically abusive and harmful to anyone in their lives. In DSM terms, this disorder is marked by a "grandiose sense of self-importance"; preoccupation "with fantasies of unlimited success"; belief that they are "special" and unique and can only be understood by, or should associate with, other special or high-status people"; low empathy; "a sense of entitlement"; and other traits that can interfere with their ability to maintain healthy relationships.

It is important to remember that emotional abuse exists and is just as psychologically harmful as physical abuse. Survivors of emotional abuse deserve to be believed about their experience, receive support and treatment for their trauma, and obtain protection from their abusers. Many trauma survivors are neurodivergent, sometimes from the trauma itself and sometimes as a result of other neurodivergence that preexisted the trauma.

With that being said, not all emotionally abusive people have narcissistic personality disorder, or any personality disorder. Additionally, narcissistic personality disorder does not cause someone to be abusive. There are neurodivergent people who are (or have been) abusive, and there are neurotypical people who are (or have been) abusive. Blaming a personality disorder for abusive behavior harms all neurodivergent people, especially anyone with a personality disorder diagnosis, as it assumes that the neurodivergence itself causes abusive behavior. It can additionally be used to downplay responsibility for abusive behavior: "He can't help it; he's a narcissist." Perpetrators of any type of abuse deserve accountability for their behavior, and blaming it on their neurodivergence suggests that they could not help themselves.

This discussion can cause defensiveness in abuse survivors. Someone whose trauma fits descriptions of narcissistic abuse may hear, "Narcissistic abuse is a harmful term," to mean, "You were not actually abused." Again, this is not the case! Their trauma is real, and their perception of their experience is valid. Using a clinical term like narcissism to describe the abuse is harmful to neurodivergent communities.

It does not help that many professionals have begun using terms like narcissistic abuse to describe emotional abuse and traumatic events that their clients experienced. When providers use this language, it lends credibility to these terms. We must make a point of using precise, accurate, and nonstigmatizing language when discussing our clients or talking about the communities we serve. This does not mean correcting a client's description of their experience during an intake, but when we write and talk about neurodivergence, we must be mindful of how our words impact the field and neurodivergent communities.

Competence and Context

Previous sections have discussed the importance of intersectionality and context in providing neurodiversity-affirming care. As stated, a provider cannot be truly neurodiversity-affirming if they are not also intersectional, including but not limited to culturally competent, antiracist, anti-ableist, antihomophobic, antitransphobic, and antimisogynistic. Unlearning internalized biases and developing understanding of a client's intersecting identities is a lifelong and never-ending process.

Please bear in mind that centering community voices includes centering voices of those marginalized by intersecting identities. The author of this text is not part of all of the intersections detailed in this book. They are included because to overlook this aspect of care would be unethical and harmful, and also it would be inappropriate to rely solely on this author to provide this education. Seek the stories of community members, and use this book merely as a starting point if you are new to neurodiversity-affirming care or as one small piece of the puzzle as you expand your knowledge.

Neurodivergence and Culture

As noted in previous sections, many providers fail to recognize how different cultures perceive neurodivergence, conceptualize differences, and interact with the mental health system. Many clients have negative experiences with medical providers due to poor accommodations related to language barriers. Stigma-reduction efforts in the United States take an approach that focuses on white, middle-class, nonimmigrant families. This outreach often overlooks anyone with a different cultural background.

While it is impossible to become an expert on every culture in the world, remain open and continue learning. Balance self-education and let the client guide you in explaining their personal experience and how their culture informs their experience in the world. Seek out continuing education to help you unlearn Western-centric conceptualizations of neurodivergence and mental health, and constantly check your own biases as you engage with your clients.

Additionally, it is perfectly valid for a client to prefer providers who share their cultural background. Keep a robust network of referral options for clients who make this request, but remember to follow their lead on this. Clients might not have this preference, which is also valid. In the same way that affirming providers can take steps to reduce barriers that prevent neurodivergent individuals from entering the mental health field, we can also offer support to potential students and break down oppressive systems that gatekeep different cultures from entering the same.

Neurodivergence and Race

We have discussed previously how research and diagnostic criteria bias, as well as individual provider bias, lead to gaps in access to mental health services and accurate diagnosis. For example, white children are diagnosed with ADHD at a higher rate than all other races, are identified at a younger age, and receive appropriate treatment sooner (Shi et al., 2021).

Those who are able to access an assessment are at higher risk for misdiagnosis compared to white peers. Additionally, heavily stigmatized diagnoses lead to increased risk of mistreatment within the system. To prevent this combination of harms at the hands of the system, a BIPOC individual who suspects neurodivergence may opt to self-identify rather than seek an official diagnosis.

Reduced support and higher risk of misdiagnosis also lead to higher risk for maladaptive coping. When an individual cannot access healthy support and coping, they are more likely to turn to unhealthy coping methods. Neurodivergent individuals are already more likely than the neurotypical population to develop substance dependence or substance use disorders, and this disparity is even more prominent for clients from marginalized racial backgrounds (McKnight-Eily et al., 2021).

Furthermore, the mental health system has historically harmed many marginalized communities, particularly Black and Indigenous populations. In the United States, involuntary hospitalization disproportionately impacts BIPOC clients. Although there may be circumstances where a hospitalization is required for a client's safety, hospitalization is incredibly stressful and can cause mistrust toward their provider and the system as a whole, and unnecessary hospitalizations can make mental health crises worse and even be traumatic. Why would these individuals seek help from a system that actively harms them?

White providers have a responsibility to provide affirming, nonharmful care to BIPOC clients. This includes acknowledging and naming the historical harm in the system and making a public commitment to antiracism in our work. It also means being open to when a BIPOC client expresses that we have made a mistake or when this happens outside of our professional role. It means using our privilege to break down barriers to our clients' access to care as well as barriers within the education system that keep the mental health field in the United States predominantly white.

It also means centering BIPOC neurodivergent voices in these conversations. Again, to fail to mention the intersection of race and neurodivergence in our clients' experiences of the world would be a gross oversight, and also this author should not be the voice of this education. Seek out education from BIPOC neurodivergent individuals about their experience and how we can best support these communities.

Neurodivergence and Physical Disability

While some neurodivergent individuals do not identify as disabled as a result of their neurodivergence, many neurodivergent individuals are disabled as a direct result of their neurotype. Even many who identify strengths related to being neurodivergent also recognize limitations and even disabilities caused by falling outside of the umbrella of neurotypical. Disability takes many forms, and all disabled individuals deserve access to appropriate support. A physically abled neurodivergent person who does not experience disability as a result of their neurodivergence is valid in their self-perception. At the same time, this does not minimize the experience of a neurodivergent person who does experience disability. Both are true and correct about their own experience, and neurodiversity-affirming care means affirming the identity and experience of each individual even if it differs from someone else's experience.

At the same time, the fact remains that *many* neurodivergent individuals are disabled, often as a direct result of their neurodivergence. Sometimes, a neurodivergent person who does not experience disability is used as an example of why another neurodivergent person is not really disabled—an excuse to deny support. This is unacceptable and must be addressed.

When discussing disability, there is often a tendency to make analogies of other disabilities. We have previously discussed the example that some with ADHD describe executive dysfunction that makes it difficult to start tasks as paralysis. Similarly, some with mood disorders that cause them to stay in bed for days at a time refer to these episodes as becoming bedridden. While these comparisons are well-intentioned, seeking to explain that behavioral neurodivergent traits are not choices or laziness, some within the physically disabled community have pointed out the harm in comparing neurodivergent disability to physical disability. An individual who feels frozen and unable to start a task does not have literal nerve damage that prevents them from moving, and someone whose depression weighs on them so heavily that they cannot get out of bed will not develop bedsores from being unable to move.

This does not mean that a neurodivergent disability is not a real disability or that these disabilities are less severe than physical disabilities. It simply means that these types of disability are different from each other. Both are valid, both are real, both are deserving of support. When the physically disabled community— which again has many neurodivergent members—expresses that these comparisons can be harmful, it is important to listen. We can articulate the challenges of neurodivergent disability without making an exact parallel to physical disability. Oppressive systems cannot be torn down if one community passes on harm to another community.

Individuals who exist at the intersection of physical and neurodivergent disability face unique challenges with advocacy, as there is often need for multiple types of accommodations and a variety of supports. It is extra isolating to exist in a world not built for you in multiple ways.

Additionally, many with an identified, diagnosed disability face barriers to accurate diagnosis of co-occurring conditions. Whether physically disabled or disabled by neurodivergence, many individuals are dismissed by providers who attempt to explain additional traits, symptoms, and concerns as related to an existing diagnosis rather than exploring other explanations. Sometimes, one diagnosis can explain emerging symptoms, but often multiple issues are present. The prevalence of co-occurring neurodivergences has previously been discussed in this text.

When a client expresses that an existing diagnosis does not fully encompass the symptoms they are experiencing, a neurodiversity-affirming provider listens and addresses these concerns, recommending additional testing when appropriate and helping the client access appropriate support.

Neurodivergence and Sexual Orientation

In addition to predominantly focusing on white experiences, research around identifying and supporting neurodivergent individuals primarily focuses on the experiences of hetero-sexual individuals. Just as Sonny Jane Wise (2023) describes "neuronormativity" as a world that assumes neurotypicality, heteronormativity is the assumption of heterosexuality unless otherwise indicated. This means that the presentations, experiences, and needs of clients who are not heterosexual and hetero-mantic will differ from the assumed majority, impacting their access to care, likelihood of accurate diagnosis, and experiences within the system.

Media treats anything different from norms around sexual orientation as deviant, reflected in portrayals of nonhetero couples as automatically sexualized even if the partners are simply holding hands. "Don't Say Gay" laws promote the idea that same-gender couples harm children simply by existing. In some ways, there has been progress, but much of this progress is presently under attack. Essentially, American society forces many who do not conform to heteronormativity to hide who they are, similar to how many neurodivergent individuals are forced to hide who they are.

For those in both marginalized groups, the message that "Who you are is fundamentally bad" can be psychologically devastating. While mental health treatment cannot fix systemic oppression, we can make space for our clients' feelings. We can come from a place of validation and understanding, helping them learn to cope with seeming impossibly situations.

And again, we can use our professional power to push for systems-level changes outside of our sessions.

Neurodivergence and Gender Identity

As noted previously, research on neurodivergence has histori-cally focused on male presentations, and clinician bias can lead to mislabeling traits even if they present in objectively similar ways. Furthermore, adults often treat children differently based on their gender. For instance, a boy who struggles to sit still and exhib-its hyperactivity might get the message that this is what boys do, while a girl is told that the behavior is "not lady-like." In response to this different treatment, girls are more likely to learn to mask neurodivergent traits in response to reprimand.

That is not to say that boys never experience pushback or reprimand for neurodivergent behaviors, of course. It simply means that boys are given more leeway to openly express these traits, making those whose neurodivergence emerges in child-hood more likely to be identified as neurodivergent at a younger age, and more likely to receive an accurate diagnosis, particularly white boys.

Differences in identification are not limited to the strict gen-der binary, however. Trans and nonbinary individuals are often left out of the conversation of gender differences and presentation, identification, and support for neurodivergence.

Children begin to recognize at an early age if they do not meet adults' expectations for their behavior and their authentic selves. They do not have the words to articulate what is happening, but there is an awareness that they do not fit expectations. For example, a survey of autistic adults found that 77% "knew I was different from an early age" (Bonnello, 2022), even if they did not know they were autistic specifically. When a child becomes aware, even subconsciously, that they do not fit in with expectations, they may begin masking or changing their behavior in an effort to fit in with these expectations. For neurodivergent individuals, including those with neurodevelopmental neurodivergence or communication differences, this can manifest as the child appearing neurotypical because they take great energy and often pains to appear the way that they feel they are supposed to.

This same thing occurs for children whose gender does not match what they were assigned. Research has shown that children as young as 2 or 3 years old express understanding of their gender identity (Murchison, 2016). If a child finds that their authentic self does not match the gender identity assigned to them, they may begin masking to perform gender in the way that is expected of them. If the child is also neurodivergent, they often use the same masking behaviors for their neurotype as well.

Not everyone masks or is even capable of masking, of course, but this tendency can inform why neurodivergent trans and nonbinary children often go unidentified.

There are many parallels to trans and nonbinary experiences of discrimination and neurodivergent experiences of ableism. For instance, while it is true that trans individuals have higher rates of depression, anxiety, and other mental health concerns compared to the cis population, this disparity is linked to discrimination and not an inherent predisposition. In fact, children and adolescents whose families accept their gender identity have comparable mental health rates regardless of gender identity (Morgan et al., 2022). Essentially, gender identity does not impact mental health, but mistreatment does. For many neurodivergent individuals, the mental health issues that go with being neurodivergent are highly correlated to lack of appropriate support rather than the neurodivergence itself.

Gender identity is still conceptualized by many as inherently pathological, with trans identities still seen as a mental health condition even if there are no additional mental health symptoms. This continues to be used as an excuse to deny gender-affirming medical care and to strip autonomy from trans individuals. When an individual is also neurodivergent, the potential for discrimination increases significantly, with increased risk for having one's autonomy denied simply for existing.

A mental health provider who is not trans-affirming cannot be neurodiversity-affirming. Even if they do not specialize in trans mental health, to deny the reality of one group's experience is to demonstrate that they are unsafe to all minoritized clients.

Conclusion

To summarize, neurodiversity-affirming mental health care is not a simple concept or marketing gimmick we can put in our directory profiles. It is not a trendy term or lip service so that we can check the boxes in our careers. It is a deep and true commitment to caring for everyone we serve, attending to all aspects of each individual's identity and acknowledging the ways that oppression impacts our clients. It requires care and attention, and it is not easy.

Despite good intentions, the field has undeniably caused harm to our clients in many ways, including rigid definitions of neurodivergence that lead to misdiagnosis and improper support, treatment protocols that objectively cause harm, gatekeeping in training, and disregarding community voices. While we cannot change the past, we can commit to a better future. This requires not only a commitment to a true understanding of our client's neurodivergence but the intersection of multiple marginalized identities, fighting oppressive systems both inside and outside of our office.

With this understanding of what it means to be neurodiversity-affirming and why this approach to mental health care is vital to the future of psychology, we can begin to formulate what our work looks like as neurodiversity-affirming providers.

4

Creating a Neurodiversity-Affirming Practice

With an understanding of the various considerations when putting this into practice, we can now begin to craft what our work looks like when we take this approach to our clients' treatment. Although it is impossible to fully understand every aspect of a client's needs, this approach allows us to reduce our risk of perpetuating systemic harm on our clients and allows for correction if this occurs. We are humans and therefore imperfect and fallible, and while we cannot prevent every mistake, we can ensure that our clients feel heard and take steps to rectify when a mistake occurs.

Since neurodiversity-affirming means an overarching approach to client interactions and support, there is not a simple checklist of changes you can make or things you can do that will make your practice affirming. You cannot complete a set of steps and be done. Instead, this is a lifelong learning process that involves continuing to listen to the communities you serve and continuing to learn for the rest of your career. It requires an ongoing commitment to justice, equal access to care, and preventing harm to our clients. It includes educating colleagues who do not provide this important level of care to their clients or who engage in nonaffirming, harmful practices. It furthermore requires an ongoing commitment to tearing down and replacing harmful, oppressive systems that impact our clients outside of their mental health care. We cannot alleviate distress and mental health issues that are caused by systems that remain in place. No matter what environment we create and maintain in our offices, if once clients leave they continue having to exist within the systems that harmed them, we can never make sustainable progress in supporting their mental health. This is why neurodiversity-affirming care requires an ongoing commitment to justice and using our professional power to make systems-level changes.

Additionally, neurodiversity-affirming care requires an individualized approach. Even two people whose neurodivergence has the same diagnostic label and who share other demographic factors can have completely different presentation, traits, needs, preferences, and values. We must take an individualized approach to meeting the need of the individual in front of us, expecting that need to be different for each client that we serve. This again means that we cannot put together a simple list of what interventions or what theoretical orientations are affirming or nonaffirming; we must have the flexibility to meet the need of each client.

This is a lifelong learning process that involves continuing to listen to the communities you serve and continuing to learn for the rest of your career."

This section aims to provide the necessary groundwork to develop a neurodiversity-affirming practice, with an understanding of all the nuance and flexibility involved. While some specific tools are offered, it is essential to remember the underlying philosophy and remain flexible. We must additionally remember that, as the world changes, our approach must shift in order to remain affirming; we must update our language and the techniques we use based on best practice and standard of care, community voices, and the resources available to us.

Neurodivergence and Trauma

Neurocognitive and neuropsychological research have shown that psychological trauma impacts our brain, rewiring and changing the brain itself (van der Kolk, 2014). Neurotypical individuals who experience trauma can become neurodivergent as a result of the traumatic event. This is known as acquired neurodivergence, when the neurodivergence is the result of an event or the environment rather than genetic or inherent to the individual's development. An individual who has experienced trauma may be neurodivergent even if no additional neurodivergences are present. At the same time, everyone experiences the world differently, and an objectively traumatic event may have a different impact on two different individuals. It is possible for a neurotypical person to experience a traumatic event and remain neurotypical, and it is possible for a neurodivergent individual to experience trauma and not develop additional neurodivergent traits as a result. However, an individual whose brain has changed as a result of their trauma is neurodivergent. Those with PTSD, C-PTSD, and other trauma-related disorders fall under the umbrella of the neurodivergent community.

The relationship between neurodivergence and trauma

extends further than this, though. As previously described, existing in a world that is not designed for your brain is stressful. Chronic stress wears us down over time and is linked to a variety of health problems. Even if an individual does not experience an immediately life-threatening event or a specific traumatic event, the chronic stress of surviving as neurodivergent in a neurotypical world can cause trauma symptoms to develop over time. Any provider who seeks to be neurodiversity-affirming must also be trauma-informed.

This does not mean that every provider needs to be a trauma therapist or specialize in treating trauma. It simply means that we must be aware of the impact of trauma and chronic stress on our clients, being prepared to address this as it comes up and take specific steps in our work to avoid retraumatizing our clients. We must recognize and name the role of trauma and stress in our clients' lives and how this impacts their experience in the world and their mental health. Whether a trauma-related disorder is formally diagnosed or not, neurodivergent individuals are at increased risk for trauma compared to the neurotypical population (Grant & Wethers, 2024).

In addition to the stress and potential trauma of existing in a world that is not designed for your brain, neurodivergent individuals are at higher risk for other traumatic events, including abuse and exploitation. Neurodivergent children are at higher risk for adverse childhood experiences (ACEs) compared to neurotypical peers (Grant & Wethers, 2024). Neurodivergent adults are also at increased risk for vulnerability (e.g., financial insecurity, underemployment, or lack of social support) that increases risk for abuse.

While this does not mean that every neurodivergent client

will have traumatic experiences, and it would be inappropriate to assume a client has trauma if the client reports that this is not their experience, it does mean that any mental health provider working with neurodivergent clients (i.e., any mental health provider) must take a trauma-informed approach to treatment.

The next section describes what it means to be trauma-informed and what this looks like in a neurodiversity-affirming clinical practice.

Trauma-Informed Care

Neurodivergent individuals often carry trauma and stress, either from specific traumatic events or simply from the challenge of being neurodivergent in the world as it presently exists. This means that mental health care must be trauma-informed in order to protect clients from retraumatization and create a safe environment.

There is misunderstanding in the field of mental health about what it means to be trauma-informed. Some providers go as far as to say that *all* mental health care is trauma-informed by definition, but this is simply not true. In fact, a provider who assumes that the care they provide is trauma-informed simply because they are a licensed mental health professional is definitely not trauma-informed because they have demonstrated a fundamental misunderstanding of what this means.

In order for care to be trauma-informed, it must involve a fundamental shift on all organizational levels, not just a change in how the provider approaches interactions with clients. A trauma-informed organization conducts training on trauma-informed care of *all* employees, not just those who work directly with clients. It involves a cultural shift that focuses on understanding and responding to the impact of trauma on all levels of care, with an awareness of the potential impact of trauma on each client's experience.

The University at Buffalo Center for Social Research's Institute on Trauma and Trauma-Informed Care details the many steps required in order to create a truly trauma-informed environment for trauma-informed treatment. They define trauma-informed care as care that "understands and considers the pervasive nature of trauma and promotes environments of healing and recovery rather than practices and services that may inadvertently re-traumatize" (What Is Trauma-Informed Care, 2023). This includes, but is not limited to, the following:

- Ensuring that all employees are committed to trauma-informed care, regardless of whether their role is client-facing.
- Training all staff on trauma-informed care.
- Establishing a trauma team to ensure all procedures are trauma-informed.
- Consulting with trained providers in evaluating services.
- Addressing policies and procedures that have the potential to be retraumatizing (but not necessarily eliminating these procedures).
- Conducting early and ongoing trauma screens and assessments for all clients, regardless of whether trauma is suspected or part of the presenting issue.

Initial steps in creating a trauma-informed environment are standard to any organizational change: getting buy-in from employees and ensuring appropriate training. An organization cannot claim to be trauma-informed if only clinicians receive training in this area, as the awareness of potential trauma and actively avoiding retraumatizing also apply to administrative staff or leadership that does not directly interact with clients but makes decisions about policies and procedures. It includes ensuring that administrative staff are trained in avoiding and responding to trauma triggers, giving clients options for waiting room space so they can select what best meets their needs, and being empathetic with different forms of communication. This goes hand-in-hand with neurodiversity-affirming mental health care; if practitioners are committed to providing affirming care, but leadership does not understand what this looks like, it is easy to implement or promote harmful policies and procedures.

Trauma-informed care in a neurodiversity-affirming environment requires special attention to the ways that the mental health system specifically may have been a source of trauma for our clients. Addressing potentially retraumatizing procedures does not automatically mean eliminating these procedures; rather, it means committing to implementing them in a way that is safe and avoids retraumatization, with informed consent, open communication, transparency, and client-centered care. For example, it is important to get a thorough history on the clients we see. A client with trauma history that they are uncomfortable discussing with a new therapist might receive a modified diagnostic interview that takes steps to avoid bringing up specific triggers before there is sufficient rapport to respond if the client becomes triggered in session. The provider would not completely waive the diagnostic interview.

Trauma-informed care additionally recognizes that, because trauma is so pervasive, there is always the possibility that a given client has trauma history even if it has not been disclosed. We recognize that a client might have memory issues around their trauma, may not conceptualize an event as traumatic at this time, or may simply not feel that they know us well enough to honestly disclose trauma. That does not mean the client was lying to us; rather, it means that we recognize that trust is earned and not automatically assumed. We acknowledge that a client might not feel comfortable disclosing trauma in the first session or during an initial trauma screen.

Similarly, neurodivergent clients who mask or camouflage their neurodivergent traits might not display these traits until farther along in treatment, when they feel safe letting the therapist see them authentically. Both trauma-informed and neurodiversity-affirming care work to build and earn our clients' trust. This will be discussed in more depth in the next section.

Addressing Retraumatization and Potential Triggers

There are times when mental health care and treatment are stressful. Clients might explore upsetting or traumatic memories or sit with intense emotions. Trauma-informed care means ensuring the client is aware of the potential for any intervention to be stressful and following the client's lead in recognizing what they are and are not ready to explore and address, as well as helping them cope with distress as it comes up.

Additionally, literally anything has the potential to be a trigger for someone. Neurodivergent individuals might have additional triggers that were not mentioned in our textbooks. The following are some true examples of uncommon triggers that might not seem obvious:

- A sexual abuse survivor whose abuser told them to "take a deep breath" right before assaulting them is triggered by interventions involving prompts to take deep breaths.
- A client with a traumatic brain injury who is triggered by scents that remind them of the foods they ate while hospitalized.
- A child with communication issues who has been bullied for their communication style who is triggered by standard greetings (e.g., "Hello" and "How are you") because they are afraid they will get the answer wrong and be teased.
- An autistic child who has gotten into trouble for struggling with transitions who becomes triggered when given time cues (e.g., "We have 5 minutes left to play today").
- A client whose previous therapist used cognitive challenging techniques to invalidate their feelings who becomes triggered when their harmful self-talk is challenged.
- A client who experienced a traumatic involuntary hospitalization who is triggered when asked about risk of harm to self due to fear of another traumatic hospitalization.

Most of these very real triggers would not show up on a standard list of potentially triggering topics or actions, and so a therapist might not think to avoid them. Many therapists have standard relaxation techniques or mindfulness scripts that start by cuing clients to "take a deep breath," and most of us likely greet our clients by saying, "Hello," at the beginning of a session. While you may find ways to work around some triggers, others are essential for quality care; for instance, it would not be best practice to simply not conduct a risk assessment because a client might find the questions triggering.

Instead, we can prepare our clients for potential triggers and have systems in place so that they can easily signal that they are beginning to struggle. When the client gives the signal, we allow them a break and help them to self-regulate using tools that work for them. When it comes to querying for trauma history, we can let them know in advance that they have the right not to disclose, to leave out details, or to decline to answer a specific question. Since some trauma survivors engage in a fawning or people-pleasing response, it is important to communicate this at the onset and reinforce any boundaries the client sets. This helps us ensure their comfort and emotional safety and teach them that they have the right to set these boundaries both in their session and elsewhere.

If a client cannot feel safe within their therapy session, where can they expect to feel safe?"

It is impossible to never experience any triggering or merely upsetting stimuli. We exist in the world, where upsetting things happen all the time, and we will never have complete control of our environment. It is healthy to be able to experience upsetting things and continue moving forward. At the same time, "That's just how the world is" is an insufficient response. If a client cannot feel safe within their therapy session, where can they expect to feel safe?

Trauma-Informed Care: Guiding Principles

Knowing that trauma-informed care involves the awareness of potential trauma and taking steps to prevent traumatization of our clients, the Institute on Trauma and Trauma-Informed Care presents five core principles that guide the practice of a trauma-informed provider (Jennings, 2015). Those principles are:

- *Safety.* This means fostering an environment that is physically, emotionally, and psychologically safe for our clients, not limited to the therapy office. It includes waiting areas, administrative spaces, and even marketing materials. Although we cannot guarantee that we prevent any possible trigger, since anything could be triggering for a given client, we can make our commitment to trauma-informed care known at all levels.

- *Choice.* The client always has the right to make decisions about the care they receive. The provider's job is to communicate what these choices are, including possible risks and benefits of each choice, and respect the client's decision.

- *Collaboration.* Trauma-informed care, like neurodiversity-affirming care, subverts the assumption of the provider as an expert who should dictate all treatment decisions. Instead, the client joins the provider in the expert role as having inside information on their personal experience. Clients deserve an active role in decision making.

- *Trustworthiness.* Trust is earned, not freely given. This includes transparency and consistency in communication and services provided. It additionally means respecting client boundaries and maintaining appropriate professional boundaries.

- *Empowerment.* While we want to support our clients and advocate for them, we also teach them self-advocacy and empower them to take charge in their healing and treatment.

According to the University at Buffalo School of Social Work, these tenets help us shift the narrative from "What is wrong with you?" to "What happened to you?" (What Is Trauma-Informed Care, 2023), validating our clients' experience and removing victim blaming from our therapeutic approaches. This not only helps us build trust with our clients by acknowledging their reality, but it helps us craft interventions that actually benefit clients rather than forcing them into yet another box.

For instance, a neurodivergent client who has consistently received the message that they are lazy or not trying hard enough is unlikely to be empowered by a therapist who encourages them to work harder to meet neurotypical standards. Instead, this approach will likely lead to burnout, including extreme fatigue and loss of skills. If a client expresses feeling unsafe due to discrimination, challenging their reality can be incredibly invalidating, as this perception is likely based on real experiences. Similarly, while it is true that many disabled individuals internalize oppressive messages and systems—often referred to as *internalized ableism*—providers must be careful not to conflate internalized ableism with expressions of frustration toward real oppressive systems. For instance, a client stating that they are struggling to receive appropriate accommodations at work is not exhibiting internalized ableism if they state that the accommodations currently in place are insufficient to meet their needs. Internalized ableism refers to when a disabled individual takes in ableist views and bias.

All mental health providers are human, and all humans make mistakes from time to time. We do not have to meet a perfect and unobtainable standard in order to serve our clients appropriately. We must simply do our best and be open and humble and listen to their feedback, making amends as needed.

Adverse Childhood Experiences

It is important to consider the impact of early childhood trauma on neurodivergent individuals. An extensive study by the Centers for Disease Control and Prevention and Kaiser Permanente found that certain experiences in early childhood correlate with negative social, psychological, and health outcomes in adulthood. The adverse childhood experiences (ACEs) study identified the following childhood stressors associated with these outcomes (summarized by Webster, 2022):

- Physical abuse
- Sexual abuse
- Emotional abuse
- Physical neglect
- Emotional neglect
- Household member with mental illness or suicidality
- Household member with substance addiction
- Domestic violence against the mother
- Household member jailed
- Parental separation, including divorce

Other risk factors, such as poverty, correlate with higher ACEs scores. Additionally, divorce can be less traumatizing than remaining in a violent home long term. Although the CDC and Kaiser did not officially recognize the stress of navigating a neurotypical world while neurodivergent as an ACE, providers can consider this added stressor on clients.

Furthermore, research shows that neurodivergence that

emerges in early childhood correlates with higher ACEs scores. For instance, both ADHD (Lugo-Candelas et al., 2021) and autistic children (Hartley et al., 2023) have higher ACEs scores on average compared to neurotypical children. The same is true of children with learning disorders (Zarei et al., 2021).

It is possible for ACEs to increase the probability for a child to become neurodivergent; for instance, the Zarei et al. (2021) study found that high ACEs scores often predate observable neurodivergent behaviors. This may be because chronic stress and traumatic events reduce some children's ability to mask or because neurological changes resulting from trauma create similar neurodivergence to these diagnoses. Regardless, providers working with neurodivergent individuals of any age would do well to understand the potential impact of ACEs on their clients' neurodivergence.

Additionally, neurodivergent children may be at higher risk for abuse by predatory adults. Predators often target children who struggle to fit in and lack adequate social support. Furthermore, as mentioned previously, behavioral interventions for children often emphasize compliance, which can teach children that abusive behavior is appropriate.

In addition to providing trauma-informed care to neurodivergent clients, it is vital that providers work to dismantle the systems that increase neurodivergent children's risk for high ACEs scores.

Affirming and Validating

There is some confusion in the mental health field about what it means to *affirm* and *validate* our clients. Unfortunately, even many licensed and seemingly qualified providers seem to believe that it means to assume that the client's perception is always 100% correct and accurate, and it is always wrong for a therapist to challenge the client in any way. This is both false and an oversimplification.

"Your feelings are valid" does not mean "Your feelings are correct," or even, "Your feelings are rational." It simply means that you are allowed to feel the way that you feel. It does not mean you can act any way that you want without consequences, but it means that you are permitted to have your feelings, regardless of what they are. It means your feelings are not bad, even if they are unpleasant, and they are not wrong or impermissible. It simply means, "You are allowed to experience that emotion."

For neurodivergent clients who have been forced to mask because their authentic selves are deemed wrong, inappropriate, or otherwise bad, the message that they are allowed to have emotions and opinions—and express these in appropriate ways—is a huge shift from being told they need to hide who they are in order to fit in with the status quo. Many can end up losing touch with their internal emotional experience as a result of compulsory masking—what is the point of being aware of my emotional experience if I am not permitted to express it, even in a healthy way? Validating emotions helps the client get back in touch with their internal emotional experience.

When feelings are ignored, they do not simply go away. Instead, they fester and often get more and more intense until they can no longer be avoided. This can lead to explosive behaviors, often in response to a trigger that may appear small if we are not aware that this process is occurring. If we consider the *feelings thermometer*, a common therapeutic tool that helps clients express emotion by indicating the feeling's intensity on a scale of 1 to 10, clients who lose touch with or deliberately ignore their internal emotional experience might not even consciously recognize their emotion until it is at a 9 out of 10. This means they have ignored many warning signs and buildup along the way, not recognizing the need to self-regulate until their distress level is incredibly high. It is easier to go from 3 or 4 back to 1 than 8 or 9. Additionally, the more intense an emotion gets, the more the amygdala activates, which can make it more difficult to use appropriate coping skills and benefit from them.

Validating feelings is core to being neurodiversity-affirming. It helps clients become aware of their emotions and needs, ask for help, and express themselves in ways that do not cause harm to themselves or others. If someone expresses a need and is met with the message that they should not have the need, and that person later hits the point of a meltdown, those who ignored the earlier request for help are responsible for failing to give support when it was requested.

Furthermore, survivors of emotional abuse are often told that their feelings are invalid, unacceptable, or incorrect. Validating their emotional experience helps build confidence and the ability to rely on their own perception, undoing damage caused by the abuse. Validation is an important component of providing trauma-informed care.

In fact, validating feelings can not only serve as a corrective emotional experience for clients who have been told throughout their lives that their emotions are wrong, but also it can help them recognize their emotional experiences that they might have previously pushed aside or repressed. We cannot begin to cope with and regulate our emotions if we do not feel that we can admit that they exist!

Similarly, affirming does not mean "Everything you think is true." It means acknowledging our clients' humanity and expressing that they are whole, worthy human beings, regardless of their ability to conform to neurotypical standards, function at a certain level, or participate in a capitalistic society. Our clients are not inherently broken or in need of repair; they are deserving of support, and they deserve to have their voices heard in determining what support is appropriate.

Providers can (and do!) affirm, validate, *and* challenge clients at the same time. We can validate our client's feelings about events while exploring their perception and challenging cognitive distortions, for instance. A client who feels sad because they made a mistake might have the thought that they are incapable of doing anything correctly. It might be true that they made mistakes, and the therapist can validate their sadness, affirm their experience, and help them recognize their strengths at the same time.

Similarly, we can validate a client's feeling of anger about being mistreated without indicating that violent behavior is an appropriate response. Feelings are valid, but that does not mean that actions do not have consequences. Clinicians must be able to hold validation and affirmation with our clients in order to not only build and maintain trust, but also help our clients heal and become their authentic selves.

Rapport

As has been discussed, traditional approaches to mental health care often emphasize the provider as an expert to whom the client should defer and listen. This often includes the assumption that the client must adhere to the provider's recommendations or else be labeled resistant, noncompliant, or defiant. Why would the client not immediately comply with the expert if they really wanted help?

When someone has experienced trauma at the hands of the health care system, they are less likely to trust future providers. They can present as guarded, or they may need a lot of reassurance and explanation. Since many neurodivergent clients also tend to communicate in ways that can be misinterpreted as hostile or rude, providers can interpret this as pushback and, if they are not careful, perceive their patients in a negative light as a result. They may then document the interaction with bias that leads other providers to make negative assumptions about the client (neurodiversity-affirming documentation will be addressed later on), perpetuating trauma and harm at the hands of the system, leading clients to further mistrust future providers, so they show up even more guarded. It is a vicious cycle, and it is our responsibility as the provider to disrupt it.

When a client enters our office and appears guarded, angry, hostile, or whatever other term seems to fit their presentation, it is tempting to become defensive. Clients might question our credentials and expertise, which we worked hard for, and we might have an emotional response to that. Just as our clients' feelings are valid, our feelings are valid as well. At the same time, my feelings being valid does not mean that it is appropriate for me to lash out in a specific way. We have a responsibility to regulate ourselves and address our emotional responses rather than taking it out on the client.

Taking a step back from the moment as it is happening in the room, consider *why* the client might present as guarded or have a lot of questions for us. A trauma-informed and neurodiversity-affirming approach to mental health care requires us to consider the possibility that the client is reacting to a truly harmful past event. Their reaction may be pointed at us, but it is not about us. Rather than becoming argumentative, the provider can identify where the client is coming from and empathize with their anger, frustration, or other emotional response.

A fictionalized example (inspired by real cases, but with details changed significantly): A parent brings their child for an evaluation due to behaviors that mimic family history of neurodivergence. The other parent was traumatized a few years ago during an involuntary hospitalization where their autonomy was stripped away, and they were given medication that harmed them as a result of misdiagnosis. The parent who requested testing wants the child to receive support early on and also wants to best understand their child's needs, and the other parent is understandably worried about how their child will be treated in the system. The second parent requests a meeting with the provider and asks extensive questions about the approach, measures used, and credentials. The provider feels attacked and can choose to argue back as the authority in the room or affirm and validate the parent's concerns, learning their history and why they feel this way.

When the provider learns the parent's history, it quickly becomes understandable why the parent is reluctant to expose their child to the same system that harmed them. They want to protect their child—is that not every parent's main job? Naming this, affirming the parent's desire to keep their child safe, and educating the parent about the provider's commitments to trauma-informed and neurodiversity-affirming mental health care made room to establish trust. By acknowledging the ways that the system does harm clients, the provider can show the steps taken to prevent this in their own practice.

Essentially, instead of approaching the parent from a standpoint of, "How dare you question my authority," meeting them where they are and saying, "I completely understand why you have these concerns. They are valid and based in system harms that exist, and harm that you experienced in the system" shows the parent that the provider is aware of these issues and taking steps to keep the child safe, while providing the child with supports that will help them.

(And by the way, that parent could go on to refer more clients!)

Another fictionalized example: a client wants to spend a portion of their intake appointment (or a consultation prior to scheduling the intake) asking questions of the provider about their treatment approaches, training, and understanding of the client's presenting concerns. The client asks several questions related to the clinician's expertise, and the clinician feels some defensiveness because it comes across that the client does not take their word that they are knowledgeable. The provider could shut down the line of questioning, asserting their credentials, or address the client's underlying concerns that different providers have different approaches, some of which have been shown to be harmful.

Recognizing that these questions are not about the provider's abilities, they can address concerns and acknowledge system harms without taking the client's questioning as an attack on their abilities or knowledge.

Regardless of our training, knowledge, experience, and so on, we are not owed rapport, trust, or respect. All clients come with their own history, leading to valid concerns about how they will be treated in the health care system. You cannot assume that it is obvious that you are one of the good ones, and it is entirely possible that you have engaged in harmful practices without intending to. When we recognize that our clients do not automatically owe us trust, we can actually build a relationship at the client's pace. This not only demonstrates that we are trustworthy, but also it aids in empowering clients and teaching self-advocacy, both of which are central to neurodiversity-affirming mental health care.

Ways to build trust and rapport without demanding them from clients include:

- Naming and validating that clients may have very real reasons not to automatically trust a provider. For instance, stating that you are aware of the prevalence of systemic harm and sharing specific steps you have taken to avoid that harm in your practice.
- Acknowledging that it is natural and expected not to trust someone you have just met. In addition to validating potential mistrust of providers, it can help to name that you are a stranger, and it makes sense to be hesitant to talk to strangers. An intake for mental health services is not a typical conversation. How often does a stranger ask about traumatic events less than an hour after meeting someone for the first time? Validate any emotional response the client has to this situation.
- Showing flexibility based on the client's self-reported needs. An intake involves many in-depth and probing questions, and especially with agency policies or payer requirements, many providers feel pressured to get all of that information right away. This is not always what is in the client's best interest, however. A neurodivergent client who has never had the space to articulate their experience

might not be able to do so in a 1-hour or 90-minute first appointment, even if they have enough comfort and trust to share it. Questions about emotional topics like trauma are likely to be even more challenging to talk about in a first appointment. Letting the client opt out of answering questions or change the subject increases a sense of safety in the moment and makes the client more likely to be forthcoming when they are ready. Give them that freedom and flexibility. This fosters empowerment and self-advocacy, teaching clients that they have the right to express their needs even with someone in a position of perceived authority.

- Naming when language or measures we use have nonaffirming language or research backing and explaining our rationale for using them. As has been discussed in depth, the present systems are severely problematic and rely on language, criteria, and assessment measures that are unambiguously nonaffirming in multiple ways. By transparently explaining to our clients which measures have the potential to have problematic and triggering language, we can prepare them to cope. For instance, a nonbinary client might be willing to complete measures that require a binary gender input if they are properly prepared to see it on the measure and understand that this limitation does not reflect the evaluator's beliefs. Another example: While it is clear that IQ tests have harmful bias and limitations in their clinical utility, many disability services will not provide support unless there is an IQ test on file. It is valid for a clinician to provide IQ tests with appropriate informed consent rather than telling a client, "I disagree with this system requirement, so I am unable to help you." Instead, we can let clients know our concerns with IQ tests as well as our commitment to helping them get the support that they need. Then, we can use our power outside the office to advocate for system changes.

- Letting the client opt out of procedures they are uncomfortable with, explaining the potential risks of opting out without pressuring them to change their mind. For example, a nonbinary client might feel uncomfortable completing assessments that rely on gendered language, or a client with trauma history might not feel able to complete a trauma screen that requires them to detail their experiences. When educating clients about the limitations and issues in the current system, we give them the option to skip measures that are nonaffirming, with appropriate information about how this might impact their access to supportive services. As noted, some clients might choose to complete the measure with appropriate consent; however, they may also choose not to move forward with that portion of the assessment. With appropriate understanding of how this might limit the conclusions the evaluator can draw, and the services the client might be able to access, it is their right to refuse any specific assessment. Additionally, part of our flexibility as clinicians includes continuously expanding our education so that we can provide as comprehensive

> *By transparently explaining to our clients which measures have the potential to have problematic and triggering language, we can prepare them to cope."*

care as possible even in situations where the information available to us is limited, either by what the client chooses to disclose or their comfort level with completing a variety of assessment measures.

A Note About Diagnosing

For providers in the United States, most payers require that a diagnosis be input in order to bill for our services. Most require that this diagnosis be input in the very first session. This increases the pressure that providers feel to gather information during an intake even if it is not in the client's best interest. Remember that clients who are seeking support almost always have some kind of clinical symptom that can be documented in a first session, even with a provisional modifier acknowledging that more information is needed to confirm. Additionally, if you are not the first mental health provider the client has seen, you can note an existing diagnosis from another provider, with a note about other possible diagnoses and symptoms you want to explore further in later sessions.

A Note About Self-Care

Mental health providers have an incredibly difficult job caring for our clients, and the more we care about doing our job well, the more draining it can be. We have the important responsibility to provide affirming and competent care, which is not an easy task. Additionally, truly understanding the potential for trauma and mistrust of the system requires us to put aside our own emotions in the moment and center our clients' needs. As noted in previous sections, clients might express anger toward the system or previous providers at the professional in the room even if that individual is not responsible for the harm and actively works to dismantle the systems that harmed the client.

Our feelings are valid, and we deserve the same care and compassion that we provide to our clients. While it may be appropriate to compartmentalize in the moment, make sure that you utilize your own coping skills and tap into your personal support systems.

Additionally, we are permitted to set boundaries, even in our professional role. We can hold compassion for our clients while recognizing that there are situations that we are not equipped to handle or for which we cannot provide the best care. In those cases, the ethical thing to do is refer the client to another provider who is more qualified to meet their needs, explaining that our motivation is helping them get the right support, even if it is not us. Of course, a client might not receive this with our true intent. Especially if they have trauma around abandonment, they might see this as another abandonment. Again, their feelings are valid, and we also still have the right to set and maintain appropriate boundaries. The recipient of a boundary does not have to like or accept the boundary for it to be valid. In fact, we have all probably received a boundary we did not like at some point!

Burnout is a serious problem in the mental health field, often causing early retirement or changes in career at best, and suicide at worst. This is true for neurotypical and neurodivergent providers alike, though neurodivergent providers face the same systemic oppression as our neurodivergent clients, which may put us at higher risk for burnout and its side effects.

While it is essential that we navigate our feelings and center our client's needs and support while in the office, we must also make sure to look out for our own needs. Take time off and set professional boundaries as needed. As author Penny Reid said, "don't set yourself on fire trying to keep others warm" (2017).

Safety Planning and Wellness Checks

Probably the biggest fear that providers report is that a client will become unsafe, and we will not appropriately protect them or intervene when we should. Caring about your clients means wanting them to be safe and not wanting harm to come to them. At the same time, the education around risk assessments and keeping clients safe is both minimal and misguided. Most education around safety focuses on provider liability rather than client well-being. In my own graduate training, the education emphasized that it was better to hospitalize a client unnecessarily than fail to hospitalize a client who ended up harming themself, with the rationale being that we cannot lose our license for acting in good faith to keep someone safe, but a client or their family could sue if the client is hurt or dies.

Forced hospitalization and other safety interventions are, on the surface, an effort to prevent suicide. However, this is not adequate prevention. This is like when a city puts up barriers on bridges to prevent jumping. While it might make it more difficult for someone to die from suicide by jumping off of that bridge, it does not address the underlying issue that someone wanted to jump off of the bridge in the first place. A safety policy that sends clients to the hospital for any mention of suicidal ideation might seem to protect the client from harming themselves, but it also serves to damage trust and makes the client less likely to be honest about their thoughts in the future.

Neurodiversity-affirming care means reevaluating how we approach safety and risk assessment. This section outlines steps any provider can take to be more neurodiversity-affirming when approaching these situations.

Suicidal Ideation and Safety

Suicidal ideation may seem like a specific term, but it can have multiple meanings. Taken broadly, the question, "Have you ever experienced suicidal ideation?" may elicit a "Yes" response from most people. Who has never had a long, difficult day, and experienced a fleeting thought of, "What if I didn't wake up in the morning?" Technically, that is a thought about one's own death.

We can approach suicidal ideation from the assumption that it is a spectrum rather than a yes or no response. One person might have zero (or almost zero) thoughts about their death, someone else might occasionally have passing thoughts, someone might have frequent thoughts and even urges that they know they will not act on, someone else might have a plan that they know they will enact at some point, and someone might have a set date and time for when they plan to end their life. Additionally, neurodivergences like obsessive compulsive disorder and posttraumatic stress disorder cause clients to experience intrusive thoughts, and sometimes those thoughts can be about self-harm or suicide. For some, the thoughts are disturbing and repulsive, not reflecting a desire to act. For even more people, suicidal thoughts can be the result of a medication side effect, which they need to report to their provider right away in order to make an appropriate adjustment. Each of these individuals has a very different level of risk.

With the approach of "It's better to overreact than underreact," most of these examples would lead to a hospitalization or other action with the intention of keeping the client safe. However, any breach of confidentiality risks the therapeutic relationship, even if we are attempting to act in our clients' best interests. When the client's well-being is at stake, this is a risk we must absolutely be willing to take, but at the same time, excessive and unnecessary breaches do more harm than good.

Passive suicidal ideation can become active over time, and addressing the passive thoughts through mental health treatment can prevent the escalation from passive to active suicidality. Furthermore, passive suicidal thoughts can be a symptom of depression, and a mental health provider cannot treat this symptom if the client does not feel safe expressing it to us. For those with intrusive suicidal thoughts that they do not want to act on, feeling unsafe to bring up these thoughts to their provider leads to further attempts to forcefully repress the thoughts, an ineffective approach to eliminating them.

Overall, there are many occasions when a client might bring up suicidal ideation but not truly be an immediate danger to themself. In these cases, it is not necessarily in the client's best interest to hospitalize or pressure them into seeking a higher level of care. If we can learn to manage their safety in an outpatient setting when appropriate, we can prevent further system harm.

Hospitalizations: Cost-Benefit Analyses

Psychiatric hospitalization is a tool intended to keep our clients safe when it is unsafe for them to not be hospitalized. At the same time, any involuntary mental health treatment is unlikely to be effective. Research shows that involuntary psychiatric admissions

(IPAs) lead to increased stigma about mental health, harm the therapeutic relationship, and decrease the client's willingness to engage in future mental health treatment (Iudici et al., 2022). A hospitalization might keep the individual physically safe from a suicide behavior in the moment, but it decreases their ability to seek effective support and treatment in the future. Again, this is not true prevention: it keeps the individual from acting on a plan in the moment without considering how they came to experience suicidal ideation in the first place, and simultaneously making them less likely to get appropriate help later on. Involuntary care is unlikely to be effective in the long term. If the client does not want to be there, they cannot meaningfully engage in treatment and progress.

With this said, there may be times when an individual truly is a danger to themselves, and the only resource available is a psychiatric hospitalization. Whenever possible, inpatient treatment should be a collaborative decision, where the client considers their available options and recognizes the need for hospitalization. Of course, there will be situations when hospitalization is the only way to keep the client physically safe, and the client will not be willing to voluntarily hospitalize. In these cases, providers must carefully consider the risks to the client versus the need for immediate support.

For a neurodiversity-affirming provider, involuntary psychiatric hospitalization is an absolute last resort, and we strive continuously to address the issues that lead to crisis, taking preventative steps to ensure that this is used as infrequently as possible.

Unfortunately, we cannot guarantee that no clients will ever die from suicide. Mental health issues, like medical illnesses, can be fatal even when treated by the most skilled clinician in the world. Additionally, we cannot therapy someone out of an oppressive system that exists to tear them down and eliminate them. What is in our control is that we can do our best to support our clients and not contribute to these harmful systems.

Safety Plans

A safety plan is a set of steps, coping skills, resources, and supports that a client can reach out to in the event that they are unsafe, either due to suicidal ideation or an external safety issue. For clients experiencing suicidal ideation, a good safety plan can help them take steps to remain safe without having to seek inpatient care. An affirming provider who has built trust with a client can encourage the client to share if they are worried that they might become unsafe and work directly with the client to put a plan in place to keep them safe without having to escalate level of care.

A safety plan is different from a safety contract. Safety contracts are often presented as a way to keep clients safe even though research shows that clients who have signed safety contracts are not less likely to experience suicidal ideation or engage in suicide behavior (Garvey et al., 2009). Essentially, a suicide contract falls back on concerns about liability. A provider whose client attempted or died from suicide can point to the contract as proof that the client had essentially promised not to engage in the behavior. Again, as such contracts are not clinically effective, they focus on concerns of provider liability rather than client well-being. Furthermore, since there is research evidencing that safety contracts do not actually keep the client safe, it is possible that the clinician could be held legally or ethically liable anyway. All it would take is an attorney or judge to ask "Why did you rely on an intervention shown to be ineffective to keep your client safe?"

An effective safety plan includes:

- Who the client can reach out to if they are becoming unsafe
- Scheduled check-ins to assess risk and safety
- Specific coping skills the client agrees to try and use as an alternative to dangerous behavior
- Triggers for the client to avoid and be mindful of
- Future-oriented prompts like things the client is looking forward to or a goal they are working toward
- Specific reasons why the client wants to follow the safety plan (these can be anything, from wanting to see how a season of their favorite show ends or spitefully wanting to outlive a politician they dislike)
- How the client will handle it if they are becoming unsafe
- What cues the client will look out for that might signal a safety concern

While the provider might make suggestions, the safety plan should be guided by the client's self-articulated needs and preferences. This increases their buy-in and the likelihood that they will follow the safety plan should the need arise.

Again, a safety plan may include circumstances under which a client does need to seek inpatient support or a higher level of care, but the goal is to empower them to take an active role in keeping themselves safe and to avoid involuntary escalations.

Nonsuicidal Self-Harm

Self-harm is a broad concept that essentially refers to any behavior that harms or significantly risks harm to the individual engaging in the behavior. It can mean many things, including but not limited to:

- Deliberately cutting, scratching, burning, or otherwise hurting the skin on part of one's body
- Banging one's head against a wall or other hard surface
- Consuming intoxicating substances in unsafe quantities
- Driving recklessly
- Consciously choosing not to take prescribed medication
- Taking medication in larger quantities than prescribed
- Instigating fights or other conflict
- Deliberately sabotaging relationships
- Bingeing or restricting food intake

Nonsuicidal self-harm, as the term suggests, refers to a behavior that is either intended to cause harm, or likely to cause harm even if this is not the direct intention, but not a deliberate attempt to end one's life. Sometimes, an individual engaging in self-harm might be aware that the behavior could potentially kill them, and they choose not to take preventative steps. Self-harm can be an attempt to cope with emotions, stressors, trauma, sensory overwhelm, and so on. While self-harm is not a healthy coping strategy, it often effectively helps the individual manage their emotions in the moment. For instance, consuming a mood-altering substance is not a healthy way to manage trauma flashbacks, but the substance will quickly change the individual's mood, making it seem like an effective solution in the short term.

Generally, nonsuicidal self-harm does not require immediate intervention unless the individual is putting themself in immediate physical danger. Safety plans can effectively manage these urges by giving the client healthier alternatives to cope in the moment.

A Note About Harm Reduction

Harm reduction refers to any intervention that aims to reduce potential danger even if the danger cannot be eliminated altogether. Everyone engages in harm reduction at some point, though it is not always labeled this way. For instance, cars are extremely dangerous. Most people ride in or drive a car sometime, despite the potential risk. Driving at safe speeds, wearing a seatbelt, and driving on roads that have been properly maintained are all harm reduction: you continue driving or riding in a car with the risks minimized to an acceptable amount.

Similarly, during Prohibition (a historic era during which alcohol was illegal in the United States), many people died or were severely injured after consuming unregulated alcohol. By selling alcohol produced under government standards for food safety, deaths resulting from alcohol reduced significantly. This is harm reduction. Ride share and taxi services that allow someone to get home without driving when they are intoxicated are harm reduction. Bars where people can consume alcohol with other people around who will notice if they become unsafe are harm reduction. All of these steps do not prevent anyone from consuming alcohol, but they make alcohol consumption safer.

Self-injury, substance use, and other potentially unsafe behaviors can all be addressed through a harm-reduction lens. Some clients might not be able to completely eliminate an unsafe behavior, and those individuals still deserve support.

Wellness Checks

A wellness check is when someone sends a third party to check on someone whom they are worried is unsafe. In theory, the goal of a wellness check is to ensure that the individual is safe and connect them with appropriate crisis resources. However, in many places around the world, wellness checks are conducted by law enforcement. Police officers rarely have appropriate training to conduct crisis interventions with neurodivergent people and often escalate the situation unnecessarily. Instead of providing appropriate resources, police intervention often leads to injury or even the death of the individual in crisis (Westervelt, 2020). This risk increases exponentially for Black, Indigenous, and other clients of color. Affirming providers prioritize client safety by avoiding using law enforcement to conduct wellness checks.

It is essential that providers compile and maintain crisis resources that do not require law enforcement involvement. Resources like Don't Call the Police (https://dontcallthepolice .com/) have alternative resources for mental health crisis services, including mobile crisis teams that do not involve law enforcement. Many jurisdictions list mobile crisis or other non-law-enforcement resources on the local health department website. Available resources can change, so maintain an updated database of resources in any jurisdiction where you practice to ensure that you have access to appropriate resources in the event that you need to check on a client for safety reasons. Carefully vet resources also, as some crisis programs that claim to be alternatives to law enforcement will still call police for a wellness check under certain circumstances. Providers can talk directly to potential resources and ask what their exact policies are for involving law enforcement in wellness checks.

Additionally, in many parts of the United States, particularly rural areas, police are the only option to conduct a wellness check. This is another reason why it is important to have policies and procedures in place for clients who might require crisis intervention. If the provider has emergency contact information, they can contact a trusted person who already knows the client to check in with them rather than having to result to contacting law enforcement.

As always, clients should have a full understanding of their provider's procedures around safety and wellness checks, and they should have an active role in determining which crisis resources best meet their needs.

New Assessment Approaches

As we have reviewed the ways in which the existing standards for assessment and diagnosis perpetuate systemic harms, it is not enough to simply get rid of those systems. To reference a previously used example, we can understand the inherent problems with IQ tests while simultaneously recognizing that many disabled neurodivergent people need access to these assessments in order to receive appropriate supportive services.

Furthermore, no societal structure would eliminate all support needs. Thus, some neurodivergent individuals will still benefit from assessment to help them determine what those needs are. Hopefully, we can one day exist in a system where those supports are available to anyone who requests them. Regardless, though, providers who conduct assessments must consciously and deliberately engage in a neurodiversity-affirming approach to evaluating our clients.

Choosing Assessments

As has been discussed, the present system often requires specific assessment measures or types of evaluation in order for clients to access appropriate care and support. This might mean that a client has to undergo testing that is inherently nonaffirming or versions of measures that are not affirming. Providers may make judgment calls about whether or not they will administer less affirming measures in order to meet client needs in a flawed system.

When it is up to the provider, we can consciously choose assessment measures with a more affirming basis. Considerations when choosing assessment measures include:

- What is the research backing for this assessment? Look into validation studies and research that contributed to the development of the assessment. Notice which populations were studied and which were left out. Assess the criteria researchers used when determining that the measure is effective.
- Who conducted the research? Different organizations have different goals and values around identifying and supporting neurodivergent individuals, with some engaging in outright eugenicist policies. If you are not familiar with the

sponsoring organization, see what the community being studied has to say.

- What bias is present in the research? Consider any research exploring what biases are present in any given measure. Although it is impossible to be completely free of bias, some assessment measures do a better job than others of addressing potential bias. Are there studies that indicate particular bias with certain populations?

- What lived experience considerations were included? Because the field of psychology has a history of dismissing community voices, many assessments do not consider lived experience when developing measures. Although no measure can be fully without bias, ignoring community voices increases risk for misdiagnosis and misunderstanding of the neurodivergent experience.

- Whose perspective is centered? While collateral information can be helpful, an assessment that completely ignores self-report or holds observational data as more valuable than self-report information is unlikely to be affirming.

- What language is used? Diagnostic criteria might require specific language, but different measures have different levels of pathologizing language and conceptualization of clients and their needs. You can assess if the measure seems to try to use affirming language whenever possible.

- Is the measure trauma-informed? In addition to attempting to use affirming language, different assessment measures can have different levels of trauma-informed language. Some questions and evaluation techniques can be triggering, and the developers can take steps to mitigate this impact.

- On what categories does the measure rely? Unfortunately, many assessments continue to require categorization of clients. Most commonly, assessments may require that clients identify their gender following a strict binary choice. This can be harmful to transgender and nonbinary clients who do not feel that the categories listed represent their experience, and it can call into question the validity of the resulting scores.

Informed Consent

The importance of informed consent has been discussed in depth, but it remains an essential component of approaching psychological assessments from a neurodiversity-affirming standpoint. This is a standard ethical requirement for all mental health providers regardless of what specific service is offered. Important points to keep in mind when developing a neurodiversity-affirming informed consent policy include:

- Potential risks of having a diagnosis in one's medical records
- Potential supports the client will have access to if they receive a diagnosis
- Limitations to the supports that can be provided
- Any limitations to the provider's scope of practice
- Specifically what diagnoses are being tested for and what diagnoses are not
- Any possible disclosure of diagnostic or other personal information, including to insurance or other payers, mandated reporting, or other required disclosures

- Potential triggers or harm from completing specific measures, such as misgendering

Age Equivalencies

Many assessment measures yield norm-referenced ratings, or scores, indicating what aspects of an individual's experience fall outside of a typical or expected range. For instance, everyone forgets or misplaces things from time to time, and not everyone has ADHD. Feeling sad from time to time is not the same as having a mood disorder. Norm-referenced ratings can help in documenting the ways that a client's experience falls outside of typical experience.

Often, norm-referenced ratings compare the client's experience to scores from others in their age range. This is because typical experiences will vary at different ages and phases of life. One's ability to tolerate distress at age 6, for example, is likely to be very different than at age 12 or age 20. Some rating scales are only appropriate for certain age ranges as well. Some traits are difficult to measure in very young children, as the range of typical can be very wide at certain points in development. For instance, ADHD can be identified as young as age four in some cases, but it is often difficult to determine what level of hyperactivity is not developmentally appropriate at that age!

Some assessments, such as adaptive behavioral measures, indicate both norm-referenced ratings and age-equivalency scores. This means that they estimate what age range is typical for the client's scores. Many neurodivergent communities and activists have pushed back on the use of age equivalencies because it literally compares adults to children based on their neurodivergence.

This practice perpetuates assumptions that neurodivergent people are not competent to be in charge of their own affairs, leading to authoritarian practices and unnecessary control of the individual.

Furthermore, age equivalency scores are not a useful measure of one's abilities, as development is so varied. Two individuals of the same age might have different skill sets and support needs even if they are both neurotypical.

Generally, assessments that measure age equivalency are not considered affirming or useful in identifying appropriate support needs. At times, they might be required for an individual to receive certain services. For instance, some disability claims require the provider to indicate an age equivalency. As always, in this situation, the provider can explain to the client why this practice is used to help them get support.

Concerns About a Diagnoses

As has been discussed, there are risks associated with being identified as neurodivergent. Clients, their legal guardians, and often the professionals supporting them express concern about the impact of having a diagnosis in the official record. These concerns come from a variety of different places, some affirming and some less so. The following are common concerns expressed and ways to explore these concerns with clients and their guardians.

"I am worried about discrimination."

This is a valid concern. Neurodivergence is not shameful or immoral, but this does not change the reality that we live in an ableist world. Discrimination happens and can have serious consequences. Someone might choose not to get an official diagnosis due to these concerns. While this might limit what supports will be available, this is an individual choice to be made based on the client's needs. Sometimes, appropriate support and accommodations can be implemented without a diagnosis being assigned, but this is often not the case. Workplace and school accommodations, for example, require a formal diagnosis.

It is important to both validate the reality of this concern and address any internalized stigma. Many neurodivergent individuals have a negative perception of themselves due to the stigma we are all exposed to simply from existing in the world. At the same time, internalized ableism and stigma are not the same thing as frustration with discrimination and oppression. Misattributing this frustration can effectively gaslight clients if we communicate that their anger at oppressive systems is actually their internalization of stigma.

Remind clients of their rights to privacy and confidentiality while realistically assessing any potential limits to confidentiality. Ideally, it should be the client's decision to disclose their diagnosis or not; while it is not shameful to be neurodivergent, it is also private, personal information that someone might choose not to share. Some people choose not to share details about their children's lives outside of the family. This does not mean they are ashamed of their children; it could simply mean they want privacy!

If a client's diagnosis will not remain confidential, they might choose not to seek an official, documented diagnosis due to privacy concerns. Ultimately, the decision based on risk of discrimination versus the benefits of a diagnosis is highly personal.

"A diagnosis could interfere with my/their career goals."

Some fields require disclosure of any history of neurodivergent diagnoses, and some jobs will not permit individuals with certain diagnoses to take on the role. At other times, the diagnosis might not automatically disqualify someone from a job but will make the hiring process much more complicated. Sometimes this is due to ableism and stigma about neurodivergence, and sometimes there are concerns about an individual's ability to do certain jobs.

For example, many government and military jobs will not allow someone with an ADHD diagnosis to apply or will require extensive reevaluation before the individual can be considered. Individuals who want to deploy with the military cannot require medication to function because soldiers are unlikely to be able to fill their prescriptions on the front line. In this case, the client would need to demonstrate that they can function without medication intervention in order to perform the role.

If appropriate support can be provided without an official diagnosis, clients might decide to forego an evaluation for this reason. However, often these government and military jobs require psychological evaluations at the time of application, so the individual could still be identified as neurodivergent.

Again, educate the client about the potential risks and benefits of a diagnosis and the support options available to them. Explain how this might impact their ability to reach their long-term goals.

"I don't want them to use it as an excuse."

This is often expressed by parents. Although well-intentioned, referring to neurodivergence as an excuse is incredibly harmful. Unfortunately, many disabled people, both neurodivergent and neurotypical, are accused of faking or exaggerating their difficulties and accused of making excuses if they require support or are unable to do certain tasks, especially if they can sometimes perform the task or could previously do it. In actuality, many neurodivergent individuals push themselves past their limits in order to meet expectations, putting them at risk for burnout. This means they might lose the ability to sustain their skills and functioning. While it is possible to recover from burnout, some neurodivergent individuals report permanent changes in their mental health following an episode of burnout (Raymaker et al., 2020).

Someone's neurodivergence does not excuse a support need; it *explains* what the need is and why the individual has this need. It provides understanding of why certain things are more challenging or even impossible, not because the individual is lazy or not trying hard enough, but because their brain is different.

It can help to have clients choose a professional athlete and look up that athlete's statistics. Most likely, the athlete does not have the same achievement every day. For example, an Olympic runner will not achieve their best time in every race they run. If they are tired or get hurt, their time will decrease significantly until they recover. Our best varies from day to day, and just because something was possible yesterday does not mean that it is possible today.

Sometimes, the concern about neurodivergence being used as an excuse refers to harmful behavior. For instance, mood episodes or sensory meltdowns can trigger behavior like damaging property or hurting someone. Neurodivergence does *not* excuse harmful behavior! If I say something cruel or physically hurt someone during an episode, I cannot simply say, "This was in the context of an episode related to my neurodivergence, and therefore you can't address it." The idea that a neurodivergent person cannot be held accountable for behavior feeds into infantilization and relies on the same assumptions that lead to stripping neurodivergent people of their autonomy.

When an individual and their support system better understand their neurodivergence, the individual can get their needs met in safe, appropriate ways, reducing the likelihood of an episode. This is not excusing behavior, but rather finding appropriate support and preventative care.

"I don't want a label."

Fear of labels is an unfortunate side effect of stigma and ableism. Two people with the same diagnostic label are still two unique individuals who happen to have a diagnosis in common. The diagnostic label opens the door for supportive services, appropriate therapy recommendations, and increased self-understanding.

Again, due to very real stigma and discrimination, clients or their parents may have very real concerns about the impact of having a label. We can unpack these concerns and address possible benefits and risks of the label, while challenging stigmatizing beliefs.

Shockingly, many providers who conduct evaluations shy away from giving a label because of these concerns. Remember that a client who comes to you for an evaluation is specifically asking you to determine which label, if any, fits the difficulties they are experiencing. They are asking you to figure out if a label is present. Deliberately choosing to avoid assigning a label means avoiding completing the task they are paying you for. Often, they are requesting an assessment for a reason. Maybe they want to better understand themselves, or maybe they want access to supportive services that require a diagnosis. Either way, refusing to assign a diagnosis when the criteria are present denies this access and perpetuates stigma when even providers cannot overcome these discriminatory attitudes!

Address your internalized bias and ableism, and consider why you struggle to assign a neurodivergent diagnosis. If it is not something you can overcome, consider if it is appropriate for you to provide evaluations as a service.

"I don't want (specific intervention)."

Decisions about interventions are very personal, and some interventions will not be the right fit for some people. Additionally, some commonly recommended interventions are not affirming and have been found to be harmful (e.g., many autistic people's experiences in ABA). While it would not be appropriate for a provider to mandate a particular intervention, sometimes having a diagnosis can lead to pressure to engage in certain forms of treatment regardless of individual preference or need.

For instance, because there is a wealth of research indicating that cognitive behavioral therapy can be an effective way to reduce anxiety symptoms in children (Whiteside et al., 2020), insurance companies may pressure parents to enroll their children in this specific method of treatment even if it is not a good fit.

If a client or their parent is concerned about pressure to engage in a certain intervention, this fear may be grounded in reality. In this case, assess the potential risks and benefits of getting an official diagnosis, and help the client determine what is best for them.

"I don't want medication."

Again, mandating that a client pursue medication options for challenges resulting from their neurodivergence would be inappropriate, and concerns that a provider would require or attempt to pressure clients into pursuing medication when they are uncomfortable are valid. At the same time, stigma around medication is also very harmful. There is a distinction between a client not feeling that medication is the right route for them and having harmful misconceptions and stigma about medication.

When exploring these concerns, make sure to take an approach of curiosity and not debate. You want to learn about the client's thought process and personal values around medication, not convince them that they are wrong. It is fine to correct misinformation, and this can be done without the end goal of necessarily changing their mind about whether or not this is an option they want to pursue.

Referral Questions

Requests for psychological evaluations come with a referral question, or the information that the client or other referral source hopes to have by the end of the assessment process. Often, requests include wanting to learn the client's accurate diagnosis (i.e., diagnostic clarification). They can also include questions about what supports are appropriate, what treatment options might be a good fit, and so on. For evaluators with forensic and other specialized training, a request can include questions like whether someone is competent to stand trial, have custody of their children, or control their own finances.

Remember that no diagnosis makes someone incompetent, and neurodiversity-affirming providers come from a place of presuming competence. We can help our clients access support that can improve their lives, and we can help other providers, caretakers, the court, or others in the client's life best understand how their neurodivergence impacts how they experience the world.

Writing Recommendations

Regardless of the referral question, assessment reports typically include specific recommendations for the client, their loved ones, and their treatment team. There are a wide variety of recommendations that can be included, and of course recommendations must always be personalized and based on the client's unique experience. As with all aspects of mental health care, the same recommendations will not apply to all clients. Two clients with the same diagnosis might have opposite needs. For example, one person with ADHD might need to work in a private room in order to focus, while another ADHD-er functions better in the presence of other people due to the effects of body doubling (having another person present while you complete a task). Explore your client's specific needs when crafting recommendations to ensure that your suggestions fit their needs.

Recommendations must always be personalized and based on the client's unique experience."

Furthermore, recommendations must be within the provider's scope of practice. For instance, a psychologist who is not a prescriber may recommend that a client speak to their prescriber about medication, but they would not recommend that the client take a specific prescription medication, as this determination is outside of their scope of practice. If the testing suggested the presence of something the provider cannot fully assess for, they may recommend further testing but not attempt to diagnose that issue. For a client who reports significant physical complaints, a mental health provider would recommend that a physician evaluate the medical condition rather than attempting to diagnose it themselves.

Recommendations can include, but are not limited to:

- Mental health treatment in the form of therapy or counseling
- Recommended goals for treatment
- Recommended therapeutic approaches or treatment programs
- Additional assessment for other diagnoses that may be present
- Referrals for medical testing or medication management
- Daily living supports and disability services
- Educational resources that are neurodiversity-affirming
- Referral information for community support
- Accommodations

Recommendations that include accommodations for things like work or school need to be worded in a specific and authoritative way. In an ideal world, those in charge of providing accommodations would want what is best for the client and go out of their way to meet needs and provide accommodations with minimal interference, reducing barriers wherever they can. Unfortunately, that is not the world we live in, and many seem to make a special effort to make the process as complicated as possible. On several occasions, I have written accommodations recommendations only to have the accommodations denied because my wording was not specific enough. For instance, I have been told that writing, "(Client) would benefit from (accommodation)" means that the accommodation is not "necessary," and therefore it was denied.

Thus, we must write our accommodation recommendations precisely and with authority: "(Client) requires (accommodation) for (specific reasons)." This makes it even more important to ensure that the specific recommendations fit the client's needs and are not general, as we do not want the client being pressured to take an accommodation that they do not feel is the right fit for them.

Examples of potential accommodations include, but of course are not limited to:

- Flexible scheduling allowing the client to work hours that fit their circadian rhythm or personal needs
- Extended deadlines for projects
- Reduced hours or workload
- Working from home to have control of the sensory environment
- All communication in writing due to an auditory processing issue
- Education for leadership around neurodivergence to improve their understanding of the client's communication style
- Modified attendance requirements
- Increased length or frequency of breaks

More Notes About Language

Some standard language and clinical terms commonly seen in medical records and assessment reports are decidedly nonaffirming and can be harmful to clients, creating additional barriers to care. When considering these terms, remember that this can not only make it more difficult for the client to trust you, but also other providers who might access the medical record might make harmful assumptions about the client and impair their ability to access care as a result of your word choice. Some terms to avoid include the following.

Noncompliant

This refers to when a client is not following treatment recommendations presented by the provider. This term assumes that the client is deliberately defying the provider, or at least making the conscious choice not to comply. It assumes that the provider is automatically correct in the recommendations they made, and the client must agree and follow through. Instead, note what the client did not follow through with, and explore it with the client from a curiosity standpoint. Is there a barrier preventing the client from engaging of which the provider is unaware? Is the recommended intervention a poor fit, and the client is uncomfortable stating this directly? Is the recommendation not possible for some reason? When we approach from curiosity, we often learn that what we perceive as noncompliance has a rea-

> *We often learn that what we perceive as noncompliance has a reasonable explanation, and we can collaborate with clients to find a better fit for their needs."*

sonable explanation, and we can collaborate with clients to find a better fit for their needs.

Malingering

Malingering is a clinical term for dishonesty. It refers to when a client is deliberately exaggerating their symptoms in order to receive a preferred outcome. While there may be clients who are dishonest with providers, coming from a standpoint of assumed deception harms the provider–client relationship significantly. Why should the client trust a provider who assumes the client is lying? Furthermore, countless clients, both neurodivergent and neurotypical, have been harmed by the health care system as a result of providers assuming they are lying when they are actually telling the truth.

Assuming dishonesty does significantly more harm than good. If there is definitive proof that the client's account of events does not match reality, providers can once again approach from a place of curiosity. As Natasha Nelson , a positive discipline educator and neurodivergent advocate, said in an interview with Elizabeth Newcamp of *Slate*: "Misbehavior is communicating unmet needs" (2023). Exploring and identifying what needs might lead to the deception can allow us to support our clients, get their needs met, and develop healthy and appropriate coping.

Resistant

Similar to noncompliant, labeling a client resistant suggests malicious intent that might not be present. Again, curiously explore the client's supposed resistance. See what barriers may be preventing them from engaging, or reasons why a given intervention or recommendation is not a good fit for their needs. Even if you feel you have fully explored this, and the client seems to resist without an apparent cause, be mindful of how it might impact their future care for other providers to see them described this way in their medical records.

Manipulative

When we refer to clients as manipulative, we are assuming malicious intent to their behaviors. Remember the quote from Natasha Nelson above. Is a client trying to indirectly solicit a specific response from the provider without stating it directly? It is possible, but consider why. Do they feel unsafe to ask you directly? Have they been taught that this is the most effective way to meet their needs? Address this gently and in an affirming way, and do not assume that you know your client's intentions behind the behavior. Again, remember how it might impact their ability to receive care if you label them with this term in their records.

Drug-Seeking

Addiction and substance dependence are widespread issues in our society. Substance use disorders (SUDs) are a form of neurodivergence, and many neurodivergent individuals with other diagnoses struggle with addiction at some point in their lives. It can be the result of attempts to self-medicate, brain chemistry that predisposes an individual to dependence, genetics, inadequate access to appropriate support, or, usually, some combination of multiple factors. Rather than making system-level changes that prevent substance dependence or appropriately support individuals who develop dependence, the existing system has put health care providers in the role of law enforcement, expecting us to detect when clients might be requesting medication that they do not really need.

First, the term itself is misleading. If an individual calls their physician because they have an infection that requires antibiotic treatment, they are technically seeking drugs. An individual who wants to discuss antidepressant options for their mental health is technically seeking drugs. But when the prescription requested is a controlled substance, such as a stimulant or an opioid, it is assumed that this intention is malicious.

Second, there is a reason why these prescriptions are legal in the first place: there are clients who need them. Assuming that clients are requesting medication due to substance dependence overlooks those with medical or mental health needs. How many clients are denied appropriate medication due to concerns of drug-seeking?

Third, the standard response when a provider assumes drug-seeking behavior is to refuse care all together. If a client is truly struggling with addiction, this is a wildly inappropriate response. Maybe prescribing the requested medication is inappropriate, but what follow-up care is offered? If you truly have clinical evidence that the client is struggling with substance dependence and that medication is contraindicated, you have a responsibility to connect the client with appropriate rehabilitation services instead of leaving them without support.

Finally, once again, indicating that a client is drug-seeking in their chart will create a barrier to accessing appropriate care, as all future providers will see them through this lens and may fail to offer appropriate support.

Nuance and Complexity

There are no absolutes, except for this one, which is not techni-cally an absolute, as it is its own exception. As has been discussed, neurodiversity-affirming mental health care requires an individu-alized approach to each client based on their needs, presentation, and self-identified values. It means that the correct approach to supporting each client is going to differ, and each case must be approached from a place of curiosity, with an openness to new ideas and strategies.

Unfortunately, our present culture tends to take extreme stances. It is easy to leap from "This did not work for me," to "This does not work at all," to "No one should ever even try this."

The same treatment option can have no impact, positive impact, or negative impact depending on the individual, and each of these outcomes is valid when it applies. For instance, therapy aimed at reducing anxiety symptoms can be wonderfully helpful to an individual with an anxiety disorder and no co-occurring condi-tions. However, if the individual also has undiagnosed ADHD and developed anxiety to compensate for their ADHD symptoms, the anxiety treatment may be ineffective, as that anxiety was meeting the need of overcoming executive functioning related to ADHD. For an individual with both ADHD and anxiety, therapeutic inter-ventions aimed at reducing anxiety might have no impact at all, or they could lead to worsening executive functioning as the anx-iety they previously used to compensate is stripped away. So, one person with anxiety might benefit greatly from this approach, one person with anxiety and ADHD might see no change, and another person with both anxiety and ADHD could feel that their prob-lematic symptoms worsened as a result of the same treatment.

All three of these individuals are valid and correct in their experience of the intervention. This does not mean the intervention should be banned for those who found it beneficial; it simply means that more options need to be available so that those for whom it was not a good fit have other choices in getting support.

This of course does not mean that inappropriate, harmful interventions do not exist. The previously mentioned treatment by hypnosis to recover repressed memories is a good example of this. Hypnosis may provide therapeutic benefit in some scenarios, but its utility for bringing up repressed memories has been disproven (Short, 2022). It is our responsibility as professionals to thoroughly vet the interventions we use and the approaches we take to treatment in order to prevent harm to our clients and avoid interventions that we know will be harmful.

At the same time, we are not immune from the tendency to shift to extremes. We need to be mindful again of our own biases and avoid a shift from "This is not something I am able to do competently" to "This should not be done ever." There are many treatment approaches that I am not trained in that still have utility, just not in my practice or with the specific populations I serve.

Medication and Psychiatry

There has been a growing movement in recent years believing that no one should receive medication intervention for a mental health issue (Fountoulakis & Fountoulakis, 2022). While medication is not a magic cure-all or the right fit for every client, many neurodivergent people benefit from psychiatric medication to alleviate mood symptoms, manage executive dysfunction and impulsivity, and treat a variety of harmful symptoms.

Accurate diagnosis is essential if a client wants to pursue medication options for symptoms they are experiencing. For example, many individuals with bipolar disorders are misdiagnosed as having a depressive disorder before learning that they are bipolar. If someone with a bipolar disorder is misdiagnosed as having a depressive disorder, their medication can cause worsening of manic or hypomanic symptoms, which can be harmful. This happened to Willa Goodfellow, who shared her experience in her book, *Prozac Monologues: A Voice from the Edge* (2020). Willa was misdiagnosed with major depressive disorder rather than bipolar II disorder, which resulted in a manic episode when she was put on antidepressant medication. This is why we need accurate diagnosis: to ensure that clients are routed to the correct medication.

Another common misdiagnosis leading to improper medication intervention is bipolar disorder versus ADHD. A person can have ADHD, or bipolar disorder, or both, and many who have ADHD are misdiagnosed as having a bipolar disorder, and vice versa. Someone who does not have bipolar disorder can have significant negative side effects if they take mood stabilizing medication that is not needed, such as heart problems, digestive issues, sexual side effects, and seizures (Himmerich & Hamilton, 2020). Similarly, someone who does not have ADHD can have significant negative effects from taking ADHD medication unnecessarily, including depressive symptoms, flattened affect, and anxiety (Ophir, 2022).

Furthermore, all medical intervention comes with risk. The professional's job and goal are to provide the client with the education they need to make an informed choice about their care, deciding which potential risks and benefits are best for them individually. For instance, surgery is always traumatic on the body.

But if a patient's appendix is inflamed, the potential damage of leaving it alone is significantly worse than the damage of removing it. Sometimes, clients choose medication, and other times they do not. Unfortunately, sometimes the decision not to pursue medication comes from internalized stigma about what it means to use medication to manage mental health, something that needs to be addressed on a societal level.

It is true that some people have negative experiences with medication. There is a history of forcing medication on individuals without their consent, particularly in institutionalized settings. This is unethical and unacceptable. It is also true that some have had harmful experiences on medication even when they fully consented based on the information that was available to them at the time. For instance, certain antipsychotic medication can cause side effects that continue even after the medication is discontinued, including weight gain and movement disorders (Leucht et al., 2012). Some who experienced negative side effects wish that they had never tried the medication in the first place.

At the same time, there is a small but vocal movement to ban all psychiatric medication because some people have been harmed. This is like saying that all vaccines should be banned because a small percentage of people have medical indications that make vaccinations dangerous to them or have an adverse reaction to the vaccine when in fact researchers indicate that these reactions are "extremely rare" (Maglione et al., 2014). People advocating against psychiatric medication have encouraged clients to go off of medication without physician supervision, which can sometimes cause dangerous withdrawals. They have coordinated harassment campaigns against prescribers or anyone who calls out misinformation. They have called licensing boards demanding that providers who admit to taking psychiatric medication be removed from the field altogether, despite the providers having done nothing unethical or illegal. These behaviors prevent people from getting the care they need, or any care at all, by creating problems that keep providers from giving full attention to clients.

Prescribers need to remain up-to-date on the benefits, risks, and side effects of all medications they prescribe, including any information about contraindications for any diagnosis. Clients deserve clear, honest communication about their options, including any potential risks and the likelihood that these risks will occur. Clients and prescribers alike need to be able to discuss side effects and possible negative impacts of medication without further stigmatizing this valid treatment option.

It is not easy to name and honor complexity. It is not easy to hold space for nuance. But it is essential.

Conclusion

The systems issues around assessing for and identifying neurodivergence are varied and significant. Although no provider can singlehandedly fix the system, we can each do our part to make small improvements and provide a neurodiversity-affirming practice. In these ways, we can provide positive system experiences for our clients, reduce instances of misdiagnosis, and help our clients receive appropriate care in other areas of the system.

CHAPTER 5

New Therapeutic Treatment Approaches

Mental health support for neurodivergent communities often starts with assessment, but this is not the only step in the process by far. Many neurodivergent individuals benefit from mental health services including therapy. For some, therapeutic approaches help them manage mental health symptoms caused by neurodivergence, such as mood or anxiety disorders. Others may not experience neurodivergent traits as mental health issues, but existing as neurodivergent in a neurotypical world is in itself a stressor that requires support. While therapy cannot fix oppressive systems by itself, it can mitigate the mental health impact of existing in these systems. Of course, this is only effective if we can provide appropriate support that meets clients' needs in a neurodiversity-affirming way.

This chapter explores how to make mental health therapy neurodiversity-affirming. As has been discussed previously, neurodiversity-affirming therapy is not one set of interventions or even one specific theoretical orientation or approach to care. It is an overarching philosophy that can be applied appropriately in many different ways depending on individual client needs. We will explore the ways that existing interventions can be approached in a neurodiversity-affirming way, and practitioners can use the skills of crafting affirming interventions in their own practices.

The Concept of Mental Illness

As noted, mental health issues are not automatically an inherent trait to neurodivergence in all cases. When conceptualizing a client's neurodivergence, we must collaborate and explore how the client views their neurodivergence and any occurring mental health issues, including whether they view any existing mental illness as inherent to their neurodivergence or as a separate trait caused by oppressive systems. Two clients with the same neurodivergent diagnosis might have opposite perceptions of their experience, both of which are valid. Providers can educate clients about their neurodivergence while empowering them to develop their own conceptualization of their experience.

Suicidality

Suicidal ideation is a common mental health symptom for many different diagnoses, including but not limited to depressive disorders, bipolar disorders, psychotic disorders, and personality disorders. The DSM considers suicidal ideation an indication of the presence of the diagnosis itself rather than a side effect of existing with the diagnosis in a problematic world.

Additionally, many neurodivergences for which suicidal ideation is not a core trait have increased risk for suicide. There is significant research supporting this trend, with studies showing that ADHD (Furczyk & Thome, 2014), autistic (Forcey-Rodriguez,

2023), and individuals with traumatic brain injuries (McIntire et al., 2021) are at higher risk for death from suicide compared to neurotypical populations. Many other neurodivergent communities exhibit similar trends.

Conducting risk assessments for suicide is standard practice for any mental health provider, as we have a responsibility to assess our clients' safety and address any safety concerns, including risks to self. Appropriate and affirming considerations in maintaining client safety have been discussed in a previous section.

Client-Centered Care

Yao and Kabir note that Carl Rogers developed the concept of *person-centered therapy*, or an approach to mental health treatment that assumes people are motivated toward self-improvement, and clients are the experts of their own lives (Yao & Kabir, 2023). Does that sound familiar?

Yao and Kabir (2023) cite what Rogers listed as essential in providing therapeutic care to clients and facilitating change:

- Contact between the therapist and client.
- The client is in a state of incongruence, or their ideal self does not match who they are.
- The therapist shows up to the relationship in a genuine, sincere manner.
- The therapist views the client with unconditional positive regard, or fully accepts the client as they are, incongruence and all.
- The therapist presents with empathy and understanding of the client's perspective.

- The client perceives and receives the therapist's unconditional positive regard and empathy.

According to Rogers, these conditions are "necessary and sufficient" (Rogers, 1957) for therapy to be effective and for the client to experience therapeutic change. This means that these components are needed, and they are *all* that is needed in therapy.

While person-centered therapy is not the only approach to mental health care that can be neurodiversity-affirming, the conditions Rogers presented are essential in providing affirming care. A therapist can be an expert on a client's specific type of neurodivergence without assuming they are the expert on the client's own experience. An affirming therapist must be mindful of the client's self-identified needs, values, and worldview, and while it can be appropriate to challenge things like internalized ableism, truly neurodiversity-affirming mental health care holds the client as the expert on themself.

Furthermore, unconditional positive regard is a central component of neurodiversity-affirming care. Mental health providers are human beings, which means we may have opinions of others that can be positive or negative; however, we inherently see each client's value as a person and show up for them with empathy and acceptance. Again, this does not mean never challenging them or not making space for therapeutic change, but it is key in maintaining trust and a positive therapeutic relationship, making room for the client to make changes as appropriate, or holding space for clients to cope with issues arising from systems issues out of their control.

Strengths-Based Care

Strengths-based therapy is an approach to mental health care that focuses on individual strengths more than symptoms or deficits. We have discussed the importance of avoiding toxic positivity when providing neurodiversity-affirming care; it can be tempting to fall into this trend when taking a strengths-based approach to supporting our clients. However, true strengths-based treatment does not ignore problematic traits or insist that they are all secretly strengths. Instead, it involves identifying strengths as well as deficits, and emphasizing how these strengths can compensate for deficits or foster the client's inherent resilience (Yuen, 2020).

While many neurodivergent individuals do not associate strengths directly resulting from their neurodivergence, therapists can still help them identify personal strengths or things they are good at. Additionally, even those who identify deficits directly resulting from their neurodivergence might still see strengths that go hand-in-hand with their neurodivergent identity. While we are not claiming that neurodivergence is secretly a superpower or denying the challenges that come with being neurodivergent, naming strengths can foster a positive sense of identity and self-esteem. Clients deserve to feel that they have value and worth regardless of their struggles, and for some, this includes awareness of their personal strengths.

Behavior Meets Needs

When exploring why clients behave in maladaptive ways or choose unhealthy coping skills, there is a tendency to label clients as noncompliant or self-sabotaging and push the client to make changes without taking the time to explore the reasons behind these behaviors. If we agree with the premise that behavior exists to meet a specific need, it is often insufficient to simply focus on changing behaviors. It is relatively simple to identify behaviors as harmful or problematic and encourage the client to stop or replace the behavior with a safer choice; however, if we do not identify the underlying need and find a healthy way to meet this need, the client might return to the avoided behavior, even if they do not consciously realize the trigger for the behavior.

There may be times when replacing behavior is appropriate, for example, finding ways for clients to cope with intense emotions with an alternative to self-harm behavior. However, if we do not also strive to identify the underlying need, we have only done half of our job. Explore the underlying needs to find solutions that meet these needs in healthy ways.

Additionally, redirecting behavior on the surface can send the message that the client is bad or wrong for engaging in the behavior. A needs-based approach expresses care and regard for the client because it shows that you want them to have what they need rather than just stop doing the harmful behavior.

Imposter Syndrome

Many neurodivergent clients experience what is often referred to as *imposter syndrome*, or the belief that they are somehow faking their neurodivergent traits, often so effectively that they do not even realize they are faking. Of course, this is not something that actually happens. The so-called disability con refers to the idea that someone would fake having a disability in order to unfairly access supportive services, financial gain, or other benefits associated with being disabled. However, a thorough analysis of existing research shows that fear of the disability con is far more rampant than actual disability (Macfarlane, 2021).

Media portrayals of faking or exaggerating disability status contribute to the conception that many pretend that they are disabled (Geiger, 2023). This leads to agencies putting significant energy into preventing fraud and causes the general public to assume that those who report that they are disabled are being dishonest (Dorfman, 2019).

While it cannot definitively be proven that no one has ever attempted to con the system and fake disability status, the research cited above suggests that this is exceedingly rare. In fact, many disabled people forego requesting benefits due to fears that they are not disabled enough to really deserve support as a result of this imposter syndrome. Additionally, concerns about faking make the process of getting support so taxing that the system is fully inaccessible to many that it claims to help. Applicants must complete complex forms, attend countless appointments, and jump through hoop after hoop in the hope that maybe they will get some support. Even if someone is approved for services, the supports available are minimal. Someone who is faking to scam the system would have to put in significant work for a payoff that is below the cost of living in most places.

In short: faking a disability is not a viable way to survive.

The assumption that many are faking disability makes it much more likely that someone will be denied needed support than that a faker will successfully game the system. The resources that go into preventing fraud could actually benefit those who are unfairly kept out by gatekeepers.

Constant messages and assumptions that many people are

faking disability feed into this imposter syndrome, causing people to believe they could somehow be faking so effectively that they do not even realize they are doing it. It discourages people from applying for services that could truly help them and feeds into a negative view of themselves.

In addition to harmful, false messages about fakers, many clients question their experience because of natural variations in functioning. In a previous section, we discussed how everyone's best varies from day to day. For some, this leads to questioning themselves on good days: "Can I really be disabled if I am doing well today?" The answer is yes! Everyone's functioning varies depending on a multitude of factors.

It hopefully goes without saying, but a neurodiversity-affirming provider does not police someone's disability claim. We do not demand that our clients prove their needs to us; rather, we help them identify and access supports that could benefit them. Additionally, we help our clients develop insight into their experiences so they can understand their needs and ask for the help that they need. This does not mean infantilizing them and insisting that they cannot do things on their own; rather, it simply means helping them identify support needs they already have and supporting them in getting those needs met.

Self-Invalidation

Some disabled neurodivergent individuals tend to invalidate their own experience, making statements like, "My difficulties aren't as bad as they could be," or, "Other people have it worse." While it might be true that someone somewhere has more difficulties or an objectively worse experience, self-invalidation can be incredibly harmful. This is similar to the imposter syndrome described above, but rather than assuming that they are not really neurodivergent, invalidation involves clients assuming that their needs do not matter or are less important than other people's needs.

While not everyone engages in self-invalidation, this is a common tendency, stemming from multiple factors. For one, many neurodivergent people are used to hearing that they are simply not trying hard enough when they struggle, or being told, "It's not that hard" when they cannot do something. They might even directly get the message that they should not accept help or support because other people have more difficult lives.

Self-invalidation can also be a misdirected attempt to cope with distress. If I convince myself that other people have it worse, I can try to believe that my problems are not as distressing as I previously believed. This dissonance does not actually alleviate my difficulties, but it can help me distance myself from them in the short term. When an individual's needs are not being met, it can be easier to find ways to fully ignore these needs rather than sitting with the discomfort of unmet needs.

When validating clients' feelings and experiences, providers must take care to provide appropriate support as the client becomes more in tune with their needs. When an individual has distanced themselves from their distress, it can be overwhelming to get back in tune with these feelings. Clients deserve to hear that their experience is valid, especially the challenges that come with being neurodivergent in a neurotypical world, and tearing down unhealthy coping skills can leave clients vulnerable to big feelings they had previously not addressed.

Psychoeducation

Whether we are assessing for and identifying neurodivergence or providing ongoing mental health support for neurodivergent clients, there will be times when the people we work with would benefit from additional information and knowledge about their experience. Although neurodiversity-affirming providers approach mental health care from a collaborative standpoint, remembering always that clients are the experts on their own experience, we can still hold our own expertise as clinicians with extensive training and help our clients obtain more information that can benefit them. Psychoeducation involves providing clients with information relevant to their diagnosis or treatment, with the goal of helping them understand themselves and make informed decisions about their needs.

Education About Education

When someone first suspects that they are neurodivergent, it is natural to want to learn more about the diagnosis, support options, and community. If a client begins wondering about neurodivergence before they are involved in the system, they might do their own research before reaching out to professionals. While this is their right, they may encounter misinformation and not have the expertise to vet their sources appropriately. Anyone can post on the internet, which means that historically marginalized voices can be heard, but also anyone can present themselves as an expert regardless of credentials and share misinformation.

At the same time, individuals can find community, particularly through social media sites and applications. In fact, websites with algorithms can match clients with other users with similar experiences, which in theory could help neurodivergent people find their communities. For example, research has shown that Facebook's algorithm can identify depressive disorders (Eichstaedt et al., 2018). Many autistic and ADHD individuals report that they first began suspecting their neurodivergence when social media apps began recommending ADHD and autistic content creators, and they found the material relatable.

(There are certainly legal, ethical, and moral concerns about a social media algorithm that can accurately identify neurodivergence, especially if the application determines that someone is neurodivergent when they do not know it themselves. This is a topic to pressure lawmakers to address and is outside the scope of this text, though it is essential to name and address.)

Search engines are another common go-to for finding information about neurodivergence. However, many search engines prioritize profit over accurate information. This means that clients are likely to find false information if it is profitable for the search engine to center misinformation. Search engines make money by selling top search result spots and by getting users to stay online and keep clicking. If I search for information and find factual, balanced articles that address my concerns appropriately, I might sign off and go on with my day. On the other hand, if the search results scare me or make me angry, I am much more likely to keep clicking.

It is not effective to tell clients to simply not use search engines. In most cases, they will search for information about their neurodivergence and need to feel safe bringing any concerns that come up with their provider, which they might not do if they worry they have done something wrong. Furthermore, no matter how knowledgeable, no provider has all of the information about any topic. Clients need the option to seek out more information. Instead, educate clients about the kinds of resources they can look for, and provide guidance for specific organizations that will give them affirming and accurate information about their diagnosis. With this groundwork, clients can find useful resources and reduce the risk of being harmed by misinformation.

Collaborative Learning

I once read an interview with someone who participated in a contest where they had to identify from a group of people who was a true expert and who was lying. They said that one way to identify the expert is to see who will admit that they do not know an answer to a question, as an imposter will simply make something up, and someone who is truly knowledgeable on a topic will be able to admit the limits to their expertise. There inevitably will be times when clients ask questions that we cannot answer, and it is both appropriate and necessary to acknowledge this.

Just as we teach clients to vet information, we can model this in real time by finding answers together when they inquire about something we do not know.

Informing Versus Advising

Mental health providers typically do not offer advice. Instead, we provide a supportive environment where our clients can determine what is the right call for themselves. When presenting educational material to clients, it can be tempting to fall into the role of expert and indicate which resources are best or guide the client toward a decision based on our own opinion. Instead, we must continue to center the client's experience and provide information that empowers them to make their own decisions.

Neurodiversity-Affirming Interventions

Now that we have laid a groundwork for what a neurodiversity-affirming mental health practice can look like, we can review some specific interventions that allow us to provide affirming care to our clients. Bear in mind that no intervention is inherently affirming if the provider is not affirming or does not present the intervention in an affirming manner, and many interventions can be affirming with an appropriate approach (Lerner et al., 2023). These examples are intended as a starting point for providers as a way to visualize specific actions they can take in sessions with their clients.

Please note that some of these activities involve helping the client become more in touch with their needs. While this is often a healthy behavior, if an individual is disengaged from their internal experiences because their needs have not been met in the past, bringing awareness to the needs can be distressing without actually helping meet the needs. Similarly, activities that help clients be more authentic and unmask can be contraindicated if the client does not feel safe unmasking in their current environment. Note what is most appropriate for the client in their current situation.

Assertiveness Training

Because many neurodivergent individuals are taught that they are too much or that they need to tone it down, they might be used to tolerating things that make them uncomfortable. They might tend to go with the flow rather than pushing back. Abusive people sometimes target and exploit neurodivergent individuals who have been taught that they are not allowed to be assertive. Assertiveness training is a set of therapeutic interventions based in cognitive behavioral therapy aimed at helping clients assert themselves.

While it is not inherently bad or negative to want to get along with other people, and compromise can be a good thing, some people fall into extreme patterns of feeling unable to assert themselves in any situation. This can lead to burnout, including loss of self-care skills, withdrawal from relationships, and disabling loss of energy, if they take on more than they can handle, feel resentment in relationships, and don't get their needs met. Assertiveness training can take many forms, including:

- *Observational exposures.* This concept is familiar to anyone with training in CBT. An exposure in therapy is when a client is exposed to a distressing stimulus until their arousal level drops, allowing them to feel safe in the situation. For assertiveness training, this could include watching videos of people arguing or managing conflict.
- *In vivo exposure.* More direct than an observation, in vivo refers to real life exposure interventions that a client completes, often in session. This might include having the client send back an item they ordered at a restaurant or disagree in a conversation.
- *Broken record.* With this technique, clients practice repeatedly declining something. Sometimes we can get better at saying "No" the first time but struggle to maintain it if the person pushes back or repeats their request. This can be a literal repetition of the initial refusal.
- *Cognitive challenging.* If a client identifies that they struggle with assertiveness because, deep down, they do not believe that they are allowed to assert themselves, they can work

with their therapist to identify and challenge thoughts
that reflect this belief. Some neurodivergent clients have
reported experiencing cognitive challenging like gaslighting, as it often includes the message that their thoughts are
wrong. Neurodiversity-affirming providers emphasize that
these thoughts may be *unhelpful* rather than telling clients
that their perception is wrong.

- *Behavior rehearsal.* Clients can share specific scenarios
that bring out their anxiety, and the therapist can help
them practice how they want to act in that situation. This
both exposes them to the distress associated with asserting themselves and helps them practice how they want to
display assertiveness.

Boundary Setting

Boundaries are a component of assertiveness. A boundary is a
limit or dividing line, and boundaries that people set are the limits individuals set for themselves and for others around what they
expect and how they will respond of these expectations are not
met. Many neurodivergent people have had boundaries crossed
in many scenarios, and so they may either not know how to set
boundaries or not realize that they deserve to have their boundaries respected. Mental health providers can help our clients set and
maintain appropriate boundaries.

Boundaries are not mandates or ultimatums, and a boundary cannot control someone else's behavior or choices. However,
a boundary might indicate how we will respond when someone
crosses a line we have drawn. Boundaries involve communicating
these limits and responding consistently if the line is crossed.

For example, telling a family member, "You cannot call me

when I am working," communicates the boundary that you do not want to receive communications when you are on the clock. However, you cannot make the family member stop calling you whenever they choose. Instead, you can choose not to check messages until after work. If that family member consistently ignores your boundaries, you might block their number or further limit their access to you.

Another example: if a friend is often highly critical, you might decide to set a boundary like, "Please do not offer feedback unless I ask for it." They might not honor the boundary, and you might end conversations when this happens. If the friend does not respect your boundaries, you might make the decision to end that friendship.

Of course, it is not always safe to set a boundary. In the first example, while it is inappropriate for an employer to expect workers to engage in work-related activities when they are off the clock, not everyone can safely call this out or set a boundary without worrying about losing their income. Similarly, those in abusive relationships might not feel safe setting boundaries, and boundaries are often ineffective with abusers. Pushing a client to set boundaries when they do not have a safe environment can do more harm than good. We can educate clients about how boundaries can help them and support them in identifying safe options for setting boundaries.

Additionally, boundaries do not control other people's decisions. Sometimes, abusive people use therapeutic language around boundaries to justify controlling behavior. For example, being told, "You are not allowed to spend time with friends," or, "I will leave you if you do not do everything I say," are not boundaries; they are control. We can help clients identify healthy boundaries that they can set for themselves.

In addition to setting boundaries, it is important to understand how to honor and respect other people's boundaries. Neurodivergent and neurotypical people can all have trouble understanding boundaries, especially if we were not taught how to appropriately respect the boundaries of others. If our boundaries have repeatedly been crossed, or we continuously witnessed boundary-crossing behavior, it may be normalized and feel appropriate.

When an individual is struggling in their relationships, they can explore disagreements and communication breakdowns from a place of curiosity and a desire to grow. This does not mean the individual is a bad person; everyone makes mistakes sometimes, and everyone has violated a boundary at some point in their life. Practice identifying ways that others have requested respect for their time and space, and practice responding appropriately when a boundary is set. This is especially important if the boundary was not the desired response, as when someone indicates that they cannot do a favor.

Changing the Environment

Many approaches to mental health care for neurodivergent individuals focus on changing the individual to fit in with neurotypical society and meet neurotypical expectations. While we cannot always control the environment, and we might not have the power to make certain changes, we can work with clients to identify specific changes that could benefit them and find ways these changes can be implemented. If the client has a legal guardian or support person/people, we can enlist them in implementing environmental changes that can better meet the client's needs.

As you work with your client to identify their unmet needs,

explore specific environmental triggers or circumstances that interfere with their ability to cope and self-regulate. If the environment cannot be tweaked in ways that benefit the client, explore alternative environments the client can spend time in that might better meet their needs. If the client has a workplace or school they attend, you can use assertiveness training to help them advocate for themselves and request appropriate accommodations or support their guardian or care person in this process.

When the environment is within the client's control, like their home and personal space, possible tweaks they can try in order to feel calmer and better supported include:

- Changing the lighting or noise level
- Adding fidget, stim (items that allow for repetitive movements that help with self-regulation), or sensory items that help with self-regulation
- Repainting or rearranging the space

Even if the client cannot avoid environments outside the home, having a safe space in the home that meets their individual needs can be great for regulation, coping, and preventing burnout.

Coping Arsenal

In the moment when someone is activated or dysregulated, choosing appropriate coping skills can be impossible. This is because when the amygdala (the part of the brain that processes emotion) is activated, the frontal lobe (the part that controls language, logic, problem solving, etc.) literally goes offline. At the same time, appropriate coping skills can be the key to reregulating during a difficult time. Because of this, developing an arsenal of coping skills during calm times can make it easier to implement them when they are needed.

Clients can practice different coping skills and see how they respond to each one. Encouraging them to bring their own ideas for skills helps ensure that they choose skills that are a good individual fit and can increase their motivation to use them. Help them craft a list of the skills they find effective, and encourage them to practice skills when they are not needed.

Clients can track skills they like using a notes application on a phone or in a physical notebook, including times when they intend to practice.

Creative Therapies

Creative expression therapies include therapeutic activities involving art, creative writing, music, and so on. Artistic expression can tap into emotions we are struggling to express with words, process feelings without having to talk about them, and foster confidence.

As with the coping skills activity above, have the client choose their preferred medium, and give them space in their session to explore this. The focus of therapeutic art is the process of creating, not the final product appearing a certain way. This means that there is no minimum skill level required in order to participate. For clients who are hesitant to engage in creative expression activities due to concerns about their skill level, we can support them in experimenting with letting go of their fears and trying something anyway, or we can support them by showing them that they are in control of the session and have the right to decline interventions.

If the client is open to implementing creative expression into their therapy, you can verbally explore their emotional experience as they complete the activity or simply share the space and process. (Therapy is not always about talking, after all!) They can even destroy what they made, to emphasize the importance of the process over the product.

Grounding Techniques

Grounding techniques are a form of mindfulness that help an individual cope with emotional distress and let go of intense feelings by refocusing their attention elsewhere. When used inappropriately, grounding exercises can lead to ignoring emotions or pushing them away; however, they can help regulate big emotions and make them more manageable. They can also help put away feelings that come up at times when we are not in a space to process them, allowing us to function for now and address them later.

In her book, *Seeking Safety: A Treatment Manual for PTSD and Substance Abuse* (2001), Lisa Najavits describes grounding as "a set of simple strategies to detach from emotional pain," which can help trauma survivors and those struggling with substance dependence distract themselves from flashbacks, harmful impulses, drug cravings, and other potentially dangerous behaviors or emotions. There are many different ways to engage in grounding, and many grounding activities do not require any particular physical resource. Najavits presents the following guidelines for grounding:

- Practice reminders to use grounding during flashbacks, dissociative episodes, substance cravings, in the presence of a trauma trigger, or during any time of intense, painful emotion.
- Remember that you are trying to distract yourself from the

big emotions, not process them, so activities like journaling about the feeling are not helpful when grounding.

- Use neutral terminology rather than labeling things as good or bad.
- Emphasize what is happening in the present moment rather than past memories or concerns about the future.
- Open your eyes, and turn on lights so that you can view your environment.

Najavits recommends rating mood and emotional intensity on a scale of 0 to 10 before and after the grounding activity. While this can be useful in identifying which grounding techniques bring down emotional pain the most, some neurodivergent individuals struggle with rating pain on a scale like this. This can be presented as an option or tool for clients who find it beneficial, but follow the client's lead if they do not find scale rankings beneficial.

Like other coping skills, grounding is most useful when it is practiced. This will help the client remember to use the skill when they need it, especially since dissociation and trauma triggers are incredibly activating and make it difficult to even remember which coping skills might be beneficial in the moment. Examples of grounding include (Najavits, 2001):

- Describing every detail in your environment, being as specific and extensive as possible.
- Choosing a category, like animals, comedy movies, or countries, and think of as many different things in that category as you can.
- Say the alphabet backwards or count backwards from 100 by sevens.

- Repeat an affirmation or quote to yourself over and over.
- Press your feet into the floor, and focus on how that feels.
- Engage in a deep breathing exercise.
- Complete a guided imagery meditation in your mind, visualizing a peaceful or calming place.

Identifying Communication Styles

As Sonny Jane Wise (2023) pointed out, neurodiversity-affirming care involves honoring all forms of communication as valid and not prioritizing one way of communicating as inherently superior to others. In a neurotypical world, though, using mouth words (speaking out loud through one's mouth) is considered the right way to communicate. Some neurodivergent individuals do not communicate this way or can only communicate this way some of the time. Autistic people, those with communication disorders, some with psychotic symptoms, and other neurodivergent communities require alternative forms of communication to express themselves.

Due to assumptions that mouth words are the best or only way to effectively communicate, many neurodivergent individuals are pressured or forced to attempt this method of communication even when it is distressing for them. For those for whom mouth words are impossible, it is often assumed that they cannot communicate. Taken a step further, it is additionally assumed that they cannot understand communication. Many nonspeaking individuals, when given access to other methods to communicate, have shared experiences of professionals and caregivers talking about them as if they are not present, ignoring efforts to communicate in other ways, and violating their autonomy.

It likely goes without saying that neurodiversity-affirming

providers do not value mouth words above other forms of communication, and we make efforts to ensure that clients can use the method of communication that works best for them.

Augmentive and alternative communication (AAC) refers to methods of communication that do not involve mouth words. This includes sign language, AAC applications on tablets or smart phones, a keyboard, or even a chart of letters that the individual uses to spell out what they want to share. Providers can keep AAC options in our offices for clients to use as needed, and we can educate caretakers on the importance of AAC for clients who are nonspeaking or who lose speech sometimes.

Identifying Your Strengths

We have discussed strengths-based therapy previously in this text, an approach to mental health treatment that focuses on an individual's inherent strengths and abilities. While not everyone identifies as having strengths, and an individual's worth is not tied to their strengths, some clients benefit from exploring what their personal strengths are. When engaging in strengths-based work, we are mindful to avoid the toxic positivity trap and note that not everything has to be positive or secretly a strength. At the same time, we can explore the ways that some traits have served us in positive ways.

For example, someone who is considered argumentative or stubborn might also be very good at asserting themselves. Some trauma survivors have engaged in survival strategies that are maladaptive now, but which helped them get through the trauma. Identifying how these patterns previously served them can help in letting go of them now. Additionally, noting how some qualities can either be strengths or cause problems depending on the context and severity can help maximize using these qualities in beneficial ways and avoid harm.

We can help clients craft a list of qualities that could be strengths with the proper context or behaviors that have served them in some way.

Interoception Training

Interoception refers to our awareness of internal sensations and experiences. Trauma survivors in particular may be less in touch with their body sensations, and other neurodivergent individuals have reported below average interoception. For some, the awareness is naturally lower, as all traits have some natural variation. For others, chronically having to ignore their needs leads to detachment. It is easier to tolerate unmet needs when we are not in touch with those needs. This can make self-care difficult; if I am not in tune with my body cues, I am more likely to forget to eat, to forego sufficient rest, or to not do other things that keep me healthy.

For these clients, activities that enhance awareness of their internal experiences can help them get in touch with their needs in a healthy way. Please be aware, however, that if the client still exists in an environment where their needs will not be met, increased interoception can be highly distressing. While detachment can be unhealthy, increased awareness without actually meeting the ignored needs is not an improvement. Screen for this before recommending these kinds of activities.

By comparison, some neurodivergent people have above average interoception and are so in tune with their internal experiences that they experience distress due to not being able to turn off their awareness. For these clients, the grounding activities described in the previous section can help move the focus from inside to outside, reducing distress.

Learning to Rest

Some neurodivergences include traits such as constantly being on the go, restlessness, difficulty settling down, and hyperfocus that causes them to remain fixated on a task for extended periods of time. Even those who do not experience this as part of their neurodivergence have received constant messages that they are lazy or that their struggles are due to not working hard enough. Additionally, capitalism requires productivity in order to survive, often requiring neurodivergent individuals to push themselves well beyond their limits to simply survive. As a result, they may overwork themselves in dangerous ways. This can lead to burnout and even suicide.

When an individual does not know how to rest, they may have to consciously learn how to engage in this practice as a component of their self-care. Be aware, however, that mental health treatment cannot fix oppressive systems. Telling a client to take time off work for their mental well-being is unhelpful for a client who will lose their home if they miss any hours at the job.

We can collaborate with clients to find their recharge. Work on fleshing out answers to questions like:

- When do you feel most at rest?
- When is the last time you felt this way?
- Make a list of activities you do most days. Which of these things drain you the most, and which drain you the least?
- What environments or activities bring you the most restful feelings?

- When do you feel the least stressed or agitated? If there are no times when these feelings are at zero, when are they at their lowest?

Once activities have been identified that either instill restfulness or are associated with the lowest amount of stress, help the client find times in their schedule when they can engage in these activities. Of course, financial constraints and resource limitations can make this difficult; again, therapy cannot fix oppressive systems, and we must rally against systemic harm while meeting our clients where they are. Even small improvements are progress, so finding tiny amounts of time and space to engage in rest can be beneficial.

Sometimes, we can stave off burnout by disengaging from our needs. Just as increasing interoception can cause harm if the individual cannot get their needs met, engaging in rest when there is not space to actually, fully rest can lead to exhaustion as their unmet needs catch up with them. Assess carefully for what interventions are appropriate and safe based on the client's environment and available resources.

Maximizing Strengths Usage

After clients have learned to identify strengths in themselves, they might need support in utilizing these strengths. Craft a list of strengths the client identifies in themself, and identify the situations when these strengths are the greatest benefit. Explore the specific ways that the client might want to use these strengths to achieve their personal goals. When making decisions, consider how different strengths will come into play.

At the same time, note the ways that the strength might have drawbacks, and explore ways to avoid falling into maladaptive patterns. If the client benefits from tracking their progress, they can document times when they use different strengths and how it goes to further explore how they can improve these skills.

Meeting the Need

Again, behavior communicates a need. Therapy that exclusively focuses on reducing a problematic behavior is inherently nonaffirming, as it emphasizes forcing the individual to change rather than addressing their support. Many of these interventions also emphasize behaviors that are not inherently unhealthy or problematic, but rather simply inconvenience others in the client's environment, are disruptive, or even just weird. Neurodiversity-affirming providers understand that behaviors that do not cause an issue do not need to be modified.

At the same time, some behaviors cause harm. They may be distressing to the client, harm their body, cause real problems to others in their environment, or damage property that cannot easily be fixed or replaced. In these cases, supporting clients in choosing different behavior can be appropriate. In the moment, this can mean redirecting. For example, a client who has an impulse to engage in self-harm behavior can be directed to another coping skill, or a client who engages in picking behavior can use a stim item (an item that allows the user to engage in repetitive movements that aid in self-regulation) that can be destroyed.

Over the long term, though, it is ineffective to simply extinguish a behavior. Behavior is communication, and behavior represents needs. An emphasis on simply eliminating a behavior does not address the underlying need. Until we identify the need, we cannot effectively find alternative ways to meet it. Of course, clients do not always have a way to understand and effectively communicate *what* that need is. The following questions can help tease out more information about the need being expressed:

- When does the behavior tend to happen?
- What times, if any, does the behavior not happen?
- What do you feel when you have an urge to engage in the behavior but do not act on it? What builds up inside of you during that time?
- When is the first time you remember engaging in the behavior?
- What is your sensory experience of the behavior?
- During what periods of time have you done the behavior more?
- During what periods of time have you done the behavior less?

If the client is comfortable with it, they may choose to document when the behavior occurs in order to better identify triggers and determine what need might be met.

Mindfulness

Mindfulness therapies are approaches to mental health treatment that direct the client to focus on the present moment. Mindfulness can increase interoception and self-awareness. There is research to suggest that mindfulness can help some neurodivergent individuals manage their mental health symptoms and cope with strong emotions (Zhang et al., 2021).

At the same time, sometimes mindfulness is presented like a magical cure-all that can be applied in any scenario for any issue.

In some circumstances, an individual might not want to be more in touch with the present moment. For example, individuals with chronic pain might experience increased painful sensations if they engage in mindfulness exercises that draw their attention to their internal experiences. Current research actually suggests that mindfulness therapies may not be effective for individuals with chronic pain (Pei et al., 2021).

As neurodiversity-affirming therapists take a collaborative approach to treatment, you can explore with each client whether or not mindfulness interventions are a good fit for them. In instances where the client wants to try mindfulness or has found it effective in the past, the following interventions might be beneficial:

- *Body scan.* This is an activity that can be done in session with the therapist narrating, or the client can mentally complete a body scan any time. It involves mentally scanning from the top of the head to the bottom of the feet, attending to any sensations, positive or negative. The goal is to nonjudgmentally bring awareness to what is happening inside the body and what needs this might be reflecting. If the scan brings the individual's attention to a body need, they can take steps to get the need met.
- *Deep breathing.* Most mental health providers have several breathing activities on hand for use with clients. The client can practice slowly and deliberately taking deep, full breaths, in and out, to deliberately regulate their nervous system and bring down big emotions.
- *Five senses game.* This game involves becoming mindfully aware of the environment. Take a moment to bring your awareness to this moment and list five things you can see,

four things you can hear, three things you can feel, two
things you can smell, and one thing you can taste.

- *Mindful seeing/hearing/feeling/eating.* Mindful sense med-
  itations involve choosing a sense and focusing intently on
  it for a short period of time. The client can choose which
  sense they prefer to focus on and mindfully tune in to that
  sense for a predetermined amount of time. When practicing,
  clients can set a timer for how long they want to focus on
  everything they can see, hear, or feel, or they can engage in
  slow, deliberate, mindful consumption of something like a
  piece of chocolate or candy. They can find free scripts to listen to or simply bring their attention to their surroundings.
- *Muscle relaxation.* A muscle relaxation exercise involves
  deliberately tensing different muscle groups and then intentionally relaxing those groups, usually from head to toe or
  from toe to head.
- *Observing your thoughts.* Metacognition refers to the practice of being aware of and observing one's thoughts. Some
  neurodivergent people (e.g., those with ADHD) experience
  racing thoughts or have difficulty shutting off their thought
  process. For these individuals, many meditation exercises
  can be frustrating because they include prompts such as
  "Empty your mind" or "Let go of all thoughts." Instead,
  they can allow their thoughts to continue and simply make
  a practice of noticing what those thoughts are. Initially this
  can be done with the intention of being aware of thoughts
  without making a judgment about the specific thoughts,
  but later on, they can begin to challenge thoughts that they
  find harmful.
- *Single-tasking.* Single-tasking refers to taking a mindful

approach to something that is usually a mundane task. Choose one single task and complete it slowly, thoroughly, and with your full attention.

Some of these mindfulness activities will not be a good fit for everyone. For example, someone with ADHD who prefers observing their thoughts over meditation exercises might struggle with single-tasking. The goal is to help the individual be more aware of the present moment and focus their attention, and whichever activity helps them reach this goal is appropriate. At the same time, some clients will prefer some activities over others or will not benefit from mindfulness at all.

Narrative Therapy

Narrative therapy refers to an approach to mental health treatment that focuses on the client's lived experience. The concept is that problems and maladaptive behaviors are separate from the client rather than inherent to them, which allows clients to approach solutions from a place of curiosity and storytelling rather than self-blame (Madigan, 2011).

Narrative therapy is based on a specific worldview and approach to supporting clients:

- Clients can create a script or narrative of their perception and view of their experience.
- These scripts can be changed and rewritten if the client desires, which can allow for reframing or creating more adaptive storylines.
- The problem is external because the client is not the problem.

- Different perspectives are appropriate, and your view is not wrong just because it differs from someone else's.
- Clients are the authors of their own stories.

This approach to supporting clients fits well into a neurodiversity-affirming paradigm, and activities like helping the client articulate their perception and experience can be empowering and can instill a sense of autonomy. At the same time, pushing clients to reframe or rescript their experience can be invalidating and so must be implemented carefully in order to keep the client's experience at the center.

PACT Goals

Many payers push for providers to have set goals for the clients we support. While this can be appropriate, and we can support our clients in making changes they desire, this emphasis on outcomes can create pressure for clients to get better. This is nonaffirming for multiple reasons. First, these goals often emphasize the importance of making the client change, fixing them, even if they do not identify as needing to be fixed. It ignores the importance of environment and identifying underlying needs in providing affirming care. Second, if a client's mental health concerns are a direct result of existing in a system not built for them, any approach to treatment that involves getting them to a point where they can tolerate this is contraindicated. Rather than actually helping the client, these approaches can only hope to teach them to mask or ignore their needs. When a systems-level change is needed, individual change is not an appropriate solution. Finally, many neurodivergent individuals have mental health issues that require lifelong support. Getting them better in order to terminate treatment is not necessarily a realistic goal.

Thus, outcome-based goals are often nonaffirming or unhelpful. It is possible to develop goals that are based on what is within the client's control. PACT goals, developed by Anne-Laurie Le Cunff (2019), are structured around the client's choices and behavior rather than outcomes. PACT goals are:

- *Purposeful.* The goal should impact the client in the long term, with the hope of improving their well-being over the rest of their life.
- *Actionable.* The goal should focus on things that are within the client's control and things that they can do to take steps toward achieving them.
- *Continuous.* The goal needs to be something they can continue to implement over time.
- *Trackable.* The client should be able to keep track of their progress in the goal.

Note that none of these steps involve making the goal dependent on the outcome. For example, an outcome-based goal might be to reduce sensory meltdowns. A PACT goal, on the other hand, would focus on supporting the client in practicing self-care skills that reduce the likelihood that they will reach the point of meltdown. The actual number of meltdowns is not measured, but the client can track which skills they practiced and how effective they were.

Positive Affirmations

Affirmations are words, statements, or quotes with a positive message that uplift or motivate. Social media influencers often share affirmations, though for therapeutic purposes, affirmations must be chosen based on individual preferences. Generalized affirmations often fall into the toxic positivity trap, especially affirmations such as "Good vibes only" or "You can do anything." As always, if a given affirmation resonates with an individual, they absolutely can use it in their own life, and those who do not find an affirmation beneficial can choose something else.

Clients can develop their own affirmation or use one they found. They can practice repeating the affirmation to themselves so that they think of it during difficult times, or they can keep it written down where they can refer to it any time.

Radical Acceptance

Radical acceptance is based in dialectical behavioral therapy (DBT) and is a practice of giving oneself full permission to feel all aspects of one's experience, positive, negative, and neutral. It does not mean that we approve of these aspects, but that we accept them, including accepting things that upset us and are outside of our control to change. This technique and the philosophy behind DBT were developed by Marsha Linehan, psychologist and professor. According to Linehan, the steps of radical acceptance are (2014):

- *Observe.* Nonjudgmentally observing that you are fighting reality, such as feeling that things shouldn't be this way.
- *The reality.* Check in with the reality of the situation, exploring what happened factually.
- *The reason.* Note that there are reasons for the way reality is, restating what occurred, not justifying that things happen for a reason.
- *Practice.* Make a point of fully accepting your entire self, using coping skills as needed.

- *List.* Create a list of what you would do if you could fully accept the facts and yourself.
- *Imagine.* Visualize or imagine mentally what it would feel and look like to accept the things you are currently struggling to accept.
- *Attend.* Mindfully notice body sensations.
- *Allow.* Make space for unpleasant feelings like sadness, anger, grief, etc.
- *Acknowledge.* Affirm that pain exists, and life has value even in the presence of pain.
- *Pros and cons.* Use a pros and cons list to work through resistance to acceptance.

As with all interventions, this can be validating to clients who are working to affirm their perception and their experience of painful experiences and emotions, though the clinician must take care to avoid pressuring the client or invalidating their perception. Remember that this does not mean being happy with reality as it is, but simply acknowledging and accepting it.

Sensory Work

Sensory sensitivity is a documented neurodivergent trait for autistic individuals. Although not listed as a diagnostic criterion, they are also common in ADHD-ers and many other neurodivergent communities. Even those who do not have clinically significant sensory issues can benefit from sensory experiences—for example, many neurotypical people enjoy professional massages. This is a sensory experience that helps them with self-care and coping.

Clients can explore what sensory experiences they enjoy, are neutral to, or dislike, and clinicians can support them in implementing activities that give them sensory joy.

Sensory-seeking may include:

- Weighted items that put pressure on the body
- Physical touch
- Movement
- Visually interesting images or objects
- Background sound
- Scented items
- Sensory-avoiding may include:
- Dimming the lights
- Reducing sound
- Wearing looser clothing
- Using noise-canceling headphones

When the client identifies their ideal level of stimulation, they can modify their environment to ensure that sensory needs are met without triggering over- or understimulation.

Strengths List

As the name suggests, this intervention involves helping the client identify their personal strengths. We have previously explored how not everyone identifies with personal strengths and how strengths-based work must be implemented carefully to avoid the trap of toxic positivity. However, when appropriate, a strengths list can help clients recognize their strengths, building self-esteem, self-confidence, and autonomy.

These questions can help clients notice their personal strengths:

- Think of times that things went well for you. What specific actions did you take that may have contributed to that outcome?
- What skills are you proud of?
- What things do you feel you do well?
- What would your friends say your strengths are?
- What positive feedback have you gotten?
- Think of a time when you were challenged. How did you overcome it?

Unmasking

Masking, also known as camouflaging, is when an individual presents in ways that are not authentic to who they truly are. Some people do not mask at all, either through conscious choice or because they are not able to camouflage their true selves. For others, masking is necessary if they do not feel safe being authentic. This is not an issue of morality. Those who cannot mask are not inferior to those who do mask, and neurodivergent people who are unable to mask often report discrimination for behavior that is perceived as unusual or weird. At the same time, while those who are able to mask are often labeled high functioning, this does not mean that choosing to mask is better than choosing not to mask. High-masking neurodivergent individuals report frequently feeling invalidated when they express support needs: "But you're so _____! What do you mean you need support?"

Masking is not a uniquely neurodivergent behavior, either. Many neurotypical individuals mask in different environments. For example, most neurotypical people who hold employment would acknowledge that they do not speak to their boss the same way that they speak to their friends.

While masking is sometimes a safety behavior, and there may be times when masking is appropriate, many neurodivergent individuals mask continuously and often unconsciously. Those whose neurodivergence emerged in early childhood may have masked for as long as they can recall. Children realize when their authentic selves do not match the expectations to which they are held by the people around them. While they do not have the language to articulate this experience, they often start to attempt to present in a way that meets these perceived expectations. (As an aside, this is also why many trans and nonbinary neurodivergent individuals are high-masking: as young children, they picked up that their authentic selves did not match the gender expectations they experienced and may have masked their gender as well as their neurotype.)

For some, any amount of masking is incredibly draining, and for others, constant masking wears them down over time. This can lead to burnout, which is why unmasking can be an appropriate way to reduce risk for developing mental health issues.

At the same time, unmasking often leads to increased interoceptive awareness, so providers must again ensure that existing needs are met before encouraging unmasking. Additionally, if the masking behavior is in place for safety reasons, we have a responsibility to ensure safety before exploring unmasking with our clients.

It can be beneficial to let caregivers know that the client might outwardly display more neurodivergent traits as they unmask, and this does not mean that they are getting worse, but rather that they are becoming more authentic. As long as the behaviors are not physically harming the individual, this should be accepted and encouraged. Note that this often requires education, as many traditional therapies for neurodivergent individuals focus on making them appear less neurodivergent, so providers, caregivers, and even clients often have to unlearn internalized ableism in order to accept the individual as they unmask.

Unmasking is a highly individualized process and experience. Since the individual may not even realize what their unmasked self looks like, it can take time to get in touch with their authentic self. Create space for them to present in whatever way feels comfortable and encourage them to take time for themselves. Ask them how they would behave if they did not have to worry about how people would respond, or if they did not have a concept of looking or feeling weird or out of place. They can experiment with different self-care behaviors and mindfully attend to what feels best.

Validation

Validation refers to affirming someone's emotions or experience. It might seem that this goes without saying in the therapy setting, but many providers forget to intentionally validate what our clients are experiencing.

> *Many providers forget to intentionally validate what our clients are experiencing."*

Many who experienced trauma, particularly childhood trauma and abuse, experienced the message that their perception of reality is wrong or that their emotions are unacceptable. As a result, they might question their experience or deny their emotional experience. In particular, many become uncomfortable with their experience of anger because they were punished for expressing angry emotions.

When we validate our clients' emotional experiences, we

allow them to get back in touch with their experience and develop confidence in their experience. This can empower them and instill a stronger sense of autonomy. We can mindfully and intentionally validate our clients' emotional experiences to bring about this emotional change.

Furthermore, when therapeutic change cannot fix system-wide issues of oppression, validating our clients' experiences can communicate to them that they are not the problem. While this does not fix the system, it can be less distressing to exist in a system when we understand that it is not our fault or that it is beyond our power to fix.

Validation can also be a powerful tool for rapport with individuals whose neurodivergence causes difficulty accurately perceiving and interpreting their reality. In the moment, it is impossible to logically talk someone out of a delusional belief or an experience that is not grounded in reality, but we can join our clients, meeting them where they are and offering appropriate support. Hannah Owens (2024), schizoaffective social worker, shared the following regarding responding to psychotic symptoms:

> If someone you know is having a delusion or hallucinating, don't tell them that it's not happening because while that may seem like it will make things better and ground them to reality, it's ignoring the fact that they are experiencing the thing as though it's real. And so acknowledging, okay, I can see that you're really scared right now. What can I do to help you, I can tell you that there's nothing to be scared of, but I see that you are scared, so let's just let me be with you while you're experiencing this thing, and once it passes we can talk

about the fact that oh maybe that wasn't actually happening. . . . But in the moment recognizing the emotion and the experience is always going to be more helpful than "that's not actually happening, that's not actually there."

Although some providers insist that validating someone's experience during this kind of episode may be enabling, Owens (2024) points out, "It's not enabling anything. It's already happening." Instead, you establish yourself as a safe person for that client and establish trust and rapport.

In these ways, validating our clients' experiences can be a powerful tool of neurodiversity-affirming care.

Whole-Person Care

Every provider has a limited scope of practice or range of issues we can diagnose, assess, treat, and support. No one is an expert on everything; this would be impossible. At the same time, human beings have complex and interconnected needs. We are doing a disservice to our clients if we are not aware of other possible needs, even if we are unable to meet all of them ourselves.

When carving our niche or developing our specialization, we can be aware of common co-occurring needs. For example, neurodivergent individuals whose neurodivergence is the result of a genetic condition are often more likely to have co-occurring medical issues compared to neurotypicals. Keep a list of things of which your clients might want to be aware.

Many neurodivergent individuals struggle to get or maintain employment. Be aware of resources that can help your clients get their financial needs met.

As always, needs will vary by individual, but we can provide our clients with superior care when we are aware of what those needs are likely to be.

Considerations With Children and Adolescents

Neurodiversity-affirming care applies to all neurodivergent clients regardless of age. However, developmental differences, laws, and considerations for best practice mean that providing affirming care will look different for minor clients. Mental health providers must follow legal and ethical parameters when working with clients who are below the age of majority (Marschall, 2023), which can complicate our ability to provide affirming care. It is still possible to be neurodiversity-affirming when working with minor clients. This section explores the considerations we must keep in mind when supporting these clients.

Privacy Concerns

In the mental health field, there is a history of denying clients access to their records, including progress notes, assessment reports, and even not telling them their diagnosis. This is a clear ethical violation, as a client cannot fully consent to treatment if they are not told what the treatment is for, and they cannot fully consent to releasing information among providers if they do not know what that information is. Part of the push for neurodiversity-affirming mental health care includes full record transparency, giving clients the right to review their records and even have copies upon request. In fact, in the United States, the current laws require providers to give clients access to records unless the provider can document an appropriate reason why the client should not have access.

This shift is positive, as it prevents providers from denying clients access to their own records and fosters trust. It also prevents medical errors, as clients can review records and note when corrections need to be made.

At the same time, for clients below the age of majority, the requirement typically means that mental health professionals are required to disclose the information to a legal guardian instead. This means that whatever the client shares with their therapist could be repeated to a parent. While there will be times when the provider coordinates with the guardian for a variety of reasons (family therapy, relationship work, making environmental changes in the home for the client's well-being), unfettered access to session content can be harmful. Reasons why a provider might feel it is unsafe or not clinically appropriate to share therapy records with a parent might include, but are not limited to:

- The minor is questioning family values or beliefs and does not feel safe expressing that to the parent. A disclosure might truly be emotionally unsafe, and even if the anxiety is unfounded, a disclosure could destroy trust in the provider, and the client might not be able to be open with them again in the future. This can also give the client the message that therapists are all untrustworthy, interfering with clients' ability to engage in treatment in the future.
- The minor discloses harm or abuse that must be reported according to the law. If the guardian is the alleged perpetrator, they could engage in more abusive behavior if they learn that the client disclosed what happened.

- The legal guardians are in a custody dispute, and there are concerns that session content could be used in the court process in a way that is harmful to the client.
- Ethical practice requires honesty, so the client must be informed about what information will be provided to the guardian. The client might not fully engage in therapy if they are concerned about disclosures; they might withhold information that could be beneficial to therapy.
- Regardless of the specific content, a client might lose trust with the therapist following a disclosure.

In various circumstances, disclosure to guardians might be necessary. For instance, if the client discloses a safety concern where the guardian is not the alleged perpetrator, the therapist might need to enlist the guardian in safety planning, which would require disclosing the safety concern. In these cases, we must attempt a collaborative approach, working with the client to ensure their safety and supporting them in using available resources, which includes the guardian.

Outside of these concerns, though, a neurodiversity-affirming provider will make it their policy not to disclose session information to the guardian. We can work with the guardian and build trust so that they know we will disclose needed information while honoring privacy as much as possible. If the law states that the guardian has the right to request records, we can craft office policies where they agree to waive this right. There may be times when we are legally required to disclose, in which case we must maintain legal and ethical standards in practice, but we can take steps to mitigate this and protect our clients.

Spanking and Other Physical Punishment

Many traditional approaches to parenting focus on behavioral models and cycles of reward and punishment that can be harmful to children regardless of neurotype. Physical punishment, for instance, is normalized in many cultures and is even legal in all 50 states under certain conditions. Spanking is permitted under specific conditions, including the child's age, what is used to hit the child, how hard the child is hit, and where on their body the parent strikes them. To be clear: there is no right way to hit your children from a moral and ethical perspective.

Although many parenting experts and social scientists continue to condone spanking in certain circumstances, long-term studies consistently show that physical punishment correlates with problematic externalized behavior such as physical aggression as well as internalized emotional issues (Ferguson, 2013). These conclusions are drawn from extensive analysis of several long-term studies.

Parenting is stressful and difficult; this cannot be denied. Parents are human beings, just like children, and experience emotions that can be difficult to manage. Even someone with full frontal lobe development will experience challenging feelings from time to time and will make mistakes, including acting out in inappropriate ways when escalated. At the same time, it is the parent's job to be an adult and model appropriate skills. This includes apologizing when they make a mistake and avoiding harmful behavior. It also means having a plan in place to mitigate mistakes that could harm the child.

Some argue that physical punishment is the only way to stop

a harmful behavior. However, we must note that every behavior toward a child teaches that child something about the world. When a child experiences physical punishment as a result of bad behavior, that child learns that it is okay for someone to strike them if they have done something to deserve it. It also teaches them that they can use hitting as a way to resolve a problem.

Instead, conceptualize discipline as a teaching tool. We are raising future adults and want to use boundaries and discipline as ways to educate children about how to be adults who have good values and strong skills. When a child engages in a behavior that is inappropriate, harmful, or otherwise not acceptable, consider two questions:

1. What unmet need is this behavior expressing? (Remember the lesson from Natasha Nelson [2023]!)
2. What skill does the child need to learn right now?

Natural consequences can teach cause-and-effect, and punishments that emphasize restorative justice (e.g., fixing damage caused by the behavior) help the child learn that they can make amends when they have made a mistake. It highlights what was wrong with the behavior and shows the child how to do better in the future, without shaming or harming them for the choice that they made.

By identifying unmet needs, parents can reduce the chances that the behavior will occur again, as they can eliminate the need that brought on the behavior initially. They can additionally improve the child's feelings of security and attachment to the parent, as it sends the message that the parent is there to help and support them rather than simply punishing misbehavior.

Neurodiversity-affirming providers can offer resources for making this shift in the household, helping parents support their children's growth, development, and attachment.

Psychoeducation With Parents

Parents are frequently on the receiving end of criticism or feedback that they did not ask for. It is considered socially acceptable to comment on people's parenting and judge parents harshly, especially if their child is exhibiting behaviors that are considered weird or otherwise inappropriate. Many parents experience feelings of defensiveness in response to feedback about their parenting choices. Build rapport with parents so they understand that your intentions as a provider are good, that you want to support them in being the best parents they can be rather than simply criticizing. Create space for open dialogue rather than lecturing them about what they are doing wrong. Point out things the parent has done well as and their positive intentions toward their child.

In addition to providing feedback to the parent, solicit feedback from them. Make sure they know they can express their feelings toward you without receiving judgment. Just like recommendations provided to neurodivergent clients, collaborative approaches to parenting recommendations can increase the likelihood that parents will implement these interventions in their home.

Abusive or Harmful Behaviors

No one wants to hear that their behavior was abusive. Reactions to cognitive dissonance can be powerful, and many parents will double down on choices about physical punishment rather than acknowledging that they should not have made that choice. We can attempt to break through this defensiveness by explaining that the parent was doing their best with the information they had at the time, and an adjustment is necessary in light of this new information.

If you have taken the time to build good rapport with the parent, they should be able to receive feedback from you about their parenting even when that feedback is difficult to hear. It may not be necessary to label behavior abusive, but rather focus on ways the parent can be more effective, be more affirming, or create a more beneficial space for their child to thrive. Additionally, if the parent is recreating harmful patterns they learned but never had the opportunity to question, the provider can support them in unlearning and applaud their efforts to break harmful intergenerational patterns.

Individual Meetings

When a provider's scope of practice includes children and adolescents, there will be times when we work directly with the parent or caregiver. This individual is highly significant in the client's life and has control over much of the client's environment. In some circumstances, a provider will work primarily with the individual. For example, an adolescent above their state's age of majority might specifically request only individual counseling, and we have a legal and ethical responsibility to honor this. In other situations, the family might see a family therapist who addresses relationships and dynamics in the household, and the client sees an individual therapist in addition to this work. In cases of high-conflict divorce, the therapist may choose to work primarily with the individual child due to restrictions imposed by a court order or concerns about the client's session information being used in a way that harms the client.

However, most of the time, a parent or guardian will be directly involved in treatment. As noted above, the provider will likely have education and feedback for the parent or guardian intended to support the child, make positive changes in the home, or build appropriate parenting skills. We might choose to have this conversation without the client present in order to fully address ways that the parent's own history might contribute to their choices and to avoid undermining the parent's position as an authority figure. At other times, a joint session to address concerns can create space for the client to express their needs directly and can make room for collaborative problem solving.

Psychoeducation With Clients

Due to the amount of maturation and brain development that occurs through childhood and adolescence, the same terminology and educational materials that adults use to understand their neurodivergence will often be inappropriate for child or teen clients. That being said, no child is too young to know their diagnosis. No one is too developmentally delayed to not have the right to their own personal information. Parents might be hesitant to tell a client their diagnosis, but it is the client's right to know about themselves.

There are many neurodiversity-affirming resources for educating children about neurodivergence. Seek out what is recommended by adults in that community, and whenever possible, use resources created by community members. These resources can help you educate the client about their neurodivergence in a developmentally appropriate way. Disclosing the diagnosis may be a component of the client's treatment, or the provider can support the parents in sharing the diagnosis with their child.

Neurodivergence and Genetics

Many neurodivergent diagnoses have a genetic component. In fact, other than certain acquired neurodivergences (e.g., traumatic brain injury or a diagnosis brought on by exposure to a substance), most neurodivergences have some genetic component. It is not a guarantee that a parent and child will share a diagnosis, and the child might inherit neurodivergence from only one parent, while the other parent is neurotypical. Furthermore, genetics are complicated—maybe the child inherited some different recessive traits, and neither parent shares their exact neurodivergent presentation.

At the same time, it is not uncommon for a neurodivergent child to have at least one neurodivergent parent. Frequently, parents will be surprised by their child's diagnosis on the grounds that "That can't be a neurodivergent trait! I do it too." You might recommend that parents get their own assessments to better understand themselves and their own needs. It can help to keep referral information for providers who specialize in assessing and supporting neurodivergent adults. All human beings deserve self-understanding. Also, a parent who better understands their own needs will be better able to show up for their child.

The Health Care System

We have previously explored how the current systems are non-affirming and harmful, and often traumatize neurodivergent clients. In this section, we will discuss steps that neurodiversity-affirming providers can take to support our clients as they navigate the existing systems. Although we cannot fix the system or prevent all clients from coming to harm at the hands of the system, we can help clients understand what resources exist, how to access them, and what barriers they are likely to face.

Advocating Versus Fostering Self-Advocacy

Professionals hold a certain privilege that comes with our education, expertise, and social status that is often granted to people with credentials after their name. As with everything, the privilege that comes with our credentials varies based on the intersecting aspects of our identity, but there are circumstances where we can speak from a place of power. Many of our clients do not hold this same privilege. This is individualized, of course, as individuals with privilege, status, and so on are often neurodivergent like any other population. We can use our privilege to advocate for our clients.

At the same time, teaching our clients skills to advocate for themselves is invaluable. It is not possible to be present with our clients all of the time, through every experience for their entire lives, and even if it were possible, it would be inappropriate. It would foster unhealthy dependence and would require clients to disclose their relationship to a mental health provider. Clients deserve the option to stand up for themselves and be their own advocates.

We can balance advocating and fostering clients' self-advocacy skills. When we advocate for them, we model what advocacy looks like and show them that they deserve support.

Additionally, we can advocate for our clients by educating them about tools and resources available to them, arming them with the knowledge to self-advocate.

Advocating for a client can look many ways, including:

- Obtaining a release of information to talk to other providers on the client's treatment team if those providers are not engaging in affirming care.
- Providing joint sessions at the client's request with people they are close to in order to educate about the client's needs, using provider privilege to help the client get their needs met.
- Providing letters of recommendation for supportive services, using provider expertise to justify the need for support.
- Providing letters of recommendation detailing the importance of maintaining the client's autonomy and independence.
- Lobbying for systems-wide changes that will benefit clients on a larger scale, using credentials, expertise, and privilege to sway those in power.

Some examples of fostering self-advocacy include:

- Giving clients the name and contact information of those who can connect them with a resource that they need.
- Educating clients about resources they can research on their own.
- Connecting clients to neurodivergent communities who understand their experience.

- Using session time for the client to practice self-advocacy through role-played conversations with the provider.

Validating Experiences

As we have discussed, each person is the expert on their own experience. This means that their perception of their experience is valid even if they struggle with perception. Furthermore, many neurodivergent individuals have had the experience of professionals telling them that their perception of their experience is bad or wrong, or that they are incapable of speaking to their own experience. Thus, validation is an essential component of neurodiversity-affirming care. With some clients, you might be the first professional to ever tell them that their experience is valid. This is powerful in supporting self-advocacy: if I recognize that my experience and needs are valid, I can start standing up for myself and asking for my needs to get met. Even before this, I can realize that I am allowed to have needs and start recognizing what they are. Validation is essential in fostering self-advocacy.

Warning Without Scaring

Neurodivergent clients will come into our care with varying levels of knowledge about their diagnosis or diagnoses, support options, rights, and personal needs. Some will be more knowledgeable about their specific neurodivergence than many professionals, and others will be just starting their journey, with very little knowledge or understanding. Both are valid—we are all in different places in our self-understanding. Ask each client about their level of understanding to avoid overexplaining things that they already know, and provide appropriate information to fill in the gaps, including resources the client can use to learn more outside of their session.

Because neurodiversity-affirming care means providing accurate, honest information, even when that information is not positive, there will be times when we give our clients information that is difficult to talk about. Neurodiversity-affirming providers avoid engaging in toxic positivity, meaning that we will not overlook the negative even though we also acknowledge strengths. We want our clients to have the information they need to self-advocate, identify their needs, protect themselves, and give informed consent to various treatment and support options. Here are some examples of difficult topics for providers to practice addressing with clients, as well as tips for engaging in these conversations.

Neurodiversity-affirming providers avoid engaging in toxic positivity, meaning that we will not overlook the negative even though we also acknowledge strengths."

Risks of an Official Diagnosis

Although it is not shameful or wrong to be neurodivergent, there are some risks of having an official diagnosis on one's medical record. In a previous section, we discussed how providers can discriminate against clients after learning that the client has a diagnosis of borderline personality disorder on their record. A client who suspects they may meet criteria for this diagnosis may choose not to be formally assessed to avoid discrimination. Autistic individuals in North Dakota, Delaware, Indiana, Utah, and other states are often put on government lists, with their identifying information, if they are officially diagnosed. Some states only require clients under a certain age to be registered, while other states require all autistic individuals to be included in the registry. Many neurodivergent disabled people have stories of being forced into conservatorships or losing custody of their children, with the diagnosis used as proof that these steps were necessary. Clients who want to relocate internationally can face barriers in countries that do not permit immigration for certain neurodivergent people.

Basically, a client who is pursuing an official diagnosis has the right to know how this diagnosis may impact them when interacting with the health care system. This might impact their choice on pursuing a diagnosis, and they need to know the potential risks of a diagnosis before being evaluated.

At the same time, as has been discussed in previous sections, there are supports and resources that might not be available without a diagnosis. It is not our job to convince someone *not* to pursue a diagnosis, but to help them come to the conclusion that is best for them.

Disclosing the Diagnosis

Neurodivergence is not bad, wrong, or shameful, and many neurodivergent individuals proudly and openly share their diagnosis. The author of this book, for example, has neurodivergent diagnoses listed in public profiles. At the same time, it is personal information, and some people are private and prefer not to share certain details with the general public. Each individual has the right to be open or private about their neurodivergence.

Even though neurodivergence is not shameful, ableism and discrimination impact many neurodivergent individuals. Clients deserve to make informed decisions about disclosures, just as they have the right to make informed decisions about getting a diagnosis in the first place. We do not want to scare clients into keeping a diagnosis private, but we want them to be aware of the risks so that they are prepared if they choose to disclose.

Requesting Accommodations

The Americans with Disabilities Act (ADA), and similar laws in other countries, entitle disabled people to reasonable accommodations in their workplace. Usually, this requires an official diagnosis to meet legal requirements. Many neurodivergent individuals benefit from accommodations. Of course, requesting accommodations involves disclosing that you have a diagnosis that qualifies for accommodations. Although many laws, including the ADA, indicate that the individual does not have to disclose their diagnosis to receive accommodations, employers often ask anyway. If the client has the legal right not to disclose, they can push back on this request, but this can lead to complications, including delaying their accommodations being approved. Plus, if the employer insists on knowing the diagnosis and the case goes to court, the judge may require the client to disclose anyway on the grounds that the employer needs to know the diagnosis in order to determine whether the requested accommodations are reasonable.

While it would not be appropriate to tell a client *not* to request accommodations, especially accommodations to which they are legally entitled, we must inform them of the potential risks and stressors that could arise as a result of making an accommodation request. We can also share the ways that we can help them advocate for themselves should they pursue accommodations.

We encourage clients to ask questions and express concerns,

and this means providing accurate and honest information in response. We are a resource to our clients, and if we do our job of building trust well, they will know that they can come to us with their concerns and questions. We can discuss topics that seem scary or are difficult to talk about.

Interactions With the System

Although many neurodivergent clients have negative experiences with the mental health system, some clients will be extremely lucky and encounter a neurodiversity-affirming provider early on in their relationship with the system. It is possible that a client will not have a history of negative or harmful experiences, which is fantastic. At the same time, many clients will interact with multiple providers in the system over the course of their lives. This means that they might experience system harm later on even if it has not happened yet when we meet them.

While it would not be appropriate to scare a client intentionally (e.g., telling them, "Other providers will harm you, and you should not trust them"), it can be beneficial to provide realistic information about challenges they may encounter on their treatment journey. This can help them prepare to cope with systemic issues if they arise later. Some examples include:

- "Some providers say insensitive things, like questioning your diagnosis when they just met you. This can be incredibly hurtful, but remember that your experience is valid even if the person questioning it has credentials."
- "Unfortunately, there are people in my line of work who have very stigmatized views of neurodivergence. This is not ethical or okay, but they sometimes end up saying harmful

things to clients. If this happens, I want you to be able to cope with any feelings it brings up for you."

- "It is my hope that I can provide you with an affirming and positive experience. There might be times when other providers are not affirming, and while I hope you never have to experience that, we can help you be prepared to deal with that if it happens."

- "We have discussed my policies for reporting safety concerns and under what circumstances I will take steps to ensure your safety, as well as what those steps are. Not every provider follows the same procedures that I do. It is a good idea to ask about policies related to safety concerns when you see a new provider so that you understand what their policies are and are not taken by surprise if they are different from mine."

We are not sugarcoating the reality of the system and potential harm from other providers, and at the same time we are not deliberately causing additional stress to our clients. These sample scripts are a starting point, and remember that this is an interactive and collaborative conversation with each client.

Behavior Rehearsal

As you have educated your client and helped them develop the skills and confidence to self-advocate, you can help them prepare for system interactions through behavior rehearsal. When clients identify a scenario they will have to navigate, you can help them practice.

A major limitation of behavior rehearsal is, of course, that we cannot know for sure how an interaction will go ahead of time.

We can guess what might happen, how someone might respond, or specific issues that may come up, but we will not know what happens until the actual interaction. At the same time, there can be benefits to practicing:

- Behavior rehearsal can reduce anxiety about difficult conversations through exposure, allowing the individual to better manage their emotions in the moment.
- Clients can explore what they imagine the worst case scenario to be and act out how they would manage the situation if it comes to pass. This can build their confidence in their ability to manage the worst possible outcome or make them realize that some of their fears may be unfounded.
- If a client is preparing for a meeting with another provider, they can use the opportunity to gather their thoughts and prepare their questions ahead of time to ensure they get what they need out of the appointment.
- Behavior rehearsal can be an effective tool to build assertiveness. Clients can bring scenarios they need to rehearse, and the therapist can take on the opposite role to let the client play out their possible experiences in a safe environment.

When systems issues impact our clients' well-being, helping clients navigate the system and learn ways to get their needs met is an essential component of care. In some situations, we may be able to step up and advocate for our clients directly. In others, we can arm them with the necessary skills to self-advocate, access the supports they need, and push for system improvements.

6

Making a Neurodiversity-Affirming Practice Visible to Potential Clients

We cannot help clients if they cannot find us to seek our services. We have to market our services in ways that let our clients know who we are and how we can help them. Mental health professionals are not taught how to market ourselves, and we often scramble to figure out how to find the clients we can help. Additionally, neurodiversity-affirming care requires commitment on every level, including marketing. There are many variables to keep in mind when marketing a neurodiversity-informed mental health practice.

Profiles and Directory Listings

There are dozens (possibly hundreds) of therapist directories to choose from, and most providers list themselves somewhere as an easy way for clients to find them. Different directories have different advantages; for instance, some directories provide resources for specific populations (e.g., Therapy for Black Girls specifically works to connect Black girls and women with therapists), and others are more general but use filtering to allow clients to narrow down the therapist pool based on things like specialization, cost, identity, and so on.

Some directories include filters specifically for neurodiversity-affirming therapists, and some even exist specifically to connect clients to neurodiversity-affirming providers (e.g., ND Therapists is a directory of openly neurodivergent therapists who have made a commitment to affirming care).

When we choose to market ourselves in a directory, we are associating ourselves with that directory. This means that we must be mindful of the directory's reputation and values. There is a well-known and highly trafficked therapist directory that has a history of publishing blogs and articles with racist and trans-phobic content. While many clients use this particular directory, meaning that the therapists listed often get a high number of referrals, the choice to be listed there could be perceived as an endorsement of those values.

The choices providers make about where we market ourselves can send a strong message about our values and morals.

Symbols

Marketing materials such as logos often contain symbols to communicate an individual's specialization and values. At the same time, some symbols have more than one meaning, and we must research thoroughly to ensure we are not inadvertently sending the wrong message with our marketing materials. For example, many organizations that claim to support the autistic community use the puzzle piece as a symbol for autism. However, this symbol was initially chosen to represent the idea that autistic people have a piece missing or are a puzzle to be fixed (Jessop, 2022). Thus, many in the autistic community have rejected this symbol. Instead, the community embraces the golden infinity symbol as a representation of neurodiversity-affirming approaches to supporting autistic people. The rainbow infinity symbol is generally considered an affirming symbol of neurodivergence as a whole.

Online Presence

It is difficult to fully avoid social media at this point. Some people pull this off, but an online presence can be an important part of helping your clients find you. Many clients research providers before reaching out to make an appointment. Remember that you are allowed to have your own professional boundaries, which can include not having an online presence or having a personal online presence rather than or in addition to a professional one.

You are not obligated to share personal information in an online presence, and in fact some clients prefer to not know these details about their provider. At the same time, some clients feel more comfortable if they can gather some information before deciding which provider to see. Both approaches are valid based on the provider's comfort and boundaries, and both preferences are valid based on the client. Clients who want to be able to vet their providers thoroughly before making first contact can seek those who have an online presence, and those who do not want this information can see providers whose boundaries are consistent with this preference.

If you choose to have a professional online presence, potential clients can use the information you share as they determine whether or not you might be a good fit and if they feel safe requesting an appointment with you. Things clients might look for in a professional online presence include, but, as always, are not limited to:

- *Confirming your credentials.* If you carry a professional license, this information will also be available on the relevant board's website. Since many clients who are not in the mental health field themselves may not know this, you can provide this information to them.
- *Assessing your political stances.* Existence is inherently political, particularly for clients whose identities are marginalized in our society. For example, a trans client might want to ensure that their provider will be affirming before scheduling an appointment. Unfortunately, even though most ethics codes speak to the importance of affirming care for trans clients, not all providers live up to this standard in their practices.
- *Assessing your identity.* A neurodivergent client might want the option to see a provider who shares their neurodivergence. Providers who are comfortable with this self-disclosure can make the information available through their online presence. (This will be discussed in more depth in the next section.)
- *Determining fit.* Rapport is key in allowing mental health care to be effective and beneficial to the client. We can only learn so much about someone from a directory profile, and an active online presence can give clients a sense for whether or not they would feel you are a good fit.

A professional online presence can be an easy way to market yourself and present your neurodiversity-affirming values and care approach. Since many neurodivergent individuals research providers before committing to an appointment, you can help them know that you strive to be a safe person that they can trust with their well-being.

Mission Statements

Many businesses have mission statements to make their stance on different important issues and their values clear. Of course, some businesses do not practice what they claim in their mission statement, but if you have a true commitment to neurodiversity-affirming care, you can put it in your business's mission statement. Leading with this statement, you can make it clear to all potential clients and anyone you employ or partner with where you stand.

If you have a true commitment to neurodiversity-affirming care, you can put it in your business's mission statement."

Since nonaffirming providers do not openly advertise the ways that their approaches to care may be harmful, clients might experience anxiety about finding the right practitioner to help them with their mental health needs. Practitioners who have intentionally developed a neurodiversity-affirming practice can make their stance clear. The way we market ourselves can signal to our clients that we have taken steps to reduce the possibility that they will come to harm in our care and to fix mistakes if and when they occur. Clients who want a neurodiversity-affirming provider can find us, and clients who do not know what it means to be affirming can learn more about approaches to care. Hopefully, these approaches can reduce the harm that far too many clients experience at the hands of the system.

Self-Disclosure: The Neurodivergent Provider

When discussing mental health care, a false dichotomy often arises between clients and providers, when in fact many mental health providers benefit from our own mental health care. Many providers are neurodivergent themselves. Although specific numbers were not available, some neurodivergent providers have stated that their own neurodivergence contributed to their career decision. Thus, mental health professionals may be more likely to be neurodivergent than the rest of the population.

As has been noted, providers have the right to make decisions about their own professional boundaries. This includes whether or not the individual feels comfortable disclosing whether or not they are neurodivergent. Some training programs teach students that any self-disclosure is a boundary violation, though this rigid assumption emphasizes a highly Westernized approach to care that is not culturally competent. In the previous section, we explored reasons why clients might need more information about a provider in order to feel safe in their care. This is valid!

Social worker Hannah Owens (2024) shared her own decision-making process, informed by her desire to fight stigma:

> I just kind of went with what I felt would be helpful at the time. I didn't understand why more people weren't very open with their mental health challenges and conditions. . . . In

my head I was like, well, that can only help us. If you're saying you want to work with people with mental illness, but we're not acknowledging our own shit. (2024)

When making decisions about self-disclosure, there are different factors to consider. This section explores these decisions. Note that there is no one right answer to this question; again, while self-disclosure can increase client comfort, providers still have the right to make decisions about professional boundaries that work for them, meaning the right to keep details private if that is what they choose. While neurodiversity-affirming providers reject the notion that self-disclosure is always bad and inappropriate, we also acknowledge that mandatory disclosure is equally problematic. Providers can use these considerations in making their own decision.

Neurotypical Self-Disclosure

As was discussed in a previous chapter, Sonny Jane Wise (2023) coined the term neuronormative to refer to the default assumption that everyone is neurotypical until proven otherwise. Before exploring considerations for neurodivergent providers who are determining whether or not they want to disclose their neurotype, it is essential to name this oppressive pattern of expecting those who divert from typical to disclose.

If a neurotypical person never deliberately discloses that they are neurotypical, this is considered standard. At the same time, a neurodivergent person who does not share their neurotype is considered to be hiding something and may risk being accused of keeping secrets if their neurodivergence is discovered later. A neurotypical person does not have to consider masking or hiding their neurotypical traits, nor do they have to consider the possible backlash of being discovered. This is an issue that must be addressed at a societal level.

Owens (2024) pointed out, "My biggest pet peeve is when people call me brave because it shouldn't have to require me being brave." A disclosure should simply be a personal choice about sharing information. Unfortunately, a single book cannot fundamentally change social norms that are this deeply embedded. This issue remains something to be aware of and speak on as we are able.

Disclosure Considerations for Students

As an undergraduate student applying for graduate programs, this author was told by more than one professor that acknowledging neurodivergence in the application was a good way to be rejected from programs. This is not automatically the case— Owens (2024) shared that she disclosed her mental health history when she applied for school, which did not prevent her acceptance. However, she experienced discrimination and was fired from an internship after she had a delusional psychotic episode in the office where she was working. In her experience, "[Disclosing] did get me into a lot of trouble . . . but at the same time it also helped me connect with people who were very understanding." When supervisors were understanding and committed to nondiscriminatory practices, she was able to thrive and connect with clients through her understanding of their lived experience.

Neurodivergence is personal, not shameful. This means that it is appropriate and acceptable to disclose if you feel comfortable doing so, and at the same time, you are not obligated to make this disclosure. For students in the United States who want to seek academic accommodations in their program, though, they will have to disclose that they have a diagnosis and will probably have to disclose what the diagnosis is.

Disclosing is completely your decision based on what is right for you. In an ideal system, students would have the option to keep their neurotype private or share it with their program and not have to worry about being mistreated, discriminated against, or denied accommodations depending on their choice.

Disclosure Considerations With Employers

Neurodivergent providers who work for organizations, agencies, group practices, and so on also find themselves having to decide whether or not to disclose neurodivergence to their employers. As with students, neurodivergent employees may be entitled to workplace accommodations if they are disabled, and requesting accommodations requires a certain amount of disclosure. Regardless of whether you need accommodations, though, you might want to advertise your neurodivergence to potential clients, which means that the employer will also likely know your diagnosis.

Hannah Owens (2024) found herself holding back until she felt she needed to disclose. She noted feeling pressure to "establish [herself] as a good worker" before sharing her diagnosis, which was influenced by very realistic concerns about judgment and stigma if her employer had a bias against schizoaffective individuals.

Hannah shared that her diagnosis helped her connect with clients whose neurodivergence was similar to hers: "It became very clear that I had kind of a knack for talking to those people because I was living it." At the same time, she shared that one of her supervisors once disclosed her diagnosis to clients without her consent. To be clear, it is *never* appropriate to share someone else's neurodivergence without their explicit consent.

While discriminating against someone on the basis of disability is illegal in the United States, most states have at-will employment laws, meaning that your employer can fire you and refuse to give the reason why. Thus, unless they say, "We are firing you because of your diagnosis," it can be impossible to prove definitively that this happened. It is valid for an individual to decide not to share their neurodivergence with employers due to discrimination concerns.

When and How to Disclose

Neurodivergent providers who choose to be open with clients about their neurotype have many options for making this disclosure. They may choose to share it on a case-by-case basis when it is appropriate, or they might put the information directly in their public profile. As has been noted previously, some clients might seek out a therapist who shares their neurotype and so may look for providers who publicly list their neurodivergence. At the same time, some providers might feel uncomfortable or simply prefer not to advertise this information.

If sharing personal information with clients during their care, be mindful of your motivation for disclosure. Any self-disclosure by a mental health professional needs to center the client's needs and treatment, as they are the focus of their appointments. If a disclosure is for your own peace of mind or well-being, keep it to yourself and address it in your own therapy or in consultation with other providers. At the same time, if it might benefit the client to know your diagnosis, it is appropriate to share.

Disclosure and Stigma

For those who choose to share their neurodivergence publicly in a way that potential clients can learn this information, there is added risk of discrimination that comes from full transparency. As has been noted previously, this author is public about being autistic and ADHD. As a result, many clients who want to see a psychologist who shares their neurotype have been able to find my practice. At the same time, strangers have made many cruel statements toward me online, including:

- "You don't have ADHD. You just want drugs."
- "Someone like you shouldn't be allowed to see clients."
- "You should be in therapy, not receiving it."
- "You should lose your license."

I have additionally witnessed providers experience complaints to their licensing board as a result of acknowledging that they take medication for neurodivergence. Again, this was from strangers, not from clients who felt that the providers were not competent to provide care. People who have never been a client will submit licensure complaints simply on the grounds that a neurodivergent person is automatically unqualified to provide care.

While public disclosure can help normalize disclosure for others, no one is obligated to share personal information, and concerns about discrimination are valid and realistic. Someone choosing to keep a diagnosis private to avoid harassment is making the best choice for themselves, and that choice must be respected.

Personal Considerations

When determining whether or not to share a diagnosis, we consider what is best for our professional role, our clients' well-being, and our own concerns about discrimination and ableism. At the end of the day, though, each person's decision about disclosing a diagnosis is personal, left up to them, and only the individual knows what is best for their life.

As Hannah shared in her interview (2024):

> Be brave, whether that means disclosing or not disclosing, or taking care of yourself because you don't feel like you can disclose yet. Be brave to do whatever feels right to you. And you don't have to use yourself as an example to teach others. That's not your responsibility. If you're in a place to be able to do that, like I feel like I am right now, that's great, but you don't owe anybody anything as a member of the mental health community who has a mental illness. You don't owe anybody anything. You don't owe anybody an explanation, you don't owe anybody the rights to know that about yourself, unless you want to share it, unless it's relevant, unless you think it will help people. If it won't help you, it doesn't matter.

Beyond the Office: Advocacy

According to the National Association of Social Workers Code of Ethics, social workers in the United States have an ethical obligation to pursue social justice and advocate for our clients. The code specifies that this is not limited to activities in the therapy office but applies also to advocacy (National Association of Social Workers, 2017).

It is not sufficient for a mental health provider to take a neurodiversity-affirming approach to treatment with clients seen in the office. As long as oppressive systems are in place that harm our clients, we have an obligation to fight these systems using our professional privilege.

The next section explores what this looks like in practice.

Vocally Opposing Unethical Laws and Policies

All providers are aware of legal and systemic requirements that violate our ethical obligations. This is a common enough occurrence that the American Psychological Association addresses it in Section 1 of its Ethics Code:

> If psychologists' ethical responsibilities conflict with law, regulations, or other governing legal authority, psychologists clarify the nature of the conflict, make known their commitment to the Ethics Code, and take reasonable steps to resolve the conflict consistent with the General Principles and Ethical Standards of the Ethics Code. Under no circumstances may this standard be used to justify or defend violating human rights. (American Psychological Association, 2017)

In other words, a psychologist must address when the law violates the ethics code, and we may not use the law as a reason to disregard ethics or violate human rights.

I have an example of such an ethical conflict in my own practice. As has previously been discussed, seven states require providers to register autistic clients with the government. When I obtained my license to practice in North Dakota, I learned of this law. I made the conflict known to the North Dakota Psychology Board and the American Psychological Association in December 2021, and as of the writing of this manuscript in March 2024, neither has responded to my concern.

Thus, I have adopted an office policy that I do not conduct autism evaluations in North Dakota, as it is impossible to do so both legally and ethically. I explain my reasoning in detail on my website and in my office policies so that clients understand how the law prevents me from practicing.

Speaking Out Against Oppression Publicly

Using the example in the previous section, I have been vocal and public about my opposition to mandatory state autism databases on public platforms, using my role and privilege as a professional to explain why these laws are harmful. I have written articles, appeared on podcasts, and spoken at lectures to bring awareness and fight against these laws. When we have the opportunity to speak out, we can use our expertise to educate the public about harms caused by the current system. Many might be unaware that these issues exist or not recognize why they are harmful.

When bringing awareness, we can provide information about actionable steps people can take to address systemic harm. It can feel hopeless to learn about oppression and not have any means of fighting it, even if one person alone would not be able to bring about change singlehandedly. Awareness is essential, but it is only the first step.

Depending on the issue being addressed, different action steps may be appropriate. These can include:

- Encouraging people to spread awareness of an issue by talking about it or sharing on social media.
- Encouraging people to contact their representatives to ask them to address harmful laws.
- Giving people specific questions they can ask or steps they can take when interacting with systems to keep themselves safe.
- Giving people resources or tools to learn more about an issue.
- Sharing information about affirming language they can use and harmful language to avoid.
- Providing education on how to support neurodivergent people.

Contacting Representatives

Many of the systemic harm that neurodivergent people experience is backed and perpetuated by laws that not only permit harm but often require harmful practices. The autism registry in North Dakota is an example of this, as it legally requires providers to violate client privacy by giving their personal and confidential information to the government. Civil disobedience can protect clients from harm caused by these laws (choosing not to register clients), but this puts the provider at risk for losing their ability to practice and support clients. Office policies of not conducting evaluations that would necessitate a report also protect clients from being reported but also take away the client's choice about whether or not they want to seek an official evaluation or receive supportive services that require a diagnosis.

The law needs to change.

Using our stance as experts, we can contact our representatives and explain why certain laws are harmful and need to be changed. This can be challenging, as representatives do not always respond to inquiries. They may also be unresponsive if you are not a constituent—when I contacted the entire state legislature in North Dakota regarding the autism registry, the few representatives who responded noted that the fact that I am not a resident of North Dakota and therefore was not a constituent would make it very difficult for my statements to have an impact.

This means that, although there are major issues around the world that we can use our privilege to address, when it comes to calling for legal changes, we may be most effective working with our local officials. As the saying goes, Think globally, act locally.

Lobbying for Legal Changes

Taking this a step farther, we can work directly with representatives to push legal changes through the legislature. This takes a specific type of temperament—this author, for example, would struggle to act with civility toward politicians if they have a history of harmful behavior, but this might be necessary when working to make changes within the system. That is a good example of how some action items might not be a good fit for your individual strengths. This is okay! No one can do everything. These are simply options, and you can determine which best fit your skill set.

A provider may partner with a legislator or multiple legislators to propose legal changes, testify at hearings to determine if these changes will be put into law, and encourage other politicians to vote in favor of the change.

Holding Colleagues Accountable

As was discussed early in this text, many providers were trained on harmful models and systems of care. While our training is not our fault, our decision about questioning our training and making changes to our practice is our responsibility. We cannot control what other providers choose to do or how they run their practice, but we can attempt to educate and correct harmful behaviors, attitudes, and practices when we see them. This can include:

- Correcting ableist and sanist language when we hear other professionals use it.
- Challenging if a colleague makes a stigmatizing statement about neurodivergent clients or any specific neurodivergent population.
- Sending colleagues resources on neurodiversity-affirming care or resources developed by and for neurodivergent communities we serve.
- Discussing the importance of neurodiversity-affirming care in consultations and supervision.
- Creating resources such as articles or continuing education trainings that emphasize neurodiversity-affirming care and

provide concrete changes our colleagues can make in order to be more affirming.

- Speaking about our own clients in affirming ways during consultation to model appropriate language choices.
- Challenging colleagues who make harmful statements about neurodivergent communities, such as if they refer to people with personality disorders as abusive.

Mental health professionals often work individually, feeling disconnected from our colleagues. Even those who work in group practices often report isolation as they spend so much of the work day meeting with clients. We are like islands separated from each other, which creates challenges to collaboration. However, the systems-wide changes that are essential to creating affirming practices for our clients will require us to work together. One person cannot change an entire system, and a large group of people will have limited success working individually rather than together. The need for collaboration is reminiscent of a quote from author Vesta M. Kelly: "Snowflakes are one of nature's most fragile things, but just look what they can do when they stick together."

If providers who are committed to neurodiversity-affirming care work to educate our colleagues on the importance of these shifts, we can work together to create an avalanche of systemic change.

CHAPTER 7

Conclusion

While one single text cannot encompass every possible scenario, situation, client presentation, diagnosis, and need, the goal of this text has been to provide readers with the groundwork to shift into a neurodiversity-affirming approach to care with clients in the mental health system. As it stands now, the existing system does not provide adequate or appropriate support to clients, and providers have an ethical responsibility to use our privilege and knowledge to demand change.

This change starts with individual shifts in our approaches to our clients, our understanding of their neurodivergence, our perception of their needs, and our goals for their mental health care. This is not an easy task, especially since each client will have a unique set of needs as well as a one-of-a-kind perception of themselves, their neurodivergence, and their personal values. However, by committing to neurodiversity-affirming care, we can make a better experience for the clients we see, and we can protect them from harm in the system. Although we may not be able to guarantee that they do not come to any harm at the hands of the system, we can prepare them for potential barriers and help them build the skills needed to advocate for themselves.

We reject the dichotomy of client and provider, recognizing that many providers are neurodivergent ourselves, and we deserve the same care and respect we offer our clients. We deserve workplace and academic accommodations, protection from discrimination, and autonomy.

Furthermore, we can call for system-wide changes using our power as professionals. It is easy for oppressive systems to ignore one voice, but if enough providers commit to advocacy outside of our offices, we can demand the changes our clients need and work toward building a better system. An individualized approach to change is not sufficient, as we are helping clients survive in the very system that harmed them in the first place. By advocating for systemic change in addition to our clinical work, we can prevent future harm to neurodivergent individuals and communities.

I hope that this book helped point you in the right direction, and I hope you will use the knowledge gained here to provide neurodiversity-affirming care to your clients and to fight oppressive systems. If you are new to the concept of neurodiversity-affirming care, I hope you are now armed with knowledge and skills to better support and serve your clients. If you were already well on your way to providing affirming care, I hope this text allowed you to enhance your existing practice, hone your skills, and develop new tools both in your clinical practice and in your advocacy work.

GLOSSARY

Abled: Someone who does not have a disability.

Ableism: Discrimination against someone based on their disability.

Accommodation: Something given to an individual to meet their needs.

Acquired neurodivergence: A form of neurodivergence that one is not born with. Brain injuries and dementia are examples of acquired neurodivergence.

Adaptive behavioral assessments: A psychological assessment tool that assesses an individual's ability to engage in various tasks of daily living. It is often used to assess support needs.

Addiction: When someone has a strong, often uncontrollable, psychological or physical drive to do something (e.g., use a substance) that is not needed for survival.

Adverse childhood experiences (ACEs): Highly stressful and potentially traumatic events occurring in childhood, which correlate with negative mental and physical health outcomes.

Advocacy: Public support for a cause. Also, actions to help an individual receive needed support.

Affirmation: A statement of emotional support.

Affirming: Providing affirmation. Also, an approach to care that validates an individual's experience and centers them as the expert on their own experience.

Age equivalency: An assessment that estimates someone's mental age based on their ability to perform certain tasks. Age equivalences are considered infantilizing and not affirming.

Anxiety: Nervousness, worry, or distress brought about by real or perceived danger. Anxiety can be a normative part of human experience, but for some it reaches a level that causes impairment and requires support.

Aphantasia: The inability to visualize images in one's mind.

Applied behavioral analysis (ABA): A treatment approach aimed at modifying behavior, often recommended for autistic children. Many autistic adults who received ABA report that the experience was abusive and often traumatic.

Asperger's syndrome: A term no longer used to describe autistic individuals who have fewer support needs than most with autism.

Assertiveness training: A treatment intervention that helps clients self-advocate and assert themselves.

Assessment: Tools, measures, and observations mental health providers use to gather information about a client's symptoms or traits, often used to make a diagnosis.

Attention-deficit/hyperactivity disorder (ADHD): A form of neurodivergence categorized as a neurodevelopmental disorder, consisting of issues with sustained attention, executive functioning, impulse control, and movement.

Augmentive and alternative communication (AAC): Methods of communication that do not involve speaking with one's mouth. This can include devices that speak for the person or sign language.

Autism: A form of neurodivergence marked by sensory sensitivities, difficulty interpreting neurotypical social cues, preference for routine, and special interests.

Autism spectrum disorder: The current diagnostic term for autism, categorized as a neurodevelopmental disorder.

Autonomy: The right to make one's own decisions about one's life and body.

Behavior rehearsal: Practicing an interaction or situation beforehand.

Bias: A distorted view or prejudice.

Bipolar disorder: A mood disorder characterized by manic or hypomanic and depressive episodes.

Black, Indigenous, and other People of Color (BIPOC): A term to encompass all racial groups that are not white.

Borderline personality disorder: A neurodivergence marked by emotional dysregulation, impulsivity, relationship difficulties, feelings of emptiness, dissociation, and other traits.

Boundaries: Limits we put forth to set expectations in relationships.

Burnout: A point of extreme exhaustion, often marked by decreased ability to engage in activities of daily living, work, and self-care.

Camouflaging: Another term for masking, camouflaging refers to when a neurodivergent person attempts to present themselves in ways that meet neurotypical expectations.

Catatonia: A symptom of neurodivergence that impacts one's awareness of and ability to respond to the world around one, including lack of movement and communication.

Cerebral palsy: A medical condition that includes neurodivergence, marked by muscle issues and often caused by brain damage before or during birth.

Cisgender: An individual whose gender aligns with what was assigned at birth.

Client-centered care: Care that prioritizes the client's specific needs, values, and goals for treatment, taking a collaborative approach rather than focusing on the provider's role as expert.

Cognitive assessments: Evaluation tools that measure cognitive ability. Many cognitive assessments have racial bias.

Cognitive behavioral therapy (CBT): An approach to therapy that involves identifying and challenging negative thought patterns that may be untrue or unhelpful in order to change unpleasant emotions and maladaptive behaviors.

Cognitive dissonance: When an individual's thoughts and beliefs do not align with themselves, causing incongruous beliefs and attitudes.

Collaboration: Working together toward a common goal.

Collateral interview: In psychological assessment, when the provider seeks information from someone other than the client regarding the client's needs, traits, symptoms, and challenges.

Communication: Any method of expressing or receiving information from someone.

Community voices: The perspectives, values, and experiences of members of a neurodivergent community.

Compassion fatigue: When a provider begins experiencing apathy toward their work and clients, often as a result of burnout or secondary trauma.

Competence: A provider's clinical skills or ability to practice effectively in a given area of treatment.

Complex PTSD: A form of posttraumatic stress involving symptoms of PTSD as well as severe emotional dysregulation, mistrust, and negative self-concept.

Conners Adult ADHD Rating Scales, Second Edition (CAARS-2): A norm-referenced assessment measure that tests for ADHD in adults.

Consent: Full permission, including agreement to participate in a type of treatment or receive certain support.

Conservatorship: A legal arrangement where the court appoints someone to manage the financial, personal, or other affairs and decisions of an individual it has deemed unable to make their own decisions.

Creative expression therapy: Therapeutic interventions that utilize artistic expression, including art, dance, music, creative writing, and so on.

Dementia: An acquired neurodivergence that usually occurs later in life, marked by a reduction in cognitive abilities like memory and reasoning and often caused by a disease in the brain.

Depression: A group of mood disorders characterized by low mood, loss of pleasure, reduced motivation, and behavior changes.

Diagnostic interview: An initial appointment where the provider gathers information about the client's history, background, and symptoms, with the goal of determining a diagnosis.

Dialectical behavioral therapy (DBT): A therapeutic approach designed to help clients cope with strong, intense emotions through interventions like radical acceptance, behavior modification, and skill building.

Disability con: A stereotype that people fake being disabled in order to access government benefits. Research shows that these are rare, and it is more likely that a truly disabled person will be denied support than that someone will successfully fake a disability.

Disabled: As defined by the ADA, "An individual with a disability is ... a person who has a physical or mental impairment that substantially limits one or more major life activities, a person who has a history or record of such an impairment, or a person who is perceived by others as having such an impairment."

Discrimination: Prejudice and unjust treatment of someone based on an aspect of their identity or a category into which they fit.

Disorder: An impairment, sometimes caused by illness, that disrupts physical or mental abilities.

Distress: Emotional suffering.

DSM-5-TR: The *Diagnostic and Statistical Manual of Mental Disorders, Fifth Edition, Text Revision*, which contains all mental health and neurodevelopmental diagnoses presently recognized. Not all neurodivergence is listed in the DSM.

Dyspraxia: A disability marked by issues with coordination and movement.

Emotional abuse: Behaviors intended to control, degrade, or isolate a victim without physically assaulting them.

Empowerment: When an individual becomes more confident and feels more capable to control their life and advocate for themselves.

Epilepsy: A neurodivergence caused by a neurological disorder, which triggers seizures.

Ethics code: The principles and aspirational goals that providers must follow as a condition of professional licensure.

Eugenics: Pseudoscientific theories about improving the human race through selective breeding, based in racist and ableist assumptions about what would improve humanity.

Executive dysfunction: Behaviors that interfere with one's ability to complete tasks and function, including distractibility, hyper-focus, impulsivity, and inability to start or complete tasks.

Exposure: A therapeutic intervention designed to alleviate an anxiety response by guiding the individual toward the anxiety-provoking stimuli until the fear response dissipates.

Fetal alcohol spectrum disorder (FASD): A form of neurodivergence sometimes accompanied by physical disability caused by exposure to alcohol in utero.

Functioning: One's ability to perform specific tasks or activities. Some neurodivergent individuals are assigned functioning labels, which are used to indicate the amount of support they need or how much control they are permitted to have over their life. Many neurodivergent communities reject functioning labels.

Gender: Social characterizations of men, women, boys, and girls, including norms for behavior and appearance.

Gender identity: An individual's innate sense of their own gender, regardless of what was assigned to them at birth.

Gender minorities: Individuals whose gender identity does not match their assigned gender at birth.

Giftedness: Abilities or potential that are above expectations.

Grounding: A therapeutic intervention intended to distract from painful thoughts or emotions.

Harm reduction: An approach to care that focuses on reducing risk associated with behaviors rather than eliminating the behavior altogether or assigning a moral judgment to the behavior.

Histrionic personality disorder: A neurodivergence marked by strong emotional reactivity and significant need for attention from other people.

Hospitalization: When an individual is admitted to the hospital for care or due to safety concerns.

Hyperactivity: Behaviors that involve excessive movement and activity, including fidgeting, restlessness, difficulty remaining seated, difficulty sitting still, and being on the go.

Hyper-focus: Complete absorption or fixation on a task to the point that other things are fully ignored or tuned out, including external stimuli and body needs.

Hypnosis: A state of being in a trance, which can resemble sleep and is induced by a hypnotist. Hypnosis has been used as a therapeutic intervention.

Identity-first language: Language that centers the identity of the individual, such as "autistic person" rather than "person with autism."

Impairment: When an individual's functioning or abilities are reduced or weakened.

Impulse control: One's ability to regulate one's behavior.

In vivo exposure: Directly encountering a feared stimulus in real life.

Infantilizing: Treating someone as a child or infant.

Intake: An initial appointment for mental health treatment.

Intellectual disability: A form of neurodivergence characterized by difficulty acquiring skills and by having cognitive impairment.

Interoception: One's ability to accurately identify and attend to one's internal body experiences.

Intersectionality: The recognition that the way an individual experiences the world is impacted by various aspects of their identity, and intersecting identities have different effects on one's experiences, including discrimination, oppression, and access to resources.

IQ tests: Cognitive assessments that evaluate intelligence quotient. While these tests can help identify some support needs, they have significant racial bias and can be unreliable. Many neurodivergent communities find them harmful.

Learning disorder: A neurodivergence manifesting as difficulty in one or more areas of learning despite appropriate access to educational resources and the absence of cognitive impairment.

LGBTQ+: An acronym for lesbian, gay, bisexual, transgender, queer, and all other identities that do not fall under cisgender, heterosexual experiences.

Lived experience: When an individual has firsthand knowledge of something because it is part of their identity and life.

Malingering: When an individual is trying to appear more disabled or disordered than they actually are.

Manipulative: When someone engages in efforts to control another person.

Marginalized: When a person or group is oppressed or treated as less than.

Masking: Hiding neurodivergent traits and attempting to present in neurotypical ways.

Medical model: An approach to care that assumes that mental health issues are the result of the brain's structure.

Meltdown: An episode that occurs when an individual is so overwhelmed that they are no longer in control of their behavior. This can manifest as crying, yelling, self-harm, and aggression.

Millon Multiaxial Clinical Inventory (MCMI): An assessment used to evaluate an individual's personality and test for clinical conditions such as anxiety, mood disorders, trauma, and psychosis.

Mindfulness: A therapeutic approach that involves helping the client become more in tune with their present moment and environment.

Minnesota Multiphasic Personality Inventory (MMPI): An assessment used to evaluate personality, mental health conditions, and interpersonal functioning.

Misdiagnosis: When an individual is diagnosed incorrectly.

Mission statement: A summary of an individual or organization's values and goals.

Mobile crisis team: A team of trained professionals who travel within a certain geographic area to support someone in crisis in person.

Multiple sclerosis: A progressive disease that causes neurodivergence as well as motor impairments and other physical disabilities.

Narcissistic abuse: A term sometimes used interchangeably with emotional abuse, which assumes that the abuser has narcissistic personality disorder. This term is not neurodiversity-affirming.

Narcissistic personality disorder: A form of neurodivergence marked by a strong need for approval and admiration from others, as well as low empathy.

Narrative therapy: An approach to therapy that sees the client as separate from their problems and helps the client craft their story.

Neurodivergence: Deviation from neurotypical expectations for brain function, perception, and behavior.

Neurodivergent: Anyone whose brain does not fall under the umbrella of neurotypical.

Neurodiversity: The range of different neurotypes and brain functioning across humanity.

Neurodiversity-affirming: An approach to care that recognizes that differences in neurotype are simply part of the range of human experience. While neurodivergent individuals may require support, an affirming provider does not assume that they are inferior or need to be fixed. Affirming providers also center the client's expertise on their own life and their lived experience.

Neuronormativity: The assumption that neurotypical is the preferred, superior neurotype.

Neurotype: The kind of brain someone has and how it impacts their communication, perception of the world, and thought process.

Neurotypical: An individual whose neurotype falls within typical expectations.

Nonbinary: When an individual's gender identity does not fit into the man/woman and boy/girl binaries.

Noncompliant: When a client does not follow the provider's treatment recommendations. This term is not affirming and overlooks causes for this behavior.

Nonspeaking: When an individual does not communicate using words articulated with their mouth. Nonspeaking individuals often use alternate forms of communication.

Obsessive compulsive disorder: A neurodivergence marked by intrusive, distressing thoughts and rumination, and/or repetitive behaviors aimed at neutralizing distress.

Official diagnosis: When an individual's neurodivergence has been confirmed by a professional.

PACT goals: An approach to goal setting where goals are purpose-ful, *a*ctionable, *c*ontinuous, and *t*rackable. This approach focuses on the journey of pursuing the goal rather than specific outcomes.

Panic attack: Sudden and acute anxious distress marked by fear, racing heart, shortness of breath, shaking, dizziness, and fear that one may be dying.

Paralysis: The loss of the physical ability to move, often as a result of illness or injury.

Parkinson's disease: A form of neurodivergence caused by a pro-gressive nervous system disease, characterized by tremors, muscle rigidity, and motor impairment.

Pathologizing: The categorization of neurodivergence as abnor-mal, often done under the medical model.

Perception: One's understanding and interpretation of the world around one.

Personality disorder: A group of neurodivergent diagnoses marked by behavior patterns that deviate from neurotypical norms and cause difficulties in relationships and functioning.

Person-centered therapy: An approach to care that assumes that clients are driven toward growth and offers unconditional positive regard.

Person-first language: Language that centers the person; for example, person with schizophrenia rather than schizophrenic person.

Physical punishment: Hitting or striking in an effort to reduce an undesired behavior. Physical punishments are abusive.

Plain language: Clear and concise wording to make the message easy to understand.

Posttraumatic stress disorder (PTSD): An acquired neurodivergence following trauma marked by intrusive memories, hypervigilance, and anxious distress.

Power dynamic: The balance of power between two people. In mental health, the provider has more power due to their authority, credentials, and control of the client's medical record.

Provisional: When a diagnosis is granted with the caveat that it may be changed as more information becomes available.

Psychoeducation: A therapeutic intervention where the provider gives the client educational information about their diagnosis, treatment, or a proposed intervention.

Psychosis: A symptom of neurodivergence manifesting as loss of contact with reality, sometimes manifesting as delusional beliefs or hallucinations.

Rapport: The strength of the relationship between a provider and client.

Reactive attachment disorder: A form of neurodivergence caused by trauma from changes in caregiver or emotional neglect in the early developmental period, often marked by reduced ability to form emotional attachments to others.

Reality testing: The ability to assess our surroundings accurately even if our perception or emotions do not fully align with what is really happening.

Reassessment: An evaluation conducted on an individual who has previously been evaluated, sometimes for the purpose of updating supports and sometimes when it is suspected that the client was previously misdiagnosed.

Records: All information in the client's chart.

Referral: When a client receives information from one about another provider who may be able to see them and help them with their needs.

Resistant: A term used to describe clients who are not following provider recommendations in treatment, which tends to overlook underlying issues that interfere with the client's ability to participate fully.

Retraumatization: When an individual with trauma history experiences symptom reactivation in response to a trigger.

Safety contract: A document that a client signs indicating that they have agreed not to engage in unsafe behaviors, often used by a provider who is concerned about liability. Safety contracts are not shown to be effective in keeping clients safe.

Safety plan: A collaborative plan developed between the client and provider with tools and steps the client can take to ensure their safety.

Sanism: Discriminatory language and behavior based on a mental health diagnosis.

Schizophrenia: A form of neurodivergence marked by hallucinations, delusional beliefs, difficulty accurately perceiving reality, and withdrawal.

Scope of practice: The skills, interventions, and types of treatment a provider is qualified to provide.

Self-advocacy: Asserting one's own rights and needs.

Self-care: Behaviors that promote one's own well-being.

Self-diagnosis: When a neurodivergent individual identifies with a specific diagnosis but has not been evaluated by a professional to confirm the diagnosis.

Self-disclosure: When a provider chooses to share personal information in a professional setting.

Self-identification: When a neurodivergent individual recognizes their neurodivergence without a mental health professional conducting an assessment.

Self-sabotaging: A behavior someone engages in knowingly that prevents them from making desired progress or achieving goals.

Social construct: An idea or norm created and perpetuated by society.

Social Responsiveness Scale, Second Edition: An assessment measure that screens for social and behavioral differences common in autistic individuals.

Stigma: Negative and unfair beliefs about a group of people based on harmful bias.

Stim: A repetitive behavior. Many autistic and ADHD individuals use stimming to self-regulate.

Strengths-based therapy: An approach to mental health treatment that emphasizes an individual's existing strengths and works to build other strengths.

Substance dependence: Physical or psychological dependence on a substance.

Substance use disorder: A form of neurodivergence that impacts the brain and behavior, preventing them from being able to control their use of a substance.

Suicidal ideation: When an individual has thought or intent to end their own life.

Support needs: The type or intensity of supportive services, help, and so on that an individual needs in order to participate in society and have quality of life.

Tone policing: Disregarding someone's experience or emotions because they did not express themselves in a tone deemed appropriate, often used as an excuse to invalidate lived experience.

Tourette syndrome: A form of neurodivergence that causes tics, including twitches, movements, or sounds, which are involuntary.

Toxic positivity: An attempt at positive reframe that invalidates painful or difficult experiences.

Trans-affirming: An approach to mental health care that affirms all clients' gender identities.

Transgender: When an individual is not aligned with the gender they were assigned at birth.

Trauma-informed: An approach to care that involves an awareness of the prevalence of trauma, the potential for each client to have trauma history, and takes steps to avoid retraumatization through system interactions.

Traumatic brain injury: An injury to the head and brain caused by a blow that leads to functional disruption.

Trigger: Something that initiates a trauma response.

Typical: Within common or expected limits.

Unmasking: Letting go of camouflaging behaviors that hide neurodivergent traits.

Validate: Indicating understanding of where someone is coming from and affirming that their experience, feelings, or perception is true for them and not right or wrong.

Wellness check: Sending someone in person to check on someone's well-being. In many areas, these are conducted by law enforcement.

REFERENCES

Afzal, T., Hipolito, J. L. & Jin, L. (2023). A systematic review of misdiagnosis of pediatric bipolar disorder: Assessments and recommendations. *Res Child Adolesc Psychopathol, 52*, 659–670. https://doi.org/10.1007/s10802-023-01163-9

American Psychological Association. (2017). *Ethical principles of psychologists and code of conduct* (2002, amended effective June 1, 2010, and January 1, 2017). https://www.apa.org/ethics/code/

Americans With Disabilities Act of 1990, 42 U.S.C. § 12101 et seq. (1990).

Anderson, L. K. (2023). Autistic experiences of applied behavior analysis. *Autism, 27*(3), 737–750. https://doi.org/10.1177/13623613221118216

Ayano, G., Demelash, S., Yohannes, Z., Haile, K., Tulu, M., Assefa, D., Tesfaye, A., Haile, K., Solomon, M., Chaka, A., & Tsegay, L. (2021). Misdiagnosis, detection rate, and associated factors of severe psychiatric disorders in specialized psychiatry centers in Ethiopia. *Annals of General Psychiatry, 20*(1), 10. https://doi.org/10.1186/s12991-021-00333-7

Barger, B. D., Campbell, J. M., & McDonough, J. D. (2013). Prevalence and onset of regression within autism spectrum disorders: A meta-analytic review. *Journal of Autism and Developmental Disorders, 43*(4), 817–828. https://doi.org/10.1007/s10803-012-1621-x

Bonati, M., Cartabia, M., & Zanetti, M. (2019). Waiting times for diagnosis of attention-deficit hyperactivity disorder in children and adolescents referred to Italian ADHD centers must be reduced.

BMC Health Services Research, 19(1), 673. https://doi.org/10.1186/s12913-019-4524-0

Bonnello, C. (2022, October 4). *Results and analysis of the autistic not weird 2022 autism survey.* Autistic Not Weird. https://autisticnotweird.com/autismsurvey/

Botha, M., Chapman, R., Giwa Onaiwu, M., Kapp, S. K., Stannard Ashley, A., & Walker, N. (2024). The neurodiversity concept was developed collectively: An overdue correction on the origins of neurodiversity theory. *Autism,* 13623613241237872. https://doi.org/10.1177/13623613241237871

Czech, H. (2018). Hans Asperger, National Socialism, and "race hygiene" in Nazi-era Vienna. *Molecular Autism, 9*(1), 29. https://doi.org/10.1186/s13229-018-0208-6

Davis, C., Cohen, A., Davids, M., & Rabindranath, A. (2015). Attention-deficit/hyperactivity disorder in relation to addictive behaviors: A moderated-mediation analysis of personality-risk factors and sex. *Front Psychiatry, 6.* https://doi.org/10.3389/fpsyt.2015.00047

Davis, L. C., Diianni, A. T., Drumheller, S. R., Elansary, N. N., D'Ambrozio, G. N., Herrawi, F., Piper, B. J., & Cosgrove, L. (2024). Undisclosed financial conflicts of interest in DSM-5-TR: Cross sectional analysis. *BMJ,* e076902. https://doi.org/10.1136/bmj-2023-076902

Dixon, J. N., Caddell, T. M., Alexander, A. A., Burchett, D., Anderson, J. L., Marek, R. J., & Glassmire, D. M. (2023). Adapting assessment processes to consider cultural mistrust in forensic practices: An example with the MMPI instruments. *Law and Human Behavior, 47*(1), 292–306. https://doi.org/10.1037/lhb0000504

Dorfman, D. (2019). Fear of the disability con: Perceptions of fraud and special rights discourse. *Law & Society Review, 53*(4), 1051–1091.

Doyle, G. [@DrDoyleSays]. (2020, September 30). *The best minds in mental health aren't the docs. They're the trauma survivors who have had to figure out how to stay alive for years with virtually no help. Wanna learn how to psychologically survive under unfathomable stress? Talk to abuse survivors.* [Post]. X. https://x.com/DrDoyleSays/status/1311196059457277952

Doyle, N. (2020). Neurodiversity at work: A biopsychosocial model and the impact on working adults. *British Medical Bulletin*, *135*(1), 108–125. https://doi.org/10.1093/bmb/ldaa021

Eichstaedt, J. C., Smith, R. J., Merchant, R. M., Ungar, L. H., Crutchley, P., Preoţiuc-Pietro, D., Asch, D. A., & Schwartz, H. A. (2018). Facebook language predicts depression in medical records. *PNAS*, *115*(44), 11203–11208. https://doi.org/10.1073/pnas.1802331115

Epps, E. G. (1973). Racism, science, and the I. Q. *Equity & Excellence in Education*, *11*(1), 35–44. https://doi.org/10.1080/0020486730110105

Ferguson, C. J. (2013). Spanking, corporal punishment and negative long-term outcomes: A meta-analytic review of longitudinal studies. *Clinical Psychology Review*, *33*(1), 196–208. https://doi.org/10.1016/j.cpr.2012.11.002

Forcey-Rodriguez, K. E. (2023). Risk factors and preventative methods of self-harm and suicidality for autistic people. *Canadian Journal of Autism Equity*, *3*(1), 12–26. https://doi.org/10.15173/cjae.v3i1.5127

Fountoulakis, K. N., & Fountoulakis, K. N. (2022). Anti-psychiatry. *Psychiatry: From Its Historical and Philosophical Roots to the Modern Face*, 523–534.

Furczyk, K., & Thome, J. (2014). Adult ADHD and suicide. *ADHD Attention Deficit and Hyperactivity Disorders*, *6*(3), 153–158. https://doi.org/10.1007/s12402-014-0150-1

Garvey, K. A., Penn, J. V., Campbell, A. L., Esposito-Smythers, C., & Spirito, A. (2009) Contracting for safety with patients: Clinical practice and forensic implications. *Am Acad Psychiatry Law*, *37*(3),363–370. PMID: 19767501.

Geiger, B. B. (2023). Suspicious minds? Media effects on the perception of disability benefit claimants. *Social Policy*, 1–21. https://doi.org/10.1017/S0047279423000399

Gnanavel, S., Sharma, P., Kaushal, P., & Hussain, S. (2019). Attention deficit hyperactivity disorder and comorbidity: A review of literature. *World Journal of Clinical Cases*, *7*(17), 2420–2426. https://doi.org/10.12998/wjcc.v7.i17.2420

Goodfellow, W. (2020). *Prozac monologues: A voice from the edge.* She Writes Press.

Granello, D. H., & Gorby, S. R. (2021). It's time for counselors to modify our language: It matters when we call our clients schizophrenics versus people with schizophrenia. *Counseling & Development,* 99(4), 452–461. https://doi.org/10.1002/jcad.12397

Grant, R. J., & Wethers, R. (2024). Trauma-Informed considerations with neurodivergent children and adolescents. In J. Stone, R. J. Grant, & C. Mellenthin (Eds.), *Trauma impacts: The repercussions of individual and collective trauma* (p. 111). Wiley.

Hartley, G., Sirois, F., Purrington, J., & Rabey, Y. (2023). Adverse childhood experiences and autism: A meta-analysis. *Trauma, Violence, & Abuse,* 15248380231213314. https://doi.org/10.1177/15248380231213314

Himmerich, H., Hamilton, A. (2020). Mood stabilizers: Side effects, contraindications, and interactions. In: Riederer, P., Laux, G., Mulsant, B., Le, W., Nagatsu, T. (Eds.). *NeuroPsychopharmacotherapy.* Springer, Cham. https://doi.org/10.1007/978-3-319-56015-1_40-1

Hoekstra, R. A., Girma, F., Tekola, B., & Yenus, Z. (2018). Nothing about us without us: The importance of local collaboration and engagement in the global study of autism. *BJPsych International, 15*(2), 40–43. https://doi.org/10.1192/bji.2017.26

Iudici, A., Girolimetto, R., Bacioccola, E., Faccio, E., & Turchi, G. (2022). Implications of involuntary psychiatric admission: Health, social, and clinical effects on patients. *Nervous & Mental Disease, 210*(4), 290–311. https://doi.org/10.1097/NMD.0000 000000001448Jennings, A. (2015). Retraumatization [PowerPoint slides]. Retrieved from http://theannainstitute.org

Jessop, P. (2022). "Autism no puzzle, nothing wrong with us." *Altogether Autism.* https://www.altogetherautism.org.nz/autism-no-puzzle-nothing-wrong-with-us/

Klein, P., Fairweather, A. K., & Lawn, S. (2022). Structural stigma and its impact on healthcare for borderline personality disorder: A scoping review. *International Journal of Mental Health Systems, 16*(1), 48. https://doi.org/10.1186/s13033-022-00558-3

KPMG. (2020). *ABA therapy M&A overview.* https://corporatefinance
.kpmg.us/insights/2020/aba-therapy.html

Kupferstein, H. (2018). Evidence of increased PTSD symptoms in autistics exposed to applied behavior analysis, *Advances in Autism,* *4*(1), 19–29. https://doi.org/10.1108/AIA-08-2017-0016

Le Cunff, A-L. (2019). *Smart goals are not so smart: Make a pact instead.* Ness Labs. https://nesslabs.com/smart-goals-pact.Lerner, M. D., Gurba, A. N., & Gassner, D. L. (2023). A framework for neurodiversity-affirming interventions for autistic individuals. *Consulting & Clinical Psychology, 91*(9), 503–504. https://doi .org/10.1037/ccp0000839

Leucht, S., Tardy, M., Komossa, K., Heres, S., Kissling, W., Salanti, G., & Davis, J. M. (2012). Antipsychotic drugs versus placebo for relapse prevention in schizophrenia: A systematic review and meta-analysis. *The Lancet, 379*(9831), 2063–2071. https://doi.org/10.1016/S0140-6736(12)60239-6

Linehan, M. M. (2014). *DBT skills training manual* 2nd ed.*).* Guilford Press.

Lugo-Candelas, C., Corbeil, T., Wall, M., Posner, J., Bird, H., Canino, G., Fisher, P. W., Suglia, S. F., & Duarte, C. S. (2021). ADHD and risk for subsequent adverse childhood experiences: Understanding the cycle of adversity. *Child Psychology & Psychiatry, 62*(8), 971–978. https://doi.org/10.1111/jcpp.13352

Luhrmann, T. (2014, July 16). *Stanford researcher: Hallucinatory "voices" shaped by local culture.* Stanford News. https://news.stanford .edu/2014/07/16/voices-culture-luhrmann-071614/

Lutz, A. S. F. (2023). An interview with neurodiversity originator Judy Singer. *Psychology Today.* https://www.psychologytoday.com /us/blog/inspectrum/202306/an-interview-with-neurodiversity -originator-judy-singer

Macfarlane, K. A. (2021). Disability without documentation. 90 Fordham L. Rev. 59. https://ir.lawnet.fordham.edu/flr/vol90/iss1/2

Madigan, S. (2011). *Narrative therapy.* American Psychological Association.

Maglione, M. A., Gidengil, C., Das, L., Raaen, L., Smith, A., Chari, R., Newberry, S., Hempel, S., Shanman, R., Perry, T., & Bidwell Goetz,

M. (2014). *Safety of vaccines used for routine immunization in the united states*. Agency for Healthcare Research and Quality. https://doi.org/10.23970/AHRQEPCERTA215

Mariani, J. J., & Levin, F. R. (2007). Treatment strategies for co-occurring ADHD and substance use disorders. *Amer J on Addictions, 16*(s1), 45–56. https://doi.org/10.1080/10550490601082783

Marschall, A. (2023). *Clinical documentation with children and adolescents*. Routledge.

McGill, O., & Robinson, A. (2021). "Recalling hidden harms": Autistic experiences of childhood applied behavioural analysis (ABA), Advances in Autism, *7*(4), 269–282. https://doi.org/10.1108/AIA-04-2020-0025

McIntire, K. L., Crawford, K. M., Perrin, P. B., Sestak, J. L., Aman, K., Walter, L. A., Page, D. B., Wen, H., Randolph, B. O., Brunner, R. C., Novack, T. L., & Niemeier, J. P. (2021). Factors increasing risk of suicide after traumatic brain injury: A state-of-the-science review of military and civilian studies. *Brain Injury, 35*(2), 151–163. https://doi.org/10.1080/02699052.2020.1861656

McKnight-Eily, L. R., Okoro, C. A., Strine, T. W., Verlenden, J., Hollis, N. D., Njai, R., Mitchell, E. W., Board, A., Puddy, R., & Thomas, C. (2021). Racial and ethnic disparities in the prevalence of stress and worry, mental health conditions, and increased substance use among adults during the Covid-19 pandemic—United States, April and May 2020. *MMWR. Morbidity and Mortality Weekly Report, 70*(5), 162–166. https://doi.org/10.15585/mmwr.mm7005a3

Morgan, H., Heritage, B., Lin, A., Perry, Y., Cook, A., Winter, S., Watson, V., Wright Toussaint, D., O'Donovan, A., Almeida, R., & Strauss, P. (2022). Factors influencing parental acceptance of trans children and young people: Findings from trans pathways. *LGBTQ+ Family: An Interdisciplinary Journal, 18*(5), 475–494. https://doi.org/10.1080/27703371.2022.2125470

Murchison, G. (2016). *Supporting and caring for transgender children*. Human Rights Campaign.

Najavits, L. M. (2001). *Seeking safety: A treatment manual for PTSD and substance abuse.* Guilford Press.

National Association of Social Workers. (2017). NASW code of ethics. Retrieved March 24, 2024, from https://www.socialworkers.org /About/Ethics/Code-of-Ethics/Code-of-Ethics-English

Newcamp, E. (Host). (2023). Mom and dad are fighting. *Slate.* https:// slate.com/podcasts/mom-and-dad-are-fighting

Nierenberg, A. A., Agustini, B., Köhler-Forsberg, O., Cusin, C., Katz, D., Sylvia, L. G., . . . & Berk, M. (2023). Diagnosis and treatment of bipolar disorder: A review. *JAMA, 330*(14), 1370–1380.

North Dakota Health & Human Services. (n.d.). Autism Spectrum Disorder (ASD) Database. https://www.hhs.nd.gov/autism-spectrum -disorder-asd-database

Odukoya, A. (2022, November 21). *Neurodivergence at a glance.* Johns Hopkins University: Integrative Learning and Life Design. https://imagine.jhu.edu/blog/2022/10/05/neurodivergence-at-a -glance/

Ophir, Y. (2022). Reconsidering the safety profile of stimulant medications for ADHD. *Ethical Human Psychology & Psychiatry, 24*(1).

Pei, J.-H., Ma, T., Nan, R.-L., Chen, H.-X., Zhang, Y.-B., Gou, L., & Dou, X.-M. (2021). Mindfulness-based cognitive therapy for treating chronic pain a systematic review and meta-analysis. *Psychology, Health & Medicine, 26*(3), 333–346. https://doi.org/10 .1080/13548506.2020.1849746

Pescosolido, B. A., Halpern-Manners, A., Luo, L., & Perry, B. (2021). Trends in public stigma of mental illness in the us, 1996–2018. *JAMA Network Open, 4*(12), e2140202. https://doi.org/10.1001/jama networkopen.2021.40202

Pfeifer, L. S., Schmitz, J., Papadatou-Pastou, M., Peterburs, J., Paracchini, S., & Ocklenburg, S. (2022). Handedness in twins: Meta-analyses. *BMC Psychology, 10*(1), 11. https://doi.org/10.1186/s40359 -021-00695-3

Prichard, D. A., & Rosenblatt, A. (1980). Racial bias in the MMPI: A methodological review. *Consulting & Clinical Psychology, 48*(2), 263–267. https://doi.org/10.1037/0022-006X.48.2.263

Raymaker, D. M., Teo, A. R., Steckler, N. A., Lentz, B., Scharer, M., Delos Santos, A., Kapp, S. K., Hunter, M., Joyce, A., & Nicolaidis, C. (2020). "Having all of your internal resources exhausted beyond measure and being left with no clean-up crew": Defining autistic burnout. *Autism in Adulthood, 2*(2), 132–143. https://doi.org/10.1089/aut.2019.0079

Reid, P. (2017). *Beard In Mind.* Cipher-Naught.

Rogers, C. R. (1957). The necessary and sufficient conditions of therapeutic personality change. *Journal of Consulting Psychology, 21*(2), 95–103. https://doi.org/10.1037/h0045357

Sandoval-Norton, A. H., Shkedy, G., & Shkedy, D. (2019). How much compliance is too much compliance: Is long-term ABA therapy abuse? *Cogent Psychology, 6*(1), 1641258. https://doi.org/10.1080/23311908.2019.1641258

Schapiro, S. J., Ellis, D., & Golden, C. (2023). MMPI: Black and white differences in the United States. *Archives of Assessment Psychology, 13*(1), 69–92.

Schomerus, G., & Angermeyer, M. C. (2017). Changes of stigma over time. In W. Gaebel, W. Rössler, & N. Sartorius (Eds.), *The Stigma of Mental Illness—End of the Story?* (pp. 157–172). Springer International Publishing. https://doi.org/10.1007/978-3-319-27839-1_9

Shi, Y., Hunter Guevara, L. R., Dykhoff, H. J., Sangaralingham, L. R., Phelan, S., Zaccariello, M. J., & Warner, D. O. (2021). Racial disparities in diagnosis of attention-deficit/hyperactivity disorder in a us national birth cohort. *JAMA Network Open, 4*(3), e210321. https://doi.org/10.1001/jamanetworkopen.2021.0321

Short, D. (2022). The aim of clinical hypnosis—Intelligence or compliance? *American Journal of Clinical Hypnosis, 64*(4), 283–289. https://doi.org/10.1080/00029157.2022.2039637

Shumaker, N., Long, T., Torres, A., Mercado, A., Marek, R. J., & Anderson, J. L. (2022). Exploring potential ethnic bias among MMPI-3 scales in assessing personality psychopathology. *Assessment*, 10731911241254341.

Singer, J. (1998). *Odd people in: The birth of community amongst people on the "autistic spectrum": A personal exploration of a new social movement based on neurological diversity.* [Bachelor's thesis, University of Technology, Sydney].

Spears, B. L. (2023). *The woman in me.* Simon & Schuster.

Stiles, C., Batchelor, R., Gumley, A., & Gajwani, R. (2023). Experiences of stigma and discrimination in borderline personality disorder: A systematic review and qualitative meta-synthesis. *Personality Disorders, 37*(2), 177–194. https://doi.org/10.1521/pedi.2023.37.2.177

Thompson, R. (2020). Disability Justice Advocate and Writer Lydia X. Z. Brown on Autism and Neurodivergence. *Room Magazine.* https://roommagazine.com/disability-justice-advocate-and-writer-lydia-x-z-brown-on-autism-and-neurodivergence-2/

U.S. Department of Health and Human Services. (n.d.). *Plain language.* National Institutes of Health. https://www.nih.gov/institutes-nih/nih-office-director/office-communications-public-liaison/clear-communication/plain-language/

van der Kolk, B. (2014). *The body keeps the score: Brain, mind, and body in the healing of trauma.* Viking.

Varshney, M., Mahapatra, A., Krishnan, V., Gupta, R., & Deb, K. S. (2016). Violence and mental illness: What is the true story? *Epidemiology & Community Health, 70*(3), 223–225. https://doi.org/10.1136/jech-2015-205546

The Vision Council. (2021). *Organizational overview.* https://thevisioncouncil.org/sites/default/files/assets/media/TVC_OrgOverview_sheet_2021.pdf

Walker, J. R. (2021). *The racist beginnings of standardized testing.* NEA. https://www.nea.org/nea-today/all-news-articles/racist-beginnings-standardized-testing

Warrier, V., Greenberg, D. M., Weir, E., Buckingham, C., Smith, P.,

Lai, M.-C., Allison, C., & Baron-Cohen, S. (2020). Elevated rates of autism, other neurodevelopmental and psychiatric diagnoses, and autistic traits in transgender and gender-diverse individuals. *Nature Communications*, *11*(1), 3959. https://doi.org/10.1038/s4 1467-020-17794-1

Webster, E. M. (2022). The impact of adverse childhood experiences on health and development in young children. *Global Pediatric Health*, *9*, 2333794X2210787. https://doi.org/10.1177/2333794X 221078708

Westervelt, E. (2020). Mental health and police violence: How crisis intervention teams are failing. NPR. https://www.npr .org/2020/09/18/913229469/mental-health-and-police-violence -how-crisis-intervention-teams-are-failing

What is trauma-informed care? (2023, October 20). University at Buffalo School of Social Work - University at Buffalo. https://socialwork .buffalo.edu/social-research/institutes-centers/institute-on-trauma -and-trauma-informed-care/what-is-trauma-informed-care.html

Whiteside, S. P. H., Sim, L. A., Morrow, A. S., Farah, W. H., Hilliker, D. R., Murad, M. H., & Wang, Z. (2020). A meta-analysis to guide the enhancement of CBT for childhood anxiety: Exposure over anxiety management. *Clinical Child & Family Psychology Review*, *23*(1), 102–121. https://doi.org/10.1007/s10567-019-00303-2

Wise, S. J. (2023, May 14). *Neurodiversity affirming practice: Core principles.* Medium. https://medium.com/@livedexperienceeducator /neurodiversity-affirming-practice-core-principles-f2c6d70661af

Yao, L., & Kabir R. (2023, Feb 9). Person-Centered therapy (Rogerian therapy). StatPearls [Internet]. StatPearls Publishing2024, Jan. https://www.ncbi.nlm.nih.gov/books/NBK589708/

Young, G. (2016). DSM-5: Basics and critics. In G. Young, *Unifying causality and psychology* (pp. 565–590). Springer International. https://doi.org/10.1007/978-3-319-24094-7_22

Yuen, E., Sadhu, J., Pfeffer, C., Sarvet, B., Daily, R. S., Dowben, J., Jackson, K., Schowalter, J., Shapiro, T., & Stubbe, D. (2020). Accentuate the positive: Strengths-based therapy for adolescents. *Adoles-*

cent Psychiatry, *10*(3), 166–171. https://doi.org/10.2174/22106766 10666200225105529

Zarei, K., Xu, G., Zimmerman, B., Giannotti, M., & Strathearn, L. (2021). Adverse childhood experiences predict common neurodevelopmental and behavioral health conditions among U.S. children. *Children*, *8*(9), 761. https://doi.org/10.3390/children8090761

Zhang, D., Lee, E. K. P., Mak, E. C. W., Ho, C. Y., & Wong, S. Y. S. (2021). Mindfulness-based interventions: An overall review. *British Medical Bulletin*, *138*(1), 41–57. https://doi.org/10.1093/bmb/ldab005

INDEX

ABOUT THE AUTHOR

Amy Marschall is a licensed psychologist and late-identified neurodivergent person. Due to rigid and biased medical model approaches to identifying neurodivergence, she went through multiple trainings in identifying ADHD and autism without realizing that she was a member of both communities, and none of her supervisors pointed it out to her. She has since devoted her energy to supporting neurodivergent communities by centering lived experience and emphasizing supporting over "fixing" different brains and experiences. She owns a private practice, Resiliency Mental Health, and is the clinical director of A Change for Better, a company that works to provide accessible, affordable, and affirming mental health care. Dr. Marschall is a speaker, writer, and advocate.